WOMEN PLAYWRIGHTS

The Best Plays
of 1998

Edited by Marisa Smith

CONTEMPORARY PLAYWRIGHTS
SERIES

SK
A Smith and Kraus Book

SMITH AND KRAUS PUBLISHERS
Contemporary Playwrights / Collections

Act One Festival '95
Act One Festival '95

EST Marathon '94: The One-Act Plays
EST Marathon '95: The One-Act Plays
EST Marathon '96: The One-Act Plays
EST Marathon '97: The One-Act Plays
EST Marathon '98: The One-Act Plays

Humana Festival: 20 One-Acts Plays 1976–1996
Humana Festival '93: The Complete Plays
Humana Festival '94: The Complete Plays
Humana Festival '95: The Complete Plays
Humana Festival '96: The Complete Plays
Humana Festival '97: The Complete Plays
Humana Festival '98: The Complete Plays
Humana Festival '99: The Complete Plays

Women Playwrights: The Best Plays of 1992
Women Playwrights: The Best Plays of 1993
Women Playwrights: The Best Plays of 1994
Women Playwrights: The Best Plays of 1995
Women Playwrights: The Best Plays of 1996
Women Playwrights: The Best Plays of 1997

If you require pre-publication information about upcoming Smith and Kraus books, you may receive our semi-annual catalogue, free of charge, by sending your name and address to *Smith and Kraus Catalogue, 4 Lower Mill Road, North Stratford, NH 03590. Or call us at (800) 895-4331, fax (603) 922-3348. WWW.SmithKraus.com.*

EDITOR'S NOTE

As we near the close of the century, it's hard to resist the tidal-like pull into the new one. Trained, as we all have been from birth to believe that the number 2000 has contained within it all the magic of life heretofore unimagined, it would be easy to dismiss the final years of the old millennium as we slide deliriously toward that new dawn. Now, however, is the time to slow things to a crawl, for these days won't come again.

1998 saw work by women playwrights as daring as any who have proceeded them. Even so, it is important to note that despite the fact that women playwrights are more empowered in their lives and in their craft than ever before, they continue to create dramatic forums for the issues and conundrums that have haunted their gender since the beginning. The exciting news, however, is that the tone of these forums is changing...evolving; taking their audiences to remote and sometimes frightening new heights from which to view them.

Indeed, to succeed in the male-dominated world of theater and playwriting, women have to be above all things *daring*. They must dare themselves to find new ways to tell new stories while daring their audiences to follow. They must dare their hearts and minds to go beyond what is safe, the tried and true, for in the daring comes the freedom to make a precious and noble gift to the audience: a new play.

The plays in this volume sing of daring hope for the future of women playwrights and indeed for the future of theater itself. Perhaps in a shared bout of pre-millennial doomsday-itis, many who write about theater have in the past year or so defined theater's future as being anything but rosy. Perhaps one of the best things about editing this particular series is that I get to see, first, that the future of theater is indeed rosy. Further, it's exciting. Thanks to the women whose work I've been so privileged to read and include, I know that Smith and Kraus will always be proving the nay-sayers wrong, because women playwrights have honed the art of daring down to a fine science.

A Smith and Kraus Book
Published by Smith and Kraus, Inc.
PO Box 127, Lyme, NH 03768
www.SmithKraus.com

First Edition: March 2000
10 9 8 7 6 5 4 3 2 1

The Library of Congress Cataloging-In-Publication Data
Women playwrights : the best plays of 1998 / edited by Marisa Smith
p. cm. — (Contemporary playwrights series)
ISBN 1-57525-181-7
1. American drama—women authors. 2. American drama—20th century. 3. Women—drama.
I. Smith, Marisa. II. Series: Contemporary playwrights series.
PS628.W6W668   1994
812'.540809287—dc20
94-10071
CIP

CONTENTS

INTRODUCTION

VOICES AT THE MILLENNIUM...WOMEN'S VOICES...

Looking back on this century and the American theater, we hear only an occasional echo of women's voices... A Lorainne Hansberry here, a Lillian Hellman there, lone voices over the decades... Not until the 1970s and early 80s with the advent of Marsha Norman, Beth Henley, Wendy Wasserstein, Tina Howe, Maria Irene Fornes, et al, did that echo become a crescendo.

And now, listening once more at the millennium, we have cause to celebrate. The disparate voices are becoming a chorus. Emily Mann, Anna Deveare Smith, Paula Vogel, Suzi Lori Park—names too numerous to mention—lead this emerging chorus of women playwrights, growing in strength and number. And Smith and Kraus Publishers is calling these new voices to our attention in their "Women Playwrights" series, initiated in 1992.

Listen to the voices of the women playwrights of 1998! Smith and Kraus has assembled rousing representation in this volume: eight vibrant voices, eight compelling plays. Dazzling in their diversity, daunting in their strength, their collective breadth and power is impressive. Common images and themes emerge—images of the body and spirit, themes of survival and triumph.

Playwright/screenwriter/editor Jocelyn Beard opens the collection with her passionate new play, *The Ornamental Hermit.* Set in 1859 in South Carolina, the play is an eloquent tale of social and spiritual liberation. A mysterious hermit comes to live on a plantation and serves as a catalyst for the community, evoking both a literal and metaphoric understanding of slavery and freedom in us all.

Playwright Val Smith also delves into history and the spiritual as a source of inspiration for her intriguing play, *Marguerite Bonet.* Set in England in 1920, a rebellious daughter of a psychic becomes the obsession of two physicists—one who is convinced Bonet can aid him in proving the existence of the spiritual realm, and the other who sees in her the connection to the deceased son he never knew. The play explores the fascinating duality of fantasy and self-deception.

Three plays in this collection concern themselves with women and their bodies. The first is *Jodie's Body,* by South African-born playwright Aviva Jane Carlin. In this brave new one-woman play, the protagonist poses nude before an art class, while discussing everything from Apartheid to her childhood and her body. In this play about imprisoning structures, both physical and political, Ms. Carlin brings a broad perspective of having lived in many lands—South Africa, Uganda, England, and now America (Seattle), and makes the enlightening connection between freedom from both political enslavement and enslavement of body image imposed by cultural values. *Jodie's Body* offers us a refreshing reappraisal of what it means to be beautiful.

Control over one's body is again the subject in Wendy MacLeod's powerful new play *The Water Children*. Here the subject is abortion—a woman is hired to act in a pro-life commercial produced by an anti-abortion group, herself having had an abortion at age sixteen. As a result, she questions her former views and faces another pregnancy with new insight into this vital question. The play recognizes the complexities of a crucial and controversial issue, one which is of deep concern to us all.

A woman and her body are yet again the subject of the daring *True Confessions of a Go-Go Girl* by Jill Morley. Filled with colorful musical interludes and striking character portrayals, this fast-paced, hard-hitting play tells the story of a woman whose lifestyle provides her with incredible power as well as a destructive dependency.

Coming of age, coming into "one's own"…the common theme of three plays in this collection. In Refuge, Jessica Goldberg tells a tender touching tale of a young woman, herself in need of care, who is charged with caring for her fragmented family and is challenged in the process by a young man who loves her. In this sensitive, contemporary story, the protagonist makes a perilous journey toward trust, love, and interdependence, a journey that all of us struggle to make.

Give Me Shelter, a spirited, new play by Wendy Weiner, chronicles a young woman's hilarious and desperate search for a livable New York City apartment. It's a lively solo performance piece, with one actress playing the parts of numerous personae who show the hapless heroine prospective new dwelling places. It's modern (wo)man's search for a suitable home and the universal search for human connection.

And finally, there is Erin Cressida Wilson's powerful, poetic, and panoramic *Hurricane.* In a steamy sequence of tempestuous scenes crisscrossing the country and culminating in Africa, women of today—of all ages and in all stages of life—struggle to make sense of their fragmented lives and find strength.

Eight vigorous voices, sounding strong on stages in New York, San Francisco, Los Angeles, Houston, Chicago, Louisville, and beyond... Some are newcomers to the American theater, some are already leaders. Some have won prizes, others will. Many have residencies in American theaters, others have been produced abroad. And all these plays and their authors have the following in common: an indomitable spirit, a humanity, a special honesty and strength that commands our attention. When it comes to 1998's women playwrights, and today's, and tomorrow's, attention must be paid.

Carol Rocamora
New York University
Tisch School of the Arts
Dramatic Writing Program

THE ORNAMENTAL HERMIT

by Jocelyn Beard

The Ornamental Hermit was produced by Imperial Granite Productions at the Schoolhouse Theatre in Croton Falls, New York in June, 1998. Directed by Jocelyn Beard. Produced by Nannette Stone. Lighting Design by Peter Petrino. Set design by Imperial Granite. Costume design by Leslie Nielson-Bowman. Sound Design by Steve Faiella.

Mehitabel	Dawn Brown Berenson
Joe	Lonnie Young
Lily Montfleurry	Tina Prestia
Mr. Seely	Richard Pettibone
Elizabeth Montfleurry	Susan Pettibone
Siegfried Von Zohar	Brian Reid
Cedric Montfleurry	Joe Harding
Jemmaline Montfleurry	Mary Ann DeRosa

The Ornamental Hermit was developed under the auspices of The Schoolhouse Playwrights Workshop, Doug Michael, Director. Lee Pope is the Artistic Managing Director of the Schoolhouse.

CHARACTERS

LILY MONTFLEURRY: a Southern Belle with attitude, 18–20

MEHITABEL: a slave; Lily's maid and best friend, 18–20

JOE: a slave; a silent enigmatic presence, 20s

MR. SEELY: the overseer; Irish, the man with the whip, 20s

ELIZABETH MONTFLEURRY: the mistress of Rivermede Plantation, a Northerner, 30s

CEDRIC MONTFLEURRY: master of Rivermede Plantation, a ridiculous though harmless pop'njay, 40s

SIEGFRIED: a mysterious foreigner, 30s

JEMMALINE MONTFLEURRY: Cedric's sister, a boozy spinster, 40–50

PLACE

The formal gardens of Rivermede Plantation near Charleston, South Carolina

TIME

Summer, 1860

ACT I

The formal gardens of Rivermede Plantation, near Charleston, South Carolina, 1860. Lights up on a section of what was to be a small, elaborate temple, constructed in the style of ancient Greece and/or Rome. It has been destroyed by hand. Huge chunks of stone have tumbled about, crushing flowers and shrubs. A large, crude mallet lies against a small marble bench nearby. A young woman, Mehitable, rushes on. She is a slave, but dressed nicely, indicating her status as a member of the household staff. She is quickly pursued by Joe, a field hand, another slave. Both are in high spirits.

MEHITABLE: You leave me be! Just leave me be!

JOE: *(Catching her in his arms.)* Not til you listen to me…

MEHITABLE: But my mistress…

JOE: Miss Lily's coach won't be here 'til after the house folk eat. It takes three, four hours to ride here from Charleston.

MEHITABLE: I know how long it takes. I just come from there yesterday.

JOE: You miss me while you in town with Miss Lily?

MEHITABLE: Miss *you?* You know I never did any such thing!

JOE: I think you did. I think you did miss Joe.

MEHITABLE: I never did! Not once. Seems to me, Joe, your head's gotten bigger since I been gone to Charlestontown.

JOE: You did miss me. I can see it right there, in your eyes…

(Joe kisses Mehitable who pulls away.)

MEHITABLE: Joe! The Missus!

JOE: The Missus is out in the cotton.

MEHITABLE: Mr. Seely…

JOE: The overseer man is out in the cotton with the Missus.

MEHITABLE: But…

JOE: Everybody's out in the cotton.

MEHITABLE: Why ain't you out in the cotton?

JOE: Because I'm here with you.

MEHITABLE: Just so you can kiss me?

JOE: That's right… *(Kisses her again.)* …but also to talk.

MEHITABLE: *(Laughing.)* Well, that's one thing you're good at, Joe. I never did know a man who liked the sound of his own voice as much as you.

JOE: I've been trying to talk to you for weeks…before you left for Charleston…

MEHITABLE: *(Suddenly afraid, lowering her voice.)* I know! At the bush meetin'! Ain't you ashamed of makin' such a big fuss?

JOE: I ain't ashamed of nothin' I done that night.

MEHITABLE: But Mammy Pam seen you kiss me!

JOE: What if she did?

MEHITABLE: Shame on you, Joe! Mammy Pam…

JOE: *(Shouting in the direction of the house.)* Is a fat old mule!

MEHITABLE: Joe!

JOE: A fat old busybody of a mule!

MEHITABLE: *(Pulling him further into the ruins.)* There you go, Big Joe! Talk, talk. All this talk is gonna get you whuped one day!

JOE: If my sayin' I love you is gonna get me whuped, then it's gonna get me whuped.

(Mehitable stares up into his face for a moment.)

MEHITABLE: What did you say?

JOE: You heard me right, girl. I love you. *(Singing it out.)* Joe loves…

MEHITABLE: *(Pulling him back.)* Then you keep quiet 'bout it!

JOE: *(A whisper.)* Joe loves Delilah. *(Suddenly intense.)* Listen to me, girl: I'm leavin'.

MEHITABLE: *(Confused.)* Leavin'? Rivermede?

JOE: *(A hiss.)* Leavin' South Carolina.

MEHITABLE: *(Panicked.)* Oh. Lord; they're sendin' you west!

JOE: No! No. No one is sendin' me anywhere.

(Mehitable stares at him until his meaning becomes clear.)

MEHITABLE: *(An indictment.)* Joe! You gonna run!

(Joe remains silent.)

MEHITABLE: *(A terrified whisper.)* You gonna run north.

JOE: And I want you to come with me…

MEHITABLE: No!

JOE: Yes! Come with me! I have…things are…arranged…

MEHITABLE: What things?

JOE: Everything! It's just that I can't…well, I can't talk about it. Too dangerous.

MEHITABLE: *(Incredulous.)* Too dangerous.

JOE: Come with me!

MEHITABLE: No!

JOE: Why not? What you got here?

MEHITABLE: I got everything here!

JOE: You got nothin'!

MEHITABLE: What do you know about what I got?

JOE: You got so much here? Bein' a slave is so likable to you that you want to stay?

MEHITABLE: I was born here at Rivermede, Joe. Right over that wall, in the quarters. This is my home. A sold slave like you wouldn't understand.

JOE: That...that's the most...ignorant thing I have ever in my life heard anyone say! Your home. You got no home, girl.

MEHITABLE: I do! This is my home right here! And Miss Lily...

JOE: Miss Lily! Miss Lily what?

MEHITABLE: Miss Lily is my...my...

JOE: Your what???

MEHITABLE: (Hotly.) My friend! Miss Lily is my friend! She needs me, Joe! Now that her mother is dead and her father marry the new missus, she needs me. I ain't gonna leave her!

(Joe regards Mehitable for a moment before collapsing on the marble bench.)

JOE: Well, ain't old Joe the biggest fool in the world.

MEHITABLE: I ain't goin' nowhere!

JOE: I see that now.

MEHITABLE: You run, you die.

JOE: (Meeting her gaze.) You stay, you die.

MEHITABLE: (Dismissively.) Not true. You know it's different here.

JOE: Different.

MEHITABLE: Specially since Mr. Seely come.

JOE: It's the same as anywhere else.

MEHITABLE: It ain't the same and you know it, Joe! How many slaves buy their freedom here last year??

(Joe remains silent.)

MEHITABLE: Six! That's how many! Here they let us have bush meetin's. They let us keep our babies! (Pointedly.) They let us have real weddin's. We wear good clothes and shoes all year long and the Missus makes sure we're fed good food...

JOE: (Putting on his "happy darkie" voice.) Just like the Massa's prize stallion.

MEHITABLE: Stop that, Joe! It's different here! It is. Over at Green Hill they lock the slaves up at night; chain 'em in like...

JOE: Like slaves!

MEHITABLE: (Starting to cry.) They got no shoes at Green Hill! They sell the babies! And Mr. Frack...

JOE: I know what goes on at Green Hill!

MEHITABLE: Then you know it's better here!

JOE: A slave is a slave. Shoes or barefoot.

MEHITABLE: Besides, here I got Miss Lily to take care of…

JOE: *(Seeing Miss Lily approach off stage.)* Miss Lily!!

MEHITABLE: She's trapped here just like the rest of us and if you dare say anything bad about her…

JOE: But, Miss Lily…

MEHITABLE: I swear I will strike you down!

JOE: She be comin'!

MEHITABLE: *(Turning to look and gasping.)* It's my mistress!

JOE: She got blood in her eye!

MEHITABLE AND JOE: *(Realizing.)* The temple!

JOE: This way!

> *(Mehitable is led quickly off by Joe.)*

LILY: *(Offstage.)* No!!! No! No! No!

> *(Lily Montfleurry rushes on stage. She is an exquisite young girl of eighteen, in her absolute youthful prime. A blonde Scarlet O'Hara, Lily is dressed in traveling clothes as befits the daughter of the owner of Rivermede Plantation, with many fussy frills. She is in a petulant rage. When she sees the destruction of her temple, she freezes, her fists slowly clenching.)*

LILY: My…my temple of Aphrodite! Who did this?

> *(She walks slowly and deliberately through the rubble, searching for a clue.)*

LILY: Who would have dared…? *(She espies the mallet.)* Aha! *(Calling.)* Mehitable! Mehitable! Come here this instant! *(Lily strides to the mallet and hefts it clumsily.)*

> *(Mehitable re-enters. She is quite nervous.)*

MEHITABLE: M-m-mistress Lily! We wasn't spectin' you 'til sugar time!

LILY: Who did this!? Who ruined my Temple of Aphrodite??

MEHITABLE: It wasn't…

LILY: Well, of course it wasn't *you*, Mehitable. *(Holding up mallet.)* It was this! This foul instrument has brought destruction to my lovely, lovely temple, and I mean to find the black devil who wielded it!

MEHITABLE: But, Mistress Lily…

LILY: Oh, I heard what Mammy Pam said about my temple! Why, she told Cordelia that my temple would be a heathen blight on Rivermede! The mark of the Devil!

MEHITABLE: She never!

LILY: With my own sweet ears I heard her say the words, Mehitable! And let me tell you I marched right into her kitchen…

MEHITABLE: You never!

LILY: I did. I marched right into her kitchen and informed everyone in earshot…

which, as you well know, always includes about ten more Negroes than you can see…that my Temple of Aphrodite was to be a symbol of the beauty of love, nothin' more, nothin' less.

MEHITABLE: But, Mammy Pam…

LILY: A lovely, magnificent symbol of the greatest of all human emotions that would outlast all our lives and serve as a reminder for future generations of Montfleurrys at Rivermede that love is the one perfect expression of the human soul! *(She pauses, caught up in the drama, and then.)* Besides, Cousin Bettina in England wrote me all about her Temple of Apollo, complete with sketches. All the young ladies in English society have temples in their gardens! Every last one! Where else can a young woman of quality meet her clandestine lover at midnight?

MEHITABLE: *(Shocked.)* Hush, Miss Lily! Mammy Pam…

LILY: Oh…fie on Mammy Pam, Mehitable! Fie! This was *my* temple! This is where I was supposed to meet with *my* clandestine lover at midnight! This was to be a place for stolen kisses, poetry and…and…for the contemplation of…life's mysteries! Look at this mess, Mehitable! What in the name of Lord Above am I supposed to contemplate in that??

MEHITABLE: Mammy Pam is gonna be contemplatin' our behinds if you don't hush!

LILY: *(Ignoring her, hefting mallet speculatively.)* It seems to me, Mehitable, that the only nigra on this plantation that could have done this evil deed is that Joe…

MEHITABLE: No!

LILY: Yes! He's the only brute of correct proportions who could have raised this mallet up over his head and brought it smashing down on my lovely temple.

(Mehitable continues to shake her head "no.")

LILY: Oh, yes, Mehitable. Big strong Joe. Put up to it by Mammy Pam and those old witches in the kitchen! Run and fetch Mr. Seely!

MEHITABLE: No! I am tellin' you that it didn't happen like…

LILY: You do as I say, Mehitable, or I'll switch you myself! Go!

(Mehitable runs off in tears.)

LILY: *(Walking slowing through the rubble, using the mallet as a walking stick.)* This is what comes from leaving Rivermede while Daddy's away. I never should have gone to Charleston! *(She pokes at a piece of the rubble with the mallet, then stoops to pick it up. It is a bas relief of Aphrodite's face.)* My poor, poor Aphrodite, what has that rough heathen done to you? Have no fear, sweet goddess. I will have that ridiculous Mr. Seely rebuild your temple from scratch, and it will be bigger and even more lovely than this one was, I promise.

(The sound of angry voices is heard off, and Lily readies herself for battle. Mr. Seely, the plantation's overseer enters, followed closely by Elizabeth Montfleurry, Lily's stepmother, a Northerner.)

ELIZABETH: Must you be such an alarmist, Mr. Seely? As you can see, Miss Montfleurry is quite hale and hardy following her journey.

MR. SEELY: *(Seeing Lily and becoming instantly relieved.)* Welcome home, Miss Lily.

LILY: Mr. Seely, thank the good Lord above that you are here!

MR. SEELY: *(Concerned.)* I'm sorry that I wasn't here to meet your coach…

LILY: Never mind that now, Mr. Seely. Surely even you can perceive that a foul crime has been committed!

ELIZABETH: What crime?

MR. SEELY: What's happened, Miss Lily? Are you hurt?

ELIZABETH: Don't be absurd, Mr. Seely, she's fit as a fiddle.

(Mehitable enters cautiously, followed by Joe, who stands with quiet ease as he watches Mr. Seely and Lily.)

LILY: There you are! Monster! Defiler of private property!

ELIZABETH: Lily, what are you raving about?

LILY: *(Whirling to face Elizabeth.)* I hear a noise…oh, it's you, Elizabeth. Standin' there like a stupid Yankee askin' a stupid Yankee question, as usual.

ELIZABETH: Yankee or not I am mistress of this plantation until your father returns from England, and I demand that you explain this outrageous behavior! Have you been at Cedric's bourbon again?

LILY: *(Stamping her foot.)* I swear on my poor dead mother's grave that this is too much for me to bear! I knew I never should have gone to Charleston!

ELIZABETH: Oh, Lily, you begged to go. You said…now let me see if I remember this correctly, oh, yes! You said—and I quote—"If I don't get to go to Cousin Fanny's cotillion, I will expire!"

LILY: And just look at what has happened in my absence!

MR. SEELY: Miss Lily, please. Has someone done something to you?

LILY: *(Twirling with arms outstretched dramatically.)* Not me, Mr. Seely, THIS! I refer to the wanton destruction of my Temple of Aphrodite! Perpetrated by that man! *(Lily points at Joe with the mallet.)*

MR. SEELY: But it wasn't…

ELIZABETH: Lily dear, it took *several* men to tear down your temple, not just Joe. *(To Joe.)* Joe, go on back to your chores.

LILY: *(Screeching.)* NO! You stay right there! Mr. Seely will deal with you!

MR. SEELY: Miss Lily…

ELIZABETH: *(Firmly.)* Go back to work. *(To Lily.)* That is quite enough, Lily. *(Joe exits.)*

LILY: *(Sputtering with fury.)* How dare you speak to me like that in front of the slaves?? You…you northern jezebel!!

ELIZABETH: That is enough! Lily, what *is* the matter with you?

LILY: My temple! It is ruined, you stupid Yankee! Have you gone blind?

ELIZABETH: *(Heaving a sigh.)* Lily. I wrote you last month of your father's plan to destroy the temple. I asked you in the letter to notify me if this was unacceptable for you. I waited several weeks for your reply, and hearing nothing from Charleston, I commissioned Mr. Seely who only yesterday had the men bring the temple down just as your father instructed. Now, if this is problematical for you, my dear, I am afraid that you will have to wait for Cedric to return from England so that you may take it up with him.

LILY: I never received any such letter from you while I was in Charleston!

MEHITABLE: *(Piping up bravely.)* Yes you did, Miss Lily.

LILY: Mehitable, you keep still!

MEHITABLE: But you did get the letter. Don't you remember, 'bout a month ago I brought it to you in Charlestontown when you sent for me to bring you the peach organdy dress for the Planters' Ball and you told me that you didn't want no letter from no northern trash? Begging your pardon, Missus 'Lizabeth.

LILY: Mehitable! You go right on back to the house and start unpackin' my things!

MEHITABLE: Yes, Miss Lily! *(Mehitable exits.)*

ELIZABETH: As usual, Lily, you have no one but yourself to blame for your woeful ignorance of the daily affairs of this plantation.

LILY: *(Somewhat cowed, but still angry.)* I still don't believe you.

MR. SEELY: *(Hating to agree with Elizabeth.)* It's true, Miss Lily. I had the men take down the temple just as your father instructed. Seems such a shame…

LILY: What!? Don't tell me that you were party to this evil scheme, Mr. Seely!

MR. SEELY: *(Pulling a few pieces of folded paper out of his pocket.)* Here are the plans your father sent to us from England, miss. They show how he wanted the temple brought down.

(Lily snatches the papers and pours over them with a frown.)

LILY: Well, this does appear to be daddy's handwriting…

ELIZABETH: Oh, for Heaven's sake!

LILY: *(Reading.)* "…but leave the cupola intact and on its side. No ruble is to be removed. Encourage weeds and other wild growth…" What in the name of Christ almighty is this supposed to mean?

ELIZABETH: I wish you would mind your language, Lily.

LILY: Oh, hush up! I just know that this is somehow your doing, Elizabeth! You have bewitched my father. You have bewitched him and everyone knows it! Why else would he have passed up an opportunity to marry that nice Letty Bascombe from Hanesport? No, you have bewitched him! And now you have plotted to destroy my temple!

ELIZABETH: Honestly, Lily. I wish you could hear how ridiculous you sound.

LILY: I do not sound ridiculous! I am surrounded by conspiracy! Even you, Mr. Seely, our loyal overseer, have stabbed me right here, in my heart!

MR. SEELY: I have done no such thing!

ELIZABETH: It seems you have forgotten who it was convinced your father to let you take over this section of the garden so you could build the blasted thing in the first place! You have also managed to conveniently disremember who bought all those books for you in New York City with drawings of Greek and Roman temples.

LILY: *(Very dramatically.)* All so you could laugh at me as I tear my heart out in the ruins!

ELIZABETH: Listen to me, you self-absorbed little fool: I have no idea why your father wanted this temple torn down. No idea whatsoever. Do you hear me? I do know, however, that he has instructed Mr. Seely to build you a new temple on whatever part of the grounds you choose. That was also in the letter I sent to Charleston which you in your petty self-indulgence deigned unfit reading. Lily, in case you have yet to take notice, most of us are quite busy here at Rivermede, which evidently exists only to provide revenue with which your father may shower you with trinkets like temples! I suggest you inform Mr. Seely of the new location for your new temple, and let us all get back to work!

(Lily gapes at Elizabeth and then "hmmphs" as she spins on her heel to turn her back on the older woman.)

ELIZABETH: Very well, you may carry on, Mr. Seely. There's still a cotton crop to tend for the next petty indulgence…a cathedral in the honeysuckle, perhaps…or a pyramid in the peonies?

(Lily "hmmphs" again as Elizabeth exits.)

MR. SEELY: *(After a moment.)* I beg your pardon, Miss Lily, but if you have no further need of me…

LILY: I *need* my temple restored to the way it *was!*

MR. SEELY: I wish I could help, miss. Truly. I know what that temple meant to you…

LILY: I swear, Mr. Seely, you are a useless as any Beaufort County dandy! Why do you bother?

MR. SEELY: *(Suddenly brusque.)* I best be returnin' to the fields.

LILY: *(Icily.)* Very well, Mr. Seely.

MR. SEELY: Unless there's anything else…

LILY: There is not.

MR. SEELY: All right, then. *(He turns to leave.)*

LILY: Wait! Mr. Seely, go to the house and tell Mehitable that I want all my things brought here directly.

MR. SEELY: Here?

LILY: That's right, Mr. Seely. I want everything brought right here. I am going to live here, in the ruins of my temple of Aphrodite until my father comes home from England.

MR. SEELY: You can't live here!

LILY: Are you now proposing to tell me what I can and cannot do, Mr. Seely?

MR. SEELY: Lily! A young lady such as yourself can't live out in the open… exposed to the elements…with the slave quarters just over there!

LILY: I will stay in these ruins, day and night and night and day until my father can explain this madness to me himself—in person.

MR. SEELY: Be reasonable, Lily. Your father said I can build you a new temple anywhere you want. I was thinking that there's a nice spot by your mother's wisteria, just below the old rock wall…near the little reflecting pool. Wouldn't that be a nice spot for a new temple? You could draw up the plans just like you did for this one and…

LILY: No! *This* was the temple I wanted, Mr. Seely! This one! I repeat: have my things brought here at once.

MR. SEELY: But, Lily…

LILY: At once means immediately, Mr. Seely! And kindly refrain from addressin' me in such a familiar tone!

MR. SEELY: *(Furious but containing it.)* Very good, miss. *(Mr. Seely exits.)*

LILY: *(Calling after him.)* And you tell that northern harpy that she is not to set foot in this part of the garden! Do you hear?
(Lily turns dramatically and trips over the mallet. She goes sprawling and her unladylike cussing fills the air as the lights fade to black.)

(Change to: the ruins, several nights later. Lily and Mehitable huddle under blankets as Lily reads aloud by lantern light. Joe sits quietly, unseen by either of the women, in the shadows.)

LILY: *(Reading.)* "No!" cried the fair Melvina as Siegfried collapsed to the floor, his hands clutching in vain at the knife that had been thrust into his beating heart…"

(Mehitable shrieks and clutches at her own chest.)

LILY: "No!" she cried again as the villain fled the turret."

MEHITABLE: He dead, Miss Lily?

LILY: *(Turning a page.)* Don't be so goulish, Mehitable! And please say, "Is he dead." Not "He dead."

MEHITABLE: Well, is he? Dead?

LILY: Of course not. *(Returning to the book.)* "Siegfried!" she gasped as she sank to the cold stone floor by his side, the blood draining from her pretty face. "Siegfried, my love! What manner of man has committed so foul a deed on this dark and dismal night? Oh, my dearest heart, Siegfried, will you not speak?"

(There is a low rumble of thunder in the distance.)

MEHITABLE: *(Looking around fearfully.)* Storm's comin'

LILY: Let it. *(Reading.)* "His eyes quivered and opened, and Melvina saw within their tortured depths the very lodestone of human despair." Oh, Mehitable, is that not the most profound turn of phrase you have ever in your life heard? "The very lodestone of human despair." Is that not eloquent to bursting?

MEHITABLE: What's it mean, Miss Lily?

LILY: It means…well, Mehitable, a lodestone is a…well, it's really more of a…oh, never mind!

(More distant thunder.)

MEHITABLE: It's gonna rain on our heads, Miss Lily.

LILY: Oh, so what if it does, Mehitable? Rain is just water and I am led to believe that we are quite filled with water so it can't possibly hurt us. Now, if you don't mind… *(She returns to reading the book.)* "Siegfried!" she gasped. "You live! Oh, my Siegfried!"

MEHITABLE: Beggin' you pardon, Mistress Lily, but why does she keep callin' him that name?

LILY: What name?

MEHITABLE: Zig-freed.

LILY: Oh, for heaven's sake. It's his name. Just like my name is Lily and yours is Mehitable.

MEHITABLE: But, my mammy named me…

LILY: I know very well what that foolish woman named you, Mehitable, and I must inform you yet again that *(Pronounced with great distaste.)* "Delilah" is an altogether inappropriate name for a young woman in your position. The Biblical Delilah was an evil temptress! Why your mammy decided to name you after such a low-born woman I'll never know. Now…

MEHITABLE: Then what about Siegfried? Who did his mammy name him after?

LILY: Mehitable, "Siegfried" is just a name. *(Lily rises and acts out all of the following, including Mehitable in her various pantomimes.)* It's passionate: "The *coup de gras* was delivered by the noble Count Siegfried," *(Lily pantomimes running Mehitable through.)* "Thunderstruck, Siegfried swept the lovely young peasant woman into his manly arms." *(Lily grabs a giggling Mehitable and sweeps her into a dip.)* It is refined: "Siegfried savored the fine claret as he considered the couples swirling around the dance floor."

(Mehitable pantomimes swaggering and sipping from a claret glass while Lily swirls around in a waltz.)

LILY: And above all, Mehitable, it's *mysterious:* Where is this man named Siegfried from? Who can say? Perhaps a remote castle high in the Prussian Alps where he broods over a lost love under stormy cold skies. *(Lily puts her arm around Mehitable and both young women gaze up into the night sky.)*

LILY: Can't you see him up there on the battlements, Mehitable? Brooding away? Or better yet in the court of a mad king, where he alone defends the crown from traitors and assassins! *En garde,* dog, and prepare to breathe your last! *(Mehitable shrieks as Lily pursues her with an invisible sword. They collapse, laughing, in the bed clothes.)*

LILY: Oh, Mehitable, Siegfried is simply the most romantic name in the world.

MEHITABLE: *(Panting and thoroughly unconvinced.)* Then how come there ain't no Siegfrieds 'round here?

LILY: You are impossible, Mehitable! *(With a casual glance in Joe's direction.)* I suppose you think "Joe" is the most romantic of all names.

MEHITABLE: *(Embarrassed.)* No, I do not!

LILY: Oh, I'm sure the feeling is mutual. I am certain that Joe thinks

Mehitable is the most romantic name in the world… *(Calling over her shoulder.)* Don't you, Joe?

MEHITABLE: Miss Lily! Please…

LILY: Oh, all right, all right, Mehitable… *(Lowering her voice.)* But you don't think he's been out here all night every night keeping watch over me, do you?

(Mehitable glances over her shoulder at Joe's dark form.)

MEHITABLE: *(Loudly.)* I swear I don't know what that stupid man thinks he's doin'. He can die from a night chill for all I think 'bout it.

LILY: Mehitable!

MEHITABLE: It's God's truth, Miss Lily! *(Making it up as she goes along.)* That old Joe is sittin' out here like a big dumb owl cause I find out that he's been keepin' time with little Gabby when me with you in Charlestontown!

LILY: What! Gabby the seamstress with the squinty eye?

MEHITABLE: He can just sit out here 'til the Lord above calls Judgment Day for all I think about it and that is the truth you can put in the ground!

LILY: My! Well, let's ignore the rogue, then, shall we?

MEHITABLE: We shall.

(Both women turn back to the book in a huff. More distant thunder.)

LILY: Back to Siegfried…where were we…here it is: "Tears slid like pearls down her fair, colorless cheeks as she clasped his bloodied hand to her heart. "Yes, my dearest Siegfried. I have escaped the unspeakable subterranean chamber of the dread Lord Montfort aided by your brother… your own dear Helmut…who gave his life this very night so that I could now hold you in my arms here in the safety of…

BOTH: *(Laughing.)* Bubenschloss!"

LILY: "The brave hero gazed into his true love's deep sapphire eyes, which brimmed with diamonds of tears…" Diamonds of tears. Is that not beautiful Mehitable? *(Back to book.)* "…which brimmed with diamonds of tears, and he was made to think of his dear, brave brother, Helmut… so tall, so noble. Dead." Is that not romantic?

MEHITABLE: Not if he's dead, Miss Lily.

LILY: *(Reading.)* "No man shall ever love as I have loved," whispered Siegfried…"

MEHITABLE: Uh-oh.

LILY: Uh-oh? What do you mean, uh-oh?

MEHITABLE: Poor Mister Siegfried's a gonner, Mistress, just like his brother: tall, noble dead Helmut.

LILY: Don't be ridiculous, Mehitable. The hero never, ever dies.

MEHITABLE: Well, this one's gonna.

LILY: He never will! Cousin Bettina sent me this book all the way from London, England, Mehitable, and she informed me in her kind letter that this particular volume is universally admired by all young ladies in London society and is generally considered to be the most romantic story ever set down on paper. Do you imagine, Mehitable, that the most romantic story ever set down on paper would include the most unfortunate detail of a deceased hero? You are simply goulish to the point of distraction! *(Returning to the book.)* Now, where the hell was I? Ah, yes. *(She takes a moment to recapture the romantic mood.)* "No man shall ever love as I have loved," whispered Siegfried. "Helmut! I follow Thee!" The brave Siegfried then gave a cry and gave himself over to greedy death while still in her trembling arms." WHAT???

(There is another rumble of thunder and the pale flash of distant lightning.)

MEHITABLE: *(Laughing.)* I told you! I told you he were a gonner! Poor Mister Siegfried. Both him and his brother be dead and fair Melvina's left all alone to cry her diamond tears.

LILY: Well this is simply the most horrible, nasty, vile book it has ever been my misfortune to read! I am going to write to Cousin Bettina first thing in the morning and tell her so! Ugh!

(She tosses the offending tome into the darkness. More distant thunder.)

MEHITABLE: Mistress Lily?

LILY: Yes, Mehitable?

MEHITABLE: I was wondren, Mistress, if you woulda really done what you said th'other day?

LILY: Done what?

MEHITABLE: Would you a switched me? Like you said you would?

LILY: Dear Lord spare me! Of course not! What a terrible thought for you to be carrying around in your heart against me!

MEHITABLE: But you said…

LILY: I know what I said, Mehitable! What you have got to understand is exactly how…how provoked I was when I saw what had been done to my lovely temple of Aphrodite.

(More thunder and lightning. The storm is getting a bit closer.)

MEHITABLE: So you didn't mean that thing you said…'bout switchin' me?

LILY: Of course not. Have I once in all my life, to your knowledge, ever switched anyone or anything besides that lazy old chestnut gelding's behind?

MEHITABLE: No…

LILY: I abhor violence. Simply abhor it! I hate the way…well, the way things are…here, well not exactly here, at Rivermede…we treat you well do we not?

MEHITABLE: Yes, mistress.

LILY: *(Lowering her voice.)* Why over at Green Hill I hear there are regular beatings now. That awful Mr. Frack once whipped a man to death! Right in front of everyone! Including the ladies!

MEHITABLE: *(Quietly.)* I heard that, too.

LILY: But we don't conduct ourselves in such a barbaric manner here at Rivermede, do we?

MEHITABLE: No, mistress.

LILY: Indeed we do not! And we never will. It isn't in our nature. That absurd Mr. Seely has suggested to me on more than one occasion that I am ignorant in such matters but I am not! I am well aware of the international debate over the keeping of slaves. I know what's being said. I hear the rattling sabers just as keenly as anyone. I know these things because I listen, Mehitable. I listen to the foolish little boys who fancy themselves young men when they gather for their cigars and their brandy. They talk and they talk about the "evil" North and its anti-slave militias and its grim little spinsters who host tea parties in Boston at which abolition is discussed like…like the weather. I know all about the abolitionist war in Kansas Territory. I have heard about the runaways who make it all the way to Canada…and I have heard about the ones who don't. Why, I'll have you know that my Cousin Odette belongs to several anti-slavery groups in Richmond and I say, good for her! *(Lowering her voice.)* Good for her. Mr. Seely is wrong, Mehitable, I do know about these things. But all the knowing doesn't do any good, does it? One deprived of power can put knowledge to little good use.

(More thunder and a flash of lightning.)

LILY: Sometimes, Mehitable, I feel the tides of an anger so vast and so consuming that it's pulling everything apart. It's a terrifying thing to think about, and the terror is made more sweet by the fact that thinking about it is all I am permitted to do! Lord help me! *(Focusing on Mehitable.)* That, however, is all besides the point Mehitable, which is that I would never, ever lay a hand on you or on anyone. Especially not you. You're my…if it wasn't for you…well, it's just that I was so angry about my temple.

MEHITABLE: You lettin' yourself get too distressed about these rocks.

LILY: That temple was the only thing in this world that was mine, Mehitable, totally mine. Who am I in this house? The useless, worthless daughter, that's who. I may as well be a house girl like you!

MEHITABLE: Now you stop that, Miss Lily!

LILY: I am an expense—just as you are. Something to be balanced against a ledger. Nothing here is mine. Nothing. But the temple. I conceived of it! I drew the plans. I directed the men…it was my accomplishment. It was something that was supposed to say something about me forever. Dear Lord above, I loved that temple!

MEHITABLE: Stop it now. You know as well as me that you can't be lovin' a pile of rocks.

LILY: *(With a sigh.)* Why not?

MEHITABLE: Ain't you never once been in love with a man, Miss Lily?

LILY: *(After a moment.)* Once. Once I was.
(More thunder.)

MEHITABLE: Who with? Ain't not a single man 'round here you spend more'n a minute in his company, beyond Mr. Seely.

LILY: Oh, that ridiculous man!

MEHITABLE: *(Excitedly.)* Who then? I can't believe that you have such a secret, Miss Lily!

LILY: Oh, all right, Mehitable! *(Settling into a special memory.)* When I was a young girl—thirteen, I was that summer—I traveled abroad with Daddy and Mother to visit Cousin Melville Montfleurry at Drummond Hall in Yorkshire. Lovely, lovely Yorkshire.

MEHITABLE: Yorkshire a nice place?

LILY: Yorkshire is…well it's another world from here, Mehitable. It's like a dream. And Drummond Hall is like the heart of a dream.

MEHITABLE: Tell me about the man, Miss Lily.

LILY: Well, One day I was out exploring the gardens. Drummond Hall is an entire universe of lovely gardens. And no slaves, Mehitable!

MEHITABLE: No slaves?

LILY: Not a one.

MEHITABLE: They got black folk in Yorkshire?

LILY: Well, no. No black folk. The British don't keep slaves as we do.

MEHITABLE: Why not?

LILY: In any case, Mehitable, it was a lovely summer day in Yorkshire. Everything was green and cool and sweet-scented. I found myself sittin' beneath an old willow tree next to a brook just thinking how lovely the world can be, when suddenly I heard a terrible commotion.

MEHITABLE: What was it?

LILY: A group of boys—savage little brutes—were chasing a tiny dog, about this big *(She extends her hands to indicate a toy sized dog.)*

MEHITABLE: Oh, Miss Lily! You know I love little dogs! What did you do??

LILY: Well, the leader of the boys, a most unpleasant red-haired youth covered in freckles, caught the dog. "Cut off its head!" one of them yelled. "Cut off its tail!"

MEHITABLE: No!

LILY: Yes! I scrambled to my feet. I was going to stop those boys…no matter what. I took a step forward, when suddenly I felt a strong hand grasp my arm. A deep voice said, "You stay here, lady."

MEHITABLE: Ooooh, Miss Lily!!

LILY: And then he was past me, moving across the brook. That terrible older boy with the freckles looked up, and the look on his cruel little pinched face…it was as if he beheld the devil himself in all his finery!

MEHITABLE: Oh, save us, Miss Lily!

LILY: And then I heard that voice again, that wonderfully deep voice. "Go home, Thomas Banks. Go home, all of you. If I catch you on Drummond land again, poaching pooches, I'll have your hides for cloth." That wretched boy dropped the dog and they just ran.

MEHITABLE: This man saved the little dog?

LILY: He did, Mehitable. As if that dog was worth all the tea in China. He picked that scared little beast up in his arms and then turned to me, smiled and just before he crossed the brook, asked "Are ye fairy or are ye angel?" "Neither of those, Sir," I replied. "Nay," he said, "I'm thinking ye be both." And off he walked, into the dappled sunlight of that summer day.

MEHITABLE: Who was he?

LILY: Benjamin Strong. A tenant on the estate. A good man. Not at all like the lazy bantycocks who strut themselves around the Carolinas. A man of feeling and substance.

MEHITABLE: *(Sagely.)* So, you're in love with Benjamin Strong.

LILY: Benjamin Strong. I never even saw his face. But yes, I suppose I am in love with him or someone like him. Someone I probably will never meet.

(More thunder and lightning.)

MEHITABLE: *(After a moment.)* I am sorry 'bout your temple. Miss Lily. It was like…the heart of a dream. *(A ray of hope.)* Mister Seely is just chompin' at the bit to build you a new one. I hate sleepin' out here in this hainty old place.

(More thunder and lightning. Closer still.)

LILY: I keep telling you it isn't haunted, isn't that right, Joe? And we have to stay here. It's a matter of pride, Mehitable.

MEHITABLE: Just look where all that pride got Mister Siegfried.

(Lily chuckles despite herself.)

MEHITABLE: *(Looking off.)* Uh-oh…here come Missus!

LILY: *(As she blows out the lantern.)* Quick, Mehitable! Pretend we're sleeping and she'll go away!

(Lily and Mehitable hunker down into their blankets. More thunder and lightning. Joe rises and takes a few steps back into the darkness. Elizabeth sweeps on followed by Mr. Seely. Both hold lanterns.)

ELIZABETH: I know that you are awake, Lily. I saw you blow out the lantern not one minute ago.

(There is no response from Lily.)

ELIZABETH: Very well. Have it your way. I will address myself to your sleeping mind with the hope that some of the knowledge I impart somehow makes it into some little corner of your brain…if there is indeed room for it amid the countless plots of revenge and…such. I have been sent out here by Mammy Pam who is, of course, furious with me for letting you and Mehitable sleep out here in your ruins these last three nights. I did my best to explain that you cannot rejoin Rivermede society until Cedric's return because you, my dear, have philosophically treed yourself. This, of course, was met with great wailing and gnashing of teeth by the entire household staff with the sole exception of Old Mars who succinctly remarked: "If dem two turkey girls is stupid 'nuff to stay out in the rain, let 'em gobble." A wise sentiment with which I tend to agree. Mammy Pam, on the other hand, was not amused and as Mister Seely has so urgently pointed out, a storm is coming.

(More thunder and lightning.)

ELIZABETH: If you stubbornly persist in your peculiar little vigil, you will inevitably become soaked which will undoubtedly result in consumption and eventually, your premature and grandly lamentable demise.

(There is a tiny gasp from Mehitable.)

ELIZABETH: As for *you*, Mehitable, Mammy Pam has instructed me to command you to return to the kitchen immediately or else.

(Elizabeth waits a moment. Neither girl moves.)

ELIZABETH: Very well. You are my witness, Mr. Seely. Please note that I did all in my power to urge these two foolish young women to return to the safety and warmth of Rivermede. I will alert Mammy Pam that her orders have been woefully ignored and that disaster is sure to follow. *(Elizabeth sweeps off.)*

MR. SEELY: She's gone. You can wake up now.
(No response.)

MR. SEELY: There's a big storm coming in off the sea. You can smell it in the air. Your step-mother is right, you're both going to get drenched if you stay out here. Please let me escort you back to the house.
(No response.)

MR. SEELY: *(Bending over Lily.)* Lily, stop this nonsense. You're only making yourself appear the fool…
(A loud fake snore escapes from Lily's perfect lips. Mr. Seely steps back, angry.)

MR. SEELY: For the love of…you are taking this thing too far!
(More snores, from both women.)

MR. SEELY: This is not amusing. It's got to be said, and I'm going to say it: you're too old to be carrying on this way. Do you know what they're saying about you in the quarters?
(More snores.)

MR. SEELY: They're sayin' that you're not right…in the head…lying out here on the hard cold ground…
(More snores.)

MR. SEELY: …readin' those foolish books to Mehitable…
(Snore and giggles.)

MR. SEELY: *(Angrily.)* Then stay out here like a couple of dumb ass turkeys!

MEHITABLE: Gobble, gobble, gobble!
(Lily howls with laughter and she and Mehitable roll gleefully in their blankets.)

MR. SEELY: We'll just see how amusing you think this when that storm breaks and no one rushes out of our warm, dry beds to help you! *(Calling into the darkness.)* I see you in there, Joe. I need you at the barn. Black mare's going to foal tonight.
(The girls laugh, gobble and snore as Mr. Seely exits. There is a particularly bright flash of lightning which illuminates Joe, who follows Mr. Seely off. The girls shriek and giggle.)

LILY: *(During a loud clap of thunder, leaping to her feet with great melodrama, calling after Mr. Seely.)* Helmut! I follow Thee!

MEHITABLE: *(With matching pathos.)* I hears you, Brother Sig-freed, and Ahs a waitin' on ya! Swing low sweet chariot! *(Mehitable dies dramatically.)*

(Both girls scream with laughter. Thunder and lightning continues as the scene fades to black.

(Change to: the ruins, one week later. Lily is lounging on the stone bench, enjoying the sunshine. Somehow, she has managed to look wonderful, despite the privations associated with her new quarters.)

MEHITABLE: *(Off.)* Miss Lily! Miss Lily!

(Lily jumps up. There is a sudden commotion. Many voices, the sound of several carriages, clomping hooves etc.)

LILY: *(As Mehitable runs on stage.)* What is it?

MEHITABLE: *(Panting.)* It's Mister Cedric! Your daddy! He's home, Miss Lily! Now we can go back into the house! Praise the Lord and baby Jesus!

LILY: *(Excitedly.)* Daddy's home?

MEHITABLE: Three, four wagons pullin' up to the house! Let's go an see, Miss Lily!

(Mehitable takes Lily's hand and pulls her in the direction of the house, but Lily resists.)

LILY: Now you just wait one moment, Mehitable! I vowed that I would not set one foot outside these ruins until my father explained himself to me...

MEHITABLE: *(Whining.)* But Miss Lily....

(There is a sudden commotion off stage and both young women shriek as a strange Man suddenly appears on top of the ruins. He is dressed as the hero of a romantic adventure; complete with boots, breeches, white poet shirt and long black cape. His hair is long and tied into a pony tail. He and Lily exchange a long, meaningful look before Mr. Seely rushes on stage.)

MR. SEELY: Get down from there!

(The man leaps dramatically off stage. Lily and Mehitable scream. The man pokes his head back through a hole in the rubble and smiles at Lily.)

MR. SEELY: Excuse me, Miss Lily!

(Mr. Seely pushes past Lily to give chase. He disappears into the rubble.)

LILY: *(Furious at being pushed—no matter how lightly.)* Mr. Seely! Mr. Seely! You come back here this instant and apologize to me!

MEHITABLE: *(Fearfully.)* Who's that man, Miss Lily?

LILY: *(Noticing a microscopic tear in a flounce.)* Look at this! That savage fiend Mr. Seely has torn my dress! *(Remembering.)* Oh! That man!

MEHITABLE: Oh Lord, he comin' back!

(The stranger rushes on stage and Mehitable shrieks. The stranger bows low to Mehitable, who shrieks more loudly. Mr. Seely rushes on. The stranger

grins apologetically at the women and runs off. Lily blocks Mr. Seely as he prepares to give chase.)

LILY: Mr. Seely! I demand an explanation!

MR. SEELY: *(As he tries to push past her again.)* Not now, Lily…

LILY: *(Exploding.)* NOT NOW "LILY?" How dare you???? How dare you address me in such an insufferably familiar tone of voice??

MR. SEELY: *(Trying again to get past her.)* I've got to stop that man!

LILY: Why? Who is that man, Mr. Seely? What makes him so important to you that you feel you must brutally manhandle me and tear my clothes in what appears so far to be a failed effort to apprehend him? Explain yourself to me, Sir.
(Mr. Seely suddenly catches Lily's wrist in a tight grip and they stare at one another like two angry bobcats.)

MR. SEELY: You spoiled little…that man—the one whom you seem determined to keep me from catching—has murdered your father, *Miss* Lily, so with your kind permission…?
(Lily gasps and steps back, allowing Mr. Seely to exit quickly. She staggers back and collapses onto the bench.)

MEHITABLE: *(Rushing to her side.)* Oh, Miss Lily! Your poor Daddy!

LILY: Oh, Mehitable! What am I to do?
(The two women commence to wailing. We hear the sound of voices raised in argument. Lily and Mehitable leap to their feet in fear.)

LILY: The murderer!

MEHITABLE: We got to hide ourselves, Miss Lily!
(Without another word, Lily and Mehitable search for a hiding place in the ruins. Unable to find a suitable spot, they climb on top of the marble bench and hug each other, hiding their faces. After a moment, Cedric Montfleurry strides on stage followed by Elizabeth.)

CEDRIC: *(Off.)* Well, where is she, Elizabeth?

ELIZABETH: *(As they enter.)* She can't have gotten far, she's on foot.

CEDRIC: *(Seeing the girls.)* Aha. I thought you said she's livin' out here with Delilah…
(Cedric lightly whacks Mehitable's fanny.)

CEDRIC: Hello, Delilah.

MEHITABLE: If you dead, let go of me!

CEDRIC: Hell, I ain't dead yet, gal!

LILY: Daddy! Daddy! Thank goodness you're alive!
(Lily rushes into Cedric's arms.)

CEDRIC: Well, of course I'm alive! Why wouldn't I be?

(Mehitable looks skeptically at Cedric.)

LILY: That absurd Mr. Seely told Mehitable and I that you had been murdered!

ELIZABETH: What?!?

LILY: That's right, murdered! He was chasing that man…

ELIZABETH: What man?

LILY: That man! The one wearing the…

CEDRIC: Hold on there, honey gal. You and I have some pressin' business.

LILY: Business?

CEDRIC: Lily Marvelle Montfleurry! Just what in the name of Sam Hill are you doing out here, girl? I have just received the beratin' of my miserable life from Mammy Pam regardin' this little campin' expedition of yours. Do you suppose that's how I was lookin' forward to bein' greeted at the door of my very own home after bein' away for so long?

ELIZABETH: What man, Cedric?

LILY: *(Ignoring her.)* Well, how do you suppose I liked coming home from my visit to Charleston to find my lovely temple of Aphrodite smashed to pieces?

CEDRIC: I have already informed you that you may build yourself a new temple! If you'd busied your foolish self with such a project instead of engagin' in this heathen behavior you would already be sittin' on your fancy behind within its walls by now.

LILY: *(Through clenched teeth.)* I don't want another temple, I want this one!

CEDRIC: Well you cannot have this one!

LILY: *(Stamping her foot.)* Why not!?

CEDRIC: *(Mimicking her foot stamp.)* Because I say so, that's why!

ELIZABETH: May we please discuss the murderer?

CEDRIC: There ain't no murderer, Elizabeth! *(To Lily.)* Hell's Bells, Lily! I shudder to think what your refined and elegant Cousin Bettina would think of you livin' out here like a wild savage. Exposin' your pretty face to the elements. *(He stoops to pick up a decanter that Mehitable has pilfered from the house.)* And drinkin' my 5-Star bourbon?!?!

MEHITABLE: It got so cold the other night, Mister Cedric…

CEDRIC: You stay quiet, Delilah. You're already in trouble up to your black fanny with Mammy Pam, don't add me to your list, girl. *(Back to Lily.)* And draggin' poor Delilah down with you. For shame, Lily. For shame. Drinkin' my best bourbon and howlin' at the moon like a couple of wild women of Borneo. Was this supposed to be a temple of Aphrodite…or Beelzebub?

LILY: *(Outraged.)* Daddy!

ELIZABETH: *(Stepping forward.)* That is quite enough of that kind of talk!

CEDRIC: *(Holding up the decanter.)* When I left for England, this decanter was full!

ELIZABETH: *(Dismissively.)* That was over five months ago…

CEDRIC: But my dear, I am the only one in residence at Rivermede who drinks spirits!

(There is a snort of derision from Lily while Mehitable clamps her hands over her mouth to keep from laughing and Elizabeth rolls her eyes.)

CEDRIC: What? Why are you three women mockin' at me?

ELIZABETH: Cedric, dear: Mammy Pam uses your bourbon all the time for cooking…

CEDRIC: What? Oh, well, that's different…

ELIZABETH: AND Jemmaline, your own sister, who has been a shadow on our doorstep since the day you left has also be known to imbibe AS WELL AS Old Mars, who visits your study at exactly…

LILY AND MEHITABLE: Two o'clock!

ELIZABETH: …every afternoon for a nip NOT TO LEAVE OUT Cousin Eugene from Charleston who stopped by a few weeks back and drank himself into a stupor before grabbing his gun and heading out to find Willie's little swamp shack…

CEDRIC: Elizabeth! Not in front of Lily!

ELIZABETH: The point is, Cedric: there are many who partake of your precious bourbon and if you must know, I sent the decanter out here to Lily. It was cold, and I didn't want her to take ill.

CEDRIC: You?

ELIZABETH: Me.

CEDRIC: I see.

LILY: Pardon me, Daddy, but I believe that you still owe me an explanation for this…this horrible act of desecration!

CEDRIC: I gave you life, girl, beyond that I owe you nothin'!

LILY: *(Pulling out all the stops, with a plaintive wail.)* Daddy! How could you speak to me like that!

(Lily collapses on the bench in tears. Mehitable goes to comfort her.)

CEDRIC: Hell!

(Lily wails louder.)

CEDRIC: Now you stop that, Lily!

LILY: *(With great anguish.)* My temple! My temple!

CEDRIC: Come on, now, baby girl…don't fuss about it…gonna make your pretty face all puckered…

(Lily wails with renewed vigor.)

ELIZABETH: Oh, for Heaven's sake, Cedric! You can at least tell the poor girl why you had the men smash her temple!

(Lily smiles gratefully through her tears at Elizabeth.)

ELIZABETH: *(Directly to Lily.)* So at the very least she'll know why she's making such a damn fool out of herself.

CEDRIC: Well, I… *(Seeing someone approaching.)* …ah, good! Here comes the very reason in person!

LILY: *(Following her father's gaze.)* In person?

CEDRIC: Now, we might finally get some peace at Rivermede! *(Over his shoulder to Lily as if this scene never happened.)* You are going to love this, honey gal!

(The stranger rushes on. He goes directly to Cedric and bows low, clicking his heels.)

CEDRIC: *(Delighted.)* I just love it when he does that!

(Mr. Seely rushes on and is clearly shocked to see Cedric.)

MR. SEELY: Mr. Montfleurry!

CEDRIC: What's the matter with you, boy? You look like you've seen a ghost! *(Laughs.)* A ghost, 'Lizbeth! Ain't that a corker?

MR. SEELY: But he said…he said…

STRANGER: *(In an exotic eastern European accent, not unlike Gary Oldman's Translyvannian Twang in "Dracula.")* Please! Allow me. *(To Cedric.)* When carriage is stopping in front of lovely house this man is surprised to see me I think rather than you, Lord Cedric. And so I am telling him your message that you are telling me to tell…but I am forgetting what is coming after "dead." *(Bowing to Mr. Seely.)* Many apologies, good Lord.

CEDRIC: *(With a loud guffaw.)* Well, howdy doo! Ain't that a corker! Mr. Seely, I told our friend, here, to tell you that I was dead *tired* and ridin' in the last carriage!

STRANGER: When this good Lord is asking me how you are being made dead, I tell him that it is my fault and like a man of justice he is chasing me. *(To Mr. Seely.)* I salute you, captain!

CEDRIC: *(Hooting with laughter.)* Seely, this man kept me up all night prayin'…

LILY: Praying? You, Daddy?

CEDRIC: Not me! Him! He prays all night! Ain't that a hoot 'n holler? So, how 'bout these ruins, son? Nice and roomy, ain't they?

(The stranger nods and bows. He begins to inspect the ruins.)

CEDRIC: Wonderful! You just make yourself at home.

ELIZABETH: *(Exasperated.)* Who is this man?

LILY: Why is he sneaking around my ruins like that?

CEDRIC: Ladies, Delilah, Mr. Seely, I present to you: The Rivermede Hermit!

(The three women gape at the man who is wandering through the ruble.)

ELIZABETH: The Rivermede Hermit?

CEDRIC: *(With great joviality, like a boy with a new toy.)* That is correct, wife! Ain't he somethin'?

ELIZABETH: *(With growing concern.)* Cedric, what is going on here?

CEDRIC: Well, you see…back in England, it's all the style…

(Lily's ears prick up.)

CEDRIC: …for country estates to have their very own hermits livin' in some old ruins or the like…

ELIZABETH: Hermits?

CEDRIC: *(Gleefully.)* Hermits, Elizabeth, hermits! Gentlemen advertise for them in the news sheets!

ELIZABETH: But…why?

CEDRIC: Oh…I dunno…gives an estate a certain air of…well, it's like a *je ne ce quois* kind of thing.

ELIZABETH: But, Cedric…

CEDRIC: Cousin Melville got one last year! Damndest fella. Sits up there in the abbey ruins…

LILY: There's never been an abbey at Drummond Hall.

CEDRIC: Oh, Melville had his men build a small abbey…

LILY: And then smashed it down, like you did to my beautiful temple???

(The Hermit bends down to pick something up, his motions blocked by the cape. When he stands, we see that he holds the face of Aphrodite.)

CEDRIC: That's right, honey gal. Melville's hermit's sworn a seven year vow of silence, just like this fella's gonna soon's he takes up residence!

LILY: *(Beginning to be swept up in the romance.)* A vow of silence? Whatever for?

ELIZABETH: But *who* is he?

CEDRIC: *(Highly amused at the concept.)* I have no idea!

ELIZABETH: What!!??

(Joe has appeared silently behind Mr. Seely. He regards the Hermit with as much obvious displeasure as the overseer.)

LILY: You don't know anything about him, Daddy?

CEDRIC: I only know this, honey gal: he answered my ad for an ornamental hermit in the Daily Mail, he prays all night and he's agreed to live in our ruins for seven years without sayin' a single word to a single soul.

ELIZABETH: *(Sputtering.)* But...but...this is preposterous! Cedric! What have you done?

CEDRIC: What's eatin' at you, woman?

ELIZABETH: You bring home a perfect stranger from across the sea...a man who could be anybody...and inform us that he will be living here at Rivermede for seven years as a hermit...

CEDRIC: An *ornamental* hermit.

ELIZABETH: *(Incredulous.)* ...an *ornamental* hermit, and you don't know anything about him???

MR. SEELY: I agree with Mistress Montfleurry, Mr. Cedric.

CEDRIC: What's that, Mr. Seely?

MR. SEELY: Well, Sir, I do not like having someone at Rivermede who none of us knows anything about. He could be nothing more than a common thief, or a highwayman...

LILY: Oh, pish-posh, Mr. Seely!

MR. SEELY: It doesn't make sense to bring a total stranger into your home!

LILY: Mr. Seely, we know everything there is to know about you, but that hasn't prevented you from wantonly tearing my good New Orleans morning dress and insultin' my honor! Spoiled indeed! I do declare, you are about the most provincial man it has ever been my displeasure to encounter!

MR. SEELY: Miss Lily, that man told me your father was dead!

LILY: Daddy! I think it's wonderful to have an ornamental hermit at Rivermede!

CEDRIC: *(Taking her hands.)* Then I am forgiven for...

LILY: *(Dismissively.)* Don't give it another thought...

ELIZABETH: NOW, JUST WAIT ONE COTTON PICKING MINUTE!!! *(All are silent.)*

ELIZABETH: Cedric Montfleurry! *I* am the mistress of this plantation. As such, I have a right to know exactly...and I do mean exactly *who* is going to live in these ruins!

CEDRIC: Now, Elizabeth...

ELIZABETH: *(Turning to face the Hermit.)* Sir! *(The Hermit turns to meet Elizabeth's gaze and bows.)*

ELIZABETH: I demand that you identify yourself.

LILY: He can not, Elizabeth! He has taken a vow of silence!

ELIZABETH: Not until he takes up residence! *(To Hermit.)* Well, sir? If you expect to live here, amongst the rubble of a young girl's fevered imagination as the *(With great scorn.)* Rivermede Hermit, you must first identify yourself to me. I will harbor no strangers at Rivermede!

CEDRIC: Elizabeth!

(But the Hermit has held up his hand. He bows low before Elizabeth.)

HERMIT: Please, Lord Cedric…allow me to ease this good Lady's fears…

LILY: Your vow! Oh, Elizabeth! You've ruined it for him!

HERMIT: *(To Lily.)* No, dear Princess, she has not done this. My vow begins when I am accepted by this house. This Lady is right to want to know that I am a good man, but it is with sorrow that I must tell you I am not.

LILY: Oh!

ELIZABETH: Be quiet, Lily! Explain yourself, sir.

HERMIT: Yes, my lady. *(With great melodrama.)* I am doing penance for a wrong committed against…against…

LILY: You poor man! Elizabeth can you not see this is causing him great pain?

HERMIT: No! I must speak now and then…never again.

LILY: Never??

HERMIT: My sin was too great.

MR. SEELY: I'm certain of that!

ELIZABETH: What exactly have you done?

CEDRIC: I don't think that's any of our affair, Elizabeth!

ELIZABETH: What if he's killed someone? Do you want a murderer living at Rivermede?

LILY: But he never…just look at him, Daddy! He never could have done such a thing!

ELIZABETH: Is that your crime?

HERMIT: No, Lady. The only life I would be capable of taking is my own. My crime was that of betrayal…of one whom I loved…deeply. For this I must do penance until God sees fit to spare me from my misery. I swear to you here and now that I mean no harm to you, or to anyone in Lord Cedric's family. There, that is all I will say. As God and his angels as my witnesses, I will say no more.

ELIZABETH: Oh, yes you will!

LILY: Elizabeth!

ELIZABETH: You will say your name! Here and now you will say it to me!

(The Hermit straightens up proudly, clicks his heels and bows again.)

HERMIT: I am Count Siegfried von Zohar.

LILY: *(A soft gasp.)* Siegfried!

CEDRIC: Siegfried?

MEHITABLE: *(Seeing the look on Lily's face.)* Uh-oh, he is rizen!

CEDRIC: This ain't no time for religion, Delilah...

LILY: Oh, Daddy! You brought home a count!

ELIZABETH: Now, listen...

LILY: I can't believe it! Our very own count! From Europe!

CEDRIC: Now tell me this wasn't worth takin' down your damn temple, honey gal!

MR. SEELY: Mr. Montfleurry, I must object to this! This man is obviously...

LILY: Oh! I have to tell Cousin Suzette at Bel Mar right away! Mehitable! Run and get my writin' things ready!

MEHITABLE: Yes, Miss Lily. *(Mehitable runs off.)*

LILY: Oh, Daddy, Rivermede will be the envy of all the great houses in the Carolinas!

ELIZABETH: THAT IS ENOUGH!

CEDRIC: Oh, for...what's got your petticoats in a twist, 'Lizbeth?

ELIZABETH: Cedric Montfleurry, I agreed to this marriage because my father thought our family coffers would benefit from an agricultural investment. You agreed to it because you were broke. May I now remind you of the actual agreement?

CEDRIC: There's no need to drag out that business now, Elizabeth...

ELIZABETH: I think there is. I think you need to be reminded who is in control of Rivermede.

LILY: Don't let her send Siegfried away, Daddy!

CEDRIC: You only control the business end! The contract I made with your daddy says nothin' about how I choose to decorate my own plantation!

ELIZABETH: Human beings are not decorations!!!

CEDRIC: They are if I say they are! This is the South, woman, don't you forget it.

MR. SEELY: This is a madhouse in the South.

CEDRIC: Now, now, Mr. Seely.

ELIZABETH: *(To Siegfried.)* Do you see what you've gotten yourself into?
(Siegfried contemplates her in silence.)

ELIZABETH: You're not a person to them, you're just a...a...diversion!

LILY: Elizabeth! That just isn't so! *(To Siegfried.)* Don't listen to her!
(Siegfried contemplates her in silence.)

CEDRIC: *(Hooting with laughter.)* Hell, he ain't gonna say nothin' honey gal, sure as his word! Ain't that a corker?

ELIZABETH: *(To Siegfried.)* If this is your penance, you must be beyond redemption. Good day, "Count."
(Elizabeth starts to exit and then turns to Mr. Seely.)

ELIZABETH: Mr. Seely?

MR. SEELY: Yes, ma'am?

ELIZABETH: You better come along with me. There's still a plantation to run.

MR. SEELY: For the moment. *(To Lily, sarcastically.)* I am sorry about your dress, Miss Lily. Hopefully you can find another that pleases you in your vast collection.

LILY: Mr. Seely, I can only hope that you may somehow be influenced by this noble man you see before you and take your own vow of silence.

ELIZABETH: Oh, and Cedric?

CEDRIC: What's that, 'Lizbeth?

ELIZABETH: Welcome home.

(Elizabeth and Mr. Seely exit.)

CEDRIC: I swear that woman could take the sparkle off a ten carat diamond!

LILY: I am so glad that you are finally home! It has been deadly here without you, Daddy. Deadly.

CEDRIC: I don't suppose you might be interested in seein' what I brought back from your Cousin Bettina's Parisian dressmaker, would you, honey gal?

LILY: *(With a squeal.)* Oh, Daddy!

CEDRIC: Well, come on! Mammy Pam's just lying in wait for you to come back in the house. Better do it on my arm than by yourself.

LILY: *(Remembering.)* Oh! The Count!

CEDRIC: What about him?

(They turn to see that Siegfried is contentedly exploring his ruins.)

LILY: *(Calling.)* Good day to you, Count Von Zohar!

(Siegfried looks up, clicks his heels and bows.)

CEDRIC: I just love it when he does that! Come on, honey gal. *(As they exit.)* We've got to do something about his clothes.

LILY: Why? What's wrong with his clothes?

CEDRIC: Well, your Uncle Melville's hermit wears himself…well, it's kind of a hair shirt *(Laughs.)* …he sits out there in the ruins scratchin' at himself all day, just like one of Jemmaline's Coon Hounds.

LILY: Oh, Daddy! Poor Count Von Zohar has already suffered enough…

CEDRIC: How about burlap?

LILY: Well…

(And they are gone. Siegfried surreptitiously watches as they depart. Now he and Joe are left alone on stage. When he is certain that the Montfleurrys are out of sight, he lets out a long breath and collapses on the bench. He reaches into his cloak and pulls out the book that Lily tossed into the ruins the night of the storm. He contemplates the cover with a smile. He looks up to see Joe

watching him intently. He smiles at Joe and salutes before settling down to read. Blackout.)

(Change to: The ruins, that night. Siegfried has struck a commanding pose in the moonlight atop the ruins. He surveys the night pensively. Joe sits in the shadows, watching him. After a moment, Lily enters carrying a basket. She looks to make sure that she hasn't been followed. Siegfried watches her in silence.)

LILY: *(Peering into the darkness and whispering.)* Count? Is that you up there, Count Von Zohar?
(Siegfried leaps down from his perch on the ruins, causing Lily to gasp. He kneels in front of her and bows his head.)

LILY: Oh! I…please, stand…your grace. Do not kneel, I beg you.
(Siegfried indicates that he should always be on his knees while in the presence of one so lovely.)

LILY: Please, sir, you are embarrassing me!
(Siegfried reluctantly rises and indicates that they should sit on the bench.)

LILY: *(Hesitating while she eyes the bench.)* Well…I…
(Siegfried indicates more firmly that she should sit.)

LILY: Very well, just for a moment. It's sugar time in the house and everyone knows I don't care for sweets after dinner, I therefore will not be missed until after Daddy's cigar, so…
(She sits, as does Siegfried. She holds the basket on her lap, all too aware of her close proximity to the handsome stranger.)

LILY: *(After a moment.)* My, it's…it's a lovely night.
(Siegfried indicates his agreement as he stares with great intensity into her eyes.)

LILY: I…it's…warm, for this time of year.
(Siegfried continues to stare with great intensity into her eyes.)

LILY: *(Faintly.)* Oh dear, they're green aren't they? *(Looking away, embarrassed.)* Does it…get this…warm where you come from? *(Before he can respond.)* Of course not. I'm certain it must be quite cold in your native…I mean the place you're from.
(Siegfried smiles and pantomimes being cold, blowing on his hands as if to warm them.)

LILY: Yes, I'm certain that it must get very cold in the Prussian Alps.
(Siegfried looks at her quizzically.)

LILY: Your native land, sir.
(Siegfried smiles and nods. He then takes Lily's hands very slowly and very

seductively in his own, raises them to his lips, and blows gently on them. Lily gives a little gasp as he gently relieves her of the basket and smiles.)

LILY: Oh! The basket. Yes, I brought it for you.

(Siegfried lifts the cloth and examines the contents.)

LILY: I knew you must be ravenous after your long journey so I had Mammy Pam make you up a supper. There's ham and some chicken, and a nice big piece of Mammy Pam's corn bread, some cheese and a slice of peach pie.

(Siegfried indicates that Lily is the best. He then pulls a dark bottle out of the basket.)

LILY: Oh, that's some of Daddy's best port.

(Siegfried indicates that Lily is the absolute best.)

LILY: I thought it would help to keep you…warm…out here in the ruins… but it seems to be fairly…warm out here, does it not?

(Without taking his eyes off Lily, Siegfried yanks the cork out of the bottle with his teeth.)

LILY: *(Transfixed.)* Oh!

(Siegfried then takes a huge gulp of the port. Some dribbles down his chin and he wipes it on his sleeve.)

LILY: *(Impulsively reaching out with hankie.)* Here, let me. *(Lily gently wipes his face with her hankie, staring helplessly into his eyes as she does so. As she cleans his face.)* I can not imagine what horrible twist of fate has brought you to Rivermede, sir, but I can assure you that we will see to your needs. You have only to ask…

(Siegfried catches Lily's hand in his own. She starts but remains glued to the bench. Slowly, he raises her hand to his lips and kisses it.)

LILY: *(Faintly.)* Oh my.

(Siegfried smiles at Lily and takes another healthy swig from the bottle. Lily has reclaimed her hand and holds it to her heaving bosom. Elizabeth enters quietly with Mr. Seely, who starts to rush to the bench and is stopped by her firm hand. She indicates for him to be quiet and listen.)

LILY: I had no idea how thirsty you are. I should have brought two bottles.

(Siegfried indicates that he thinks that's a pretty good idea.)

LILY: After all, why shouldn't you enjoy a little wine in your silence?

(Siegfried indicates "exactly.")

LILY: *(As Siegfried moves in to kiss her.)* Especially on such a warm…hot night…

(Siegfried is just about to kiss Lily.)

MR. SEELY: *(Unable to restrain himself.)* That tears it!

(Mr. Seely rushes at the bench. Lily utters a shriek and leaps to her feet. Siegfried has spun to face Mr. Seely with a smile, indicating that he'd love an opportunity to settle their differences, as in: "you wanna a piece of me? go for it!")

ELIZABETH: Stop this!

MR. SEELY: You've had this coming, Hermit!

(Mr. Seely prepares to charge, but Lily forces herself between the two snarling men.)

LILY: No! I will not have this, Mr. Seely!

MR. SEELY: Stand aside, Miss Lily. This is between me and your father's hermit!

LILY: Stop this at once!

MR. SEELY: *(Focusing on Lily.)* I implore you, Lily, stand aside. Stand aside or I shall be forced to…to…

LILY: To what, Mr. Seely? Hold your breath until your face turns blue?

MR. SEELY: Or I will be forced to manhandle you!

LILY:	MR. SEELY:
Oh! You impertinent, odious, ridiculous…	What you need is a spanking!

ELIZABETH: That is quite enough!

LILY:	MR. SEELY:
A spanking! How dare you?!?	I'd love to do it myself!

ELIZABETH: Mr. Seely, kindly escort Miss Lily back to the house.

LILY:	MR. SEELY:
You can't expect me to…	I'm not a nursemaid…

ELIZABETH: ENOUGH!! Lily, return to the house immediately. Mr. Seely, go with her and make sure she avoids further trouble.

MR. SEELY: *(Sputtering.)* But this man…

ELIZABETH: Is to be left to me, Mr. Seely. Do you understand? To me.

MR. SEELY: But…

ELIZABETH: Mr. Seely! If you cannot comprehend such a simple instruction, I must confess my doubt as to whether or not you are capable of performing the duties of overseer of Rivermede Plantation. Do you or do you not understand what I require?

MR. SEELY: *(With great spleen, through clenched teeth.)* I understand.

ELIZABETH: Good! Now, take Miss Lily and make sure that she goes in the house and into the parlor before Cedric finishes his cigar. Lily?

(Lily turns to Siegfried.)

LILY: I wish to apologize for the barbaric actions of Mr. Seely.

(Siegfried indicates that no harm was done.)

LILY: Good night, then, Your Grace.

MR. SEELY: Oh, for the love of…

ELIZABETH: Now, Mr. Seely.

MR. SEELY: *(To Siegfried.)* This isn't over, Hermit.

ELIZABETH: It is for tonight, Mr. Seely. Now take Miss Lily to the house.

MR. SEELY: *(To Joe.)* Joe, walk along with us, boy. There's a loose shutter bangin' on Mr. Cedric's study.

JOE: Yassuh.

LILY: *(To Siegfried.)* Good night.

(Siegfried bows to Lily. She turns to leave and freezes when she sees that Mr. Seely and Joe are waiting for her.)

LILY: You may both walk behind me. I will not be escorted to my very own home like a prisoner being dragged to the guillotine in shackles! *(Lily sweeps by the men and exits.)*

(Mr. Seely gives Siegfried a last pointed look and exits with Joe. Elizabeth watches them for a moment and then turns to confront Siegfried, who is eyeing her speculatively.)

ELIZABETH: You and I must achieve an understanding

(Siegfried continues to stare expectantly at Elizabeth.)

ELIZABETH: Let us put our cards on the table…you do understand the metaphor?

(Siegfried slowly nods.)

ELIZABETH: *(Taking a step closer to Siegfried.)* Good. Then here is my hand: I run this plantation. Not Cedric, not Mr. Seely not some unknown male person whom you haven't yet encountered. Me. This is my…investment, my fiefdom.

(Siegfried smiles at the word "fiefdom.")

ELIZABETH: Because he is my husband, I feel qualified to offer the following: Cedric Montfleurry is a jackass…no, he's like a magpie, do you know what a magpie is?

(Siegfried shakes his head "no.")

ELIZABETH: Oh, it's a big fancy black bird that talks and talks and likes shiny things. A magpie will swoop into an open window if he sees something shiny inside. A magpie's nest is chockablock full of shiny, useless things. *(She begins to move closer to Siegfried.)* Now, you are Cedric's newest shiny thing, aren't you? He's brought you back to his nest at great cost and great risk. After all, you simply responded to his ad in a London news sheet. You could be anyone, couldn't you? Anyone in the world…with one definite exception. *(She is now standing directly in front of Siegfried, their bodies are nearly touching.)* You are certainly not a count and your real name certainly isn't Siegfried von Zohar. My guess, is that you are some petty criminal—a pickpocket, or a burglar, perhaps—undoubtedly from the East End of London, who found a discarded news sheet one day and saw an opportunity to improve his lot and did so. This makes you a man who simply takes what he wants, and therefore a dangerous individual.

(Both Elizabeth and Siegfried are concentrating intently on the other, both trying to get a reading.)

ELIZABETH: I will host no dangerous individuals here at Rivermede, so you may consider yourself on borrowed time. I will rid myself of you at my first opportunity. Am I clear?

(Siegfried continues to study her face.)

ELIZABETH: In the meantime, you are to avoid Lily. You will shun her company as if she had the plague…or worse. I see that it has taken you less than five hours to assess and exploit the foolish girl's romantic nature and I simply will not stand for it.

(Siegfried begins to indicate his innocence, but Elizabeth continues like a steamroller.)

ELIZABETH: Fortunately, *I* have no such nature, so similar chicanery will *not* work on me.

(They stare at one another for a moment, each assessing the other. Elizabeth's gaze is bold and determined whereas Siegfried's is intense and without emotion.)

ELIZABETH: Very well, then. I have done you the courtesy of revealing my hand. You have heard and understood my intention of expelling you from the plantation as soon as our magpie grows weary of his new shiny thing and that, sir, may happen far more quickly than you may think. *(She espies the basket sitting by the bench.)* In the meantime, you won't be needing this. *(She retrieves the basket.)* Cedric has declared that you are to enjoy a purely vegetarian diet—to hasten the purification of your soul. *(She holds out a small sack.)* Collard greens, turnip roots and a few carrots, I believe. Oh, and you'll find plenty of water in the well by the slaves' quarters.

(When Siegfried doesn't make a move to accept the sack she shrugs and tosses it onto the bench.)

ELIZABETH: There you are, sir. Good night to you.

(Before Elizabeth can turn to leave, Siegfried's arm shoots out of his cape and captures her in a vise-like grip.)

ELIZABETH: Let go of me!

(Siegfried ignores this and pulls Elizabeth roughly to him, so that their bodies are touching. He gazes down into her face and regards her mounting fury with amusement. Without taking his eyes off of hers, Siegfried reaches into the basket and skillfully removes the bottle of port. He then releases the sputtering Elizabeth and bows mockingly.)

ELIZABETH: If...if you ever touch me again..

(Siegfried indicates that he is shocked and hurt that she would think so poorly of him. He's just a nice boy from the Prussian Alps, after all.)

ELIZABETH: *(Collecting herself.)* I repeat myself: You are on borrowed time.

(Elizabeth turns and begins to march off the stage.)

(Siegfried begins to laugh. Elizabeth whirls around, enraged.)

ELIZABETH: Don't you dare laugh at me!

(He continues to laugh as he takes a swig from the bottle. Elizabeth's eyes narrow and she takes a step back toward Siegfried.)

ELIZABETH: All right, laugh. Laugh all you want, but remember this: just because you're a nice white boy doesn't mean you're going to have an easy time of it here in the South, especially when you're wandering our country roads, destitute and homeless. You are a world away from wherever it was that you started. You are going to discover that our funny little caste system is far more complex than the one participated in by the Hindu people of the Queen's India. The day you leave Rivermede you will do so with empty pockets and an empty stomach. What you will be forced to do in order to fill them could easily break a pretty-faced petty thief like you. I have no idea what you were endeavoring to escape when you fooled Cedric into bringing you here, but I can tell you this: you headed in the wrong direction. This is South Carolina, sir, and we have more slaves here in our tiny little district than anywhere else on earth. You have landed inside a powder keg. This, my friend, is Hell on earth. Let me be the first to bid you welcome. *(Elizabeth turns and exits.)*

(Siegfried has stopped laughing. He watches Elizabeth as she departs and then walks thoughtfully to the bench. He sets the bottle down and picks up the sack of vegetables. He reaches in and pulls out a sorry-looking carrot. He turns to look after Elizabeth, smiles and takes a bite. Blackout.)

END OF ACT I

ACT II

The ruins. The next day. It is early in the morning. We hear a commotion in the distance. After a moment, Siegfried rushes on stage pursued by Mr. Seely.

MR. SEELY: Come back here, Hermit!
(Siegfried quickly climbs up the side of the ruined temple and brandishes a large piece of marble.)

MR. SEELY: Come down from there, boy!
(Siegfried raises the piece of marble higher.)

MR. SEELY: Go ahead and throw it. Come on!
(Siegfried hesitates.)

MR. SEELY: That's right. If you miss, you have no options. The way I see things, Hermit, you have no options anyway. Now get on down from there and hand over what you stole.
(Siegfried maintains his position.)

MR. SEELY: You don't understand the way things work around here, do you?
(Siegfried remains silent.)

MR. SEELY: Then let me tell you the way things work. I am Mr. Seely, the overseer. You know what that means? They have overseers where you come from, Hermit?
(After a moment, Siegfried shakes his head "no.")

MR. SEELY: Don't give me that. I know exactly where you're from, Hermit. I'm a country boy meself—in case you couldn't tell—and I know the look of the old sod when I see it. Where's your family, Hermit? Cork? Donegal?
(Siegfried shakes his head no.)

MR. SEELY: Have it your way, Hermit. I know who and what you are. Who I am is Mr. Seely. What I am is the overseer, and that makes me just like the master of the county workhouse back home, only here, in the Carolinas, the overseer tends to slaves. Slaves run the Carolinas, who in turn feed the cotton mills back home. Slaves, boy. Working the cotton, cooking their food wiping their babies' behinds…and it's my job—the overseer's job—to make sure that the slaves do what they're supposed to. If they laze, run or steal, they get this. *(He touches the bullwhip strapped to his side.)* Now, the way I figure things, you were bought by Mr. Montfleurry just the same as any slave. That makes you my responsibility, boy-o. Mine.

(Without warning, Siegfried leaps down from his spot to confront Mr. Seely, whom he happens to tower over. The two men begin to circle each other.)

MR. SEELY: You're just a pet around here. Around *here!* Right here, these ruins, Hermit. You leave the ruins, you're mine, understand? You go creeping and crawling up at the main house like you did this morning and you're mine! You steal something from the main house like you did this morning and you taste this!

(Mr. Seely pulls the whip from his waist. He draws back the whip and cracks it, but Siegfried catches it easily and yanks it out of the younger man's grasp.)

MR. SEELY: Damn you!

(Siegfried considers the bullwhip with distaste.)

LILY: *(Offstage.)* Mr. Seely!

(Both men turn and look in the direction of the main house. Siegfried hands the whip back to Mr. Seely with an evil grin and immediately assumes a kneeling position before him, hands clasped in front of him in a gesture of beseeching. Lily rushes on in her elaborate night gown and shawl followed by Mehitable.)

LILY: Mr. Seely! What in the name of God above are you doing to this poor man? *(Seeing the whip.)* Mr. Seely! *(She grabs the whip.)* Why you…barbarian! How dare you? How dare you whip this poor man after all he's been through?

MR. SEELY: But, Miss Lily…

LILY: Don't you "Miss Lily" me, you…you…libertine! It's you who should be whipped!

MEHITABLE: Miss Lily!

LILY: What is it, Mehitable?

MEHITABLE: It's your Daddy, Miss Lily! He's a comin' along with Missus!

(Lily whirls to look where Mehitable is pointing.)

LILY: Good! Let them come! Let my father see what a violent criminal he has in his employ!

MR. SEELY: Listen to reason, Lily, for once in your life…

LILY: Listen to what? When have you ever once had anything remotely interesting to say, Mr. Seely?

(Cedric stomps on followed by Elizabeth. Cedric is dressed in a nightshirt and dressing robe whereas Elizabeth is already dressed for the day.)

CEDRIC: Lily! Just what the hell do you think you are doin' out here paradin' around these young men in your private pieces?

LILY:	MR. SEELY:
Daddy! Mr. Seely was trying to…	Mr. Montfleurry, this hermit of yours was…

CEDRIC: Hold on there! Hold on! Now don't go jabberin' at me like a pack of hyenas! Lily! What are you don' out here in your never-sees? Delilah, run and fetch somethin' for Miss Lily to wear!

MEHITABLE: Yes, sir. *(Mehitable exits.)*

LILY: *(With a disdainful sniff for Mr. Seely.)* Father, I was awakened this morning by the sound of a struggle...

CEDRIC: A struggle you say?

LILY: Yes, Daddy, a struggle.

CEDRIC: What kind of a struggle...

ELIZABETH: Oh, let her tell the damn story!

CEDRIC: Elizabeth, I must object to your use of profanity in my presence!

ELIZABETH: *(In exasperation, imitating Lily.)* Oh, Cedric honey, let her tell the silly old story.

CEDRIC: That's better. Lily?

LILY: I heard a struggle, Daddy. Just a plain old struggle.

CEDRIC: Where?

LILY: In the house.

CEDRIC: In the house, you say?

LILY: Yes, Daddy, in the house.

CEDRIC: What part of the house?

LILY: The kitchen, I think.

CEDRIC: The upper kitchen or the lower...

ELIZABETH: Oh, for the love of...Mr. Seely, will you kindly explain?
(Mehitable enters with dress for Lily. She helps her into it over the following.)

MR. SEELY: Yes, ma'am. This morning, when I was heading out to the east field...

LILY: I'm sure whatever this man has to say is a lie.

ELIZABETH: Lily...

MR. SEELY: I am certain that Mr. Montfleurry knows that I would never mis-speak the truth.

CEDRIC: If there's one thing about this boy, it's that he don't speak nothin' unless it's the truth.

LILY: No matter how un-fascinating it is.

ELIZABETH: Will you please continue, Mr. Seely...disregarding further interruptions, if you please?

MR. SEELY: When I was heading out to the east fields this morning, I saw this man sneaking around the side of the house...

CEDRIC: The house?

ELIZABETH: Yes, Cedric! He said the house!

MR. SEELY: I followed along after him, and caught him trying to climb in the kitchen window.

CEDRIC: The upper kitchen or the…

ELIZABETH: Cedric!

MR. SEELY: I saw him grab something that must have been just inside the window, and then I made my presence known. We struggled…

CEDRIC: Aha! A struggle! You hear that, 'Lizbeth? Most likely the very struggle that woke you up, Lily darlin'.

MR. SEELY: …and I chased him here…

LILY: Where you commenced to bullwhippin' the poor man!

MR. SEELY: I never did!

LILY: Liar! I saw you with my own eyes!

MR. SEELY: Mehitable!

MEHITABLE: Yes, suh?

MR. SEELY: You were right behind Miss Lily, did you see me use the whip?

LILY: Don't you dare say a word, Mehitable!

CEDRIC: Besides, if she was behind Lily, she couldn't have seen anything…

ELIZABETH: *(Zeroing in on Siegfried.)* You!
(Siegfried leaps to his feet and bows formally in front of Elizabeth.)

ELIZABETH: Have you been whipped?
(Siegfried catches Mr. Seely's eye and winks before shaking his head "no.")

ELIZABETH: Well, that's a relief.

LILY: I am sure this brave man is just trying to save Mr. Seely's honor, such as it is.

ELIZABETH: *(Ignoring Lily.)* Were you trying to get in the kitchen?
(Siegfried thinks and then nods "yes.")

ELIZABETH: Why?
(Siegfried begins an elaborate pantomime.)

ELIZABETH: You were looking for Mr. Cedric?
("No." More pantomime.)

ELIZABETH: Did you wish to speak to someone?
("No." More pantomime.)

LILY: Don't be ridiculous, Elizabeth. He's taken a vow of silence, he can't speak to anyone!
(More pantomime.)

ELIZABETH: Were you looking for something to write on?
("No." More pantomime.)

LILY: Did you want a book to read? Rivermede has a well-stocked library, though we're weak in the classics…

("No." More pantomime.)

ELIZABETH: What then? Why were you trying to climb in the kitchen window?

("I wasn't trying to climb in the window.")

ELIZABETH: Then what were you trying to do?

("I was trying to find…")

CEDRIC: *(Highly amused.)* Damn, this boy is a three-cent hoot! Ain't he, honey girl?

ELIZABETH: What? What were you trying to find?

MEHITABLE: *(Suddenly realizing.)* He's prayin'!

("That's it! You got it!")

LILY: Praying?

MEHITABLE: Mr. Siegfried be lookin' for a place to say his prayers.

("BINGO!")

LILY: Of course! You were looking for a chapel!

("Bingo again!")

CEDRIC: That's unfortunate, son. We ain't got us a chapel here at Rivermede. Gonna have to do your prayin' out here in God's glory.

LILY: No! We can build a chapel!

ELIZABETH: Oh, for heaven's sake.

LILY: We can, we can! Daddy said I could build a new temple, so that's what I'm going to do! *(Turning to Mr. Seely.)* I've decided that I want a nice small chapel built on the other side of the garden, Mr. Seely. I will begin drawing up the plans today.

MR. SEELY: What?! You can't believe this…this stranger, Miss Lily! I tell you he was sneakin' around the house! If all he wanted was a place to pray, why didn't he just walk right up to the front door?

(Siegfried pantomimes sleeping.)

LILY: Because, unlike some people, Count Von Zohar doesn't enjoy rousing young ladies from their early morning sleep!

MR. SEELY: Then why did he steal something from inside the kitchen?

LILY: You have no proof that he did any such thing! Honestly, Mr. Seely! I wouldn't blame the Count if he challenged you to a duel this very day! *(Siegfried holds up his hands. He then reaches into his cloak and withdraws a piece of cornbread.)*

LILY: There! There you are, Mr. Seely! Pilfered corn bread…

CEDRIC: Corn bread, you say?

LILY: Yes, Daddy. Cornbread from the big pan Mammy Pam makes for the field workers every single morning!

CEDRIC: Now hold on there. Cornbread ain't officially sanctioned dietary material for the Rivermede Hermit!

LILY: *(To Siegfried.)* May I, sir?

CEDRIC: Just roots…for purification!

(Siegfried hands the cornbread to Lily with a bow.)

LILY: Thank you, Sir. I will personally see to it that you are fed a proper breakfast. *(Whirling to face a stricken Mr. Seely.)* Here! Take it!

(When Mr. Seely fails to respond, Lily takes his hand and presses the cornbread into it.)

LILY: The stolen property, Mr. Seely! The impure non-sanctioned dietary material! I have recovered it for you! Now, be a good boy and take it back to Mammy Pam who I am certain is in a state for want of this piece of cornbread!

CEDRIC: Looks like you stepped in it boy!

LILY: Come, Mehitable. We must arrange for the Count's meals and then get started on plans for his chapel.

ELIZABETH: *His* chapel?

MR. SEELY: I will not waste men and materials building a chapel for a thief and a liar!

LILY: You will do as I say, Mr. Seely!

MR. SEELY: I will not!

CEDRIC: Now, now…

LILY: Daddy, this man has insulted the very heart of me!

CEDRIC: Come on, honey gal. You know this boy's the best overseer we've ever had at Rivermede.

LILY: He's a beast!

MR. SEELY: Spoiled brat!

ELIZABETH: This is giving me a headache.

JEMMA: *(Off.)* Hoo-hoo! Cedric!

LILY: Speakin' of headaches.

JEMMA: *(Off.)* Hoo-hoo!

CEDRIC: What…? *(Squinting.)* Who's that sposed to be?

LILY: *(Glumly.)* It's Aunt Jemmaline.

CEDRIC: Who?

ELIZABETH: Your sister.

CEDRIC: Hell, woman! I've been gone from my home for half a year! None of you look the way I remember!

(Jemmaline Montfleurry enters hurriedly. She is in quite a state.)

JEMMA: Cedric! My god, Cedric!

CEDRIC: *(Opening his arms.)* My darlin' little sister!

JEMMA: *(Catching her breath, ignoring his offer of embrace.)* I came as soon as I heard! Terrible, terrible news. Hello, Lily…Elizabeth.

LILY: You are looking quite fetching today, Aunt Jemma.

JEMMA: What? Oh, this? Last year's finery, my dear. But, my goodness let me get it out! Terrible, terrible news. I came as soon as I… *(Noticing Siegfried.)* …as I…well, now. Just who in the hell is this?

ELIZABETH: That is the Rivermede Hermit.

CEDRIC: Ain't he a corker, sister?

LILY: He's a count.

MR. SEELY: *(Muttering under his breath.)* And I'm a the Duke of shagging Gloucester.

JEMMA: *(Not able to take her eyes off Siegfried.)* A who?

LILY: From the Prussian Alps.

JEMMA: *(Accepting this last bit as definitive.)* Oh. Well, my…oh yes! I came to tell you the terrible, terrible news…it's just a dreadful shock… *(Back to Siegfried.)* Oh, my. The Prussian Alps, did you say?

ELIZABETH: What terrible news?

JEMMA: *(Taking Siegfried's arm and beginning to stroll.)* You know, I once knew a man who was from the alps…

CEDRIC: Good Lord, not the alps!

JEMMA: …but I do not believe they were Prussian…Westfalian, perhaps… yes, Westfalian. Cedric, do you remember that charming man we encountered at that spa father took mother to for treatment of her little rash thing…oh, yes! Of course. *(With a harsh pronunciation.)* Herr Schlagger, was the man's name. Otto…or something to that effect, yes. Pippo, perhaps? Does that sound like an alpine name to you, Count? Pippo Schlagger? Do you remember him, Cedric? He wore that funny green hat with a peacock's feather and had that adorable little monkey that he kept in his…oh! Do you suppose it was the monkey whose name was Pippo? That would certainly seem to…of course. I remember now. They used to come to dinner together as Msrs. Otto und Pippo Schlagger! Remember, Cedric? The major domo would call it out…oh, what a ghastly little man he was! Remember, Cedric? He had absurdly red hair and that frightening mole…or was it a growth? Well, it was right on his forehead, wasn't it? In any case, he would call out their names, Otto's and Pippo's, every night when they arrived in the dining room! Otto and the monkey would sit quite happily by themselves and share every bite of that awful Teutonic food…oh, Count, I mean no disrepect to your native cuisine, but...*dampfnoodle* is quite a culinary tragedy, is it not? How the monkey ever managed to get it down...oh, but of course he had his own little beer stein! We just laughed and laughed, remember? Ah, well. That was a long time ago, when laughter sprang so naturally from our lips. I don't suppose you know Herr Schlagger, do you Count...? No, of course you would not, after all, you are from the Prussian Alps and he was from the Westfalian Alps. Cedric and I were introduced to him when we were quite young and you seem to be quite young now, so you couldn't possibly be acquainted with him, or with his monkey. His children, perhaps...or the monkey's. Monkey's do have children, do they not? Yes, I am quite certain that poor Herr Schlagger is quite deceased by this time, and Pippo, if that was his name, as well, of course...although one can never be too certain in these matters, don't you agree?

(Everyone has been rendered mute by Jemma's diatribe.)

ELIZABETH: *(Recovering.)* What terrible news, Jemmaline?

JEMMA: What's that, Elizabeth?

CEDRIC: Why, Jemmaline you came a scamperin' into the garden not five minutes ago jabberin' and snackin' your jaw about something...

JEMMA: Cedric Montfleurry! That is certainly no way to conduct your verbal self whilst in the presence of a guest...a Prussian count, to say the very least!

CEDRIC: Oh, he ain't no guest, sister...

LILY: Count Von Zohar has taken a vow of silence, Aunt Jemmaline.

JEMMA: A who? Shout into this ear, child.

LILY: A vow of silence!

CEDRIC: He's my new ornamental hermit! First one in Beaufort County!

JEMMA: An ornamental hermit?

CEDRIC: That's the ticket.

JEMMA: Not a practical hermit?

CEDRIC: Nope. Ornamental.

JEMMA: Who doesn't say anything?

CEDRIC: Correct.

JEMMA: Who is also a count from the Westfalian Alps?

LILY: Prussian.

MR. SEELY: The man's a common thief!

JEMMA: A what?

LILY: Mr. Seely! Kindly refrain from expressing yourself in what is obviously a family discussion! Have you no cotton crop to tend?

MR. SEELY: But the man is a thief!

LILY: Of a tiny little piece of cornbread! Why, I once stole an entire cigar from Daddy's humidor...

CEDRIC: What's that?? A cigar, you say??

LILY: Yes, Daddy, from Cuba! I think that makes me worse than this poor man, don't you agree, Mr. Seely? A cornbread thief and a cigar thief all in the same place! Watch out that you all aren't found dead in your beds by morning!

JEMMA: Well, that certainly isn't encouraging...Oh! Yes, I nearly forgot! Cedric! I came as soon as I heard...

ELIZABETH: *(Nearing exhaustion.)* Finally.

CEDRIC: What's gotten you spooked, Jemma gal? You look as though you've seen Uncle Bouvier's shade!

JEMMA: Oh, is he still floatin' around? I thought he passed over!

ELIZABETH: Please, Jemmaline, try to concentrate.

JEMMA: I remember when he appeared in the ballroom that night at Marshwood, why I thought I would expire!

ELIZABETH: Jemma...

JEMMA: I mean, he was floatin' above the parquets with those awful red glowin' eyes...

CEDRIC: The news, woman!

JEMMA: What?

ELIZABETH: The terrible, terrible news?

JEMMA: Oh, yes! Tragedy has struck Beaufort County!

LILY: What?

JEMMA: Poor Adele and Deliah MacGregor!

LILY: The twins??

JEMMA: The very same! Those poor twin girls...

CEDRIC: All right, then! This sounds like women's talk. Come along, Mr. Seely...

JEMMA: No! Cedric, wait! This concerns everyone!

ELIZABETH: Is there any way we could entice you to simply tell us what has happened, Jemmaline?

JEMMA: Well, certainly, Elizabeth. No need for Northern airs.

LILY: Oh, please tell us what has happened, Aunt Jemma!

JEMMA: Well, those two poor girls were coming home in the early hours after the Spinner's Summer Ball...

LILY: *(Aghast.)* There was a ball at Rock Hill??

JEMMA: Oh, yes indeed, Lily. Night before last. It was lovely.

LILY: Why was I not invited???

JEMMA: I have no idea, Lily. It's a shame, though, for I cannot recall ever seeing Rock Hill look so...well, it was enchanted, I suppose that is the word, enchanted.

LILY: But Sally Spinner always invites me to functions at Rock Hill!

JEMMA: Come to think of it, Lily, people were remarking at your absence.

ELIZABETH: Lily, I'm sure that your invitation to the Spinner's ball was with the letters I sent to you in Charleston...

LILY: Another empty victory for you, Elizabeth!

JEMMA: Let me tell it! Let me tell it!

CEDRIC: Tell it, sister!

JEMMA: Well, I left Rock Hill well after midnight, but the young people, including poor Adele and Deliah were still dancing. By the time the MacGregor girls headed home it was nearly dawn.

LILY: What happened to them?

JEMMA: Just as their carriage was passing over the creek down by Johnson's old sheep meadow a man stepped into the road on the other side of the bridge and shouted "Stand and deliver!"

CEDRIC: Stand and deliver? Stand and deliver what?

ELIZABETH: *(Shooting a quick look at Siegfried.)* He was robbing them, Cedric.

JEMMA: Indeed he was!

LILY: Robbing them of what?

JEMMA: Why, their jewels, Lily, dear.

LILY: Oh, no! Adele wasn't wearing that heavy blue sapphire, was she?

JEMMA: The very same. He jumped right into the carriage and...and...well, he helped himself.

CEDRIC: To what? The jewels or...

JEMMA: *(Tragically.)* Both! After his gloved hands removed their jewels from their ears, necks and...

LILY: He...touched them??

JEMMA: *(Erotically thrilled by the thought.)* Yes! What is worse is that after he had helped himself to their treasured possessions...he...he...kissed them...

LILY: Kissed them???

JEMMA: On the lips...and said, "Thank you, lovely ladies, go home to your beds and dream of me."

LILY: He said that?

JEMMA: He did! He then leaped from the carriage and said, "For I will be visiting the womenfolk of Beaufort County until my needs are met."

CEDRIC: (Outraged.) His needs???

ELIZABETH: Surely those girls were being driven by someone! Why didn't the driver come to their aid?

JEMMA: This is the worst part…except for those two poor girls being ravaged…the poor old nigra, a free man, who was driving them had himself a heart attack when the bandit rose out of the darkness on the other side of that bridge. Fell over dead.

LILY: Dead!

JEMMA: Those poor girls had to drive themselves all the way back to Mount Royale, and you know Angus MacGregor's horses! Why, that roan gelding of his near killed six men on that awful day, remember, Cedric? The one with the white blaze and the piebald eye? Such a mean-spirited animal, and certainly not fit for a lady to drive!

CEDRIC: Am I to understand that this…robber made a boast of robbin' more women of this county?

JEMMA: He practically kicked the entire stable down! Remember? Angus had to call slaves in from the fields to help hold him.

MR. SEELY: Has the law been brought into this?

JEMMA: Dreadful, evil creature. Never trust an animal with a piebald eye.

ELIZABETH: Is anybody doing anything about the bandit, Jemmaline?

JEMMA: What? Oh, indeed they are, Elizabeth. Angus and his brother Edgar MacGregor are talking about forming a gentleman's…what did he call it? A posse! Doesn't that sound…exotic? Posse? A posse to hunt for the Kissing Bandit.

LILY: *(Enthralled.)* The Kissing Bandit!

CEDRIC: Funny, that reminds me that there was a fella robbin' coaches near to Cousin Melville in Yorkshire…

JEMMA: Well, of course there was, Cedric. Someone's always robbing coaches in England, Cedric. This, however, is Beaufort County, South Carolina! The cavalier's must rise and ride!

ELIZABETH: *(Looking directly at Siegfried.)* I'd wager that there hasn't been a single robbery of any kind in Yorkshire since the day you left, Cedric.

JEMMA: I will be moving in with you, Cedric, dear, until this…this…violent offender has been brought to justice.

CEDRIC: Moving in?

LILY: Here?

JEMMA: I can't be expected to keep my own company out at Marshwood! Why, it's so isolated in that tiny little corner of the county that all the women folk out my way are at risk!

CEDRIC: I thought you said this rogue was a "kissing" bandit.

JEMMA: So I did!

CEDRIC: Honey, there ain't no white woman anywhere near Marshwood under the age of fifty!

JEMMA: Honestly, Cedric! Everybody in Beaufort County knows that I inherited mama's jewels, including the black pearls.

LILY: Black pearls?

ELIZABETH: *(Without taking her eyes off Siegfried.)* I certainly hope you haven't brought them here, Jemmaline.

JEMMA: Well, of course I have, Elizabeth! I wasn't going to just leave them at Marshwood for the first Kissing Bandit who comes along! Although… perhaps it's the kissing the man likes and not specifically the jewels in which case the black pearls would be perfectly safe at Marshwood with me not bein' there to tempt the bandit…

LILY: What black pearls?

CEDRIC: Those damn things are worth a king's ransom, sister! I can't believe that you just trotted them out in the light of day all the way up from Marshwood with a bandit of any kind runnin' around! Where are they? In your caboose??

ELIZABETH: *(Before Jemmaline can answer.)* Cedric, dear! Let's not discuss that here and now.

LILY: I want to see them!

CEDRIC: *(Looking about in a paranoid fashion.)* Hush up, Lily! What if that bandit's a skulkin' about?

MR. SEELY: Oh, I am certain that he is, Mr. Cedric.

ELIZABETH: For once we are in agreement, Mr. Seely.

CEDRIC: Meanin'?

LILY: Oh, these two nervous nellies obviously think that poor Count Von Zohar is the bandit.

CEDRIC: My hermit?

ELIZABETH: An examination of the facts…

MR. SEELY: Can you account for your hermit's whereabouts in the wee hours of the morning?

CEDRIC: Well…

LILY: Is your spiteful nature a bottomless pit, Mr. Seely?

ELIZABETH: This man *(Indicates Siegfried.)* is obviously a pretender! There is no Count Von Zohar!

(Siegfried indicates that he is cut to the quick.)

CEDRIC: Hold on, now! I traveled with this man from London to Rivermede and I tell you that one, he ain't no robber and two, he is Count Von Zohar!

MR. SEELY: How do you know?? What proof did he offer?

CEDRIC: Well, of course I didn't do any thing so vulgar as to ask this fine and sufferin' gentleman for proof! What kind of a poorly-bred inebriate do you take me for, sir??

JEMMA: Now, now, stop this fussin' immediately! It most certainly could not have been your hermit, Cedric, dear.

ELIZABETH: Why not?

JEMMA: In the first place, Elizabeth, the MacGregor girls said that the Kissing Bandit spoke like an Irishman…

MR. SEELY: Irish?

LILY: There's nothin' worse than an Irish rogue, don't you agree, Mr. Seely?

JEMMA: Well, this poor man is from the Spanish Alps, is he not?

ELIZABETH: He is not!

JEMMA: Besides, he doesn't look anything like an Irishman.

CEDRIC: Well, all this squabblin' is gettin' us nowhere. Mr. Seely!

MR. SEELY: Yes, sir?

CEDRIC: Have them bring Jupiter around the house for me. I'm going to ride over and see Angus, join up with that gentleman's brigade, which reminds me, 'Lizbeth?

ELIZABETH: Yes?

CEDRIC: I'll be wantin' my father's sword from the war of 18 and 12.

ELIZABETH: Cedric you cannot be thinking about galloping around the countryside on Jupiter, who hasn't been ridden since you left, brandishing that sword!

CEDRIC: Ain't you been listenin'? There's a Kissin' Bandit on the loose! Threatenin' the good women of this county…oh, and you, too, 'Lizbeth. It's a gentleman's responsibility to the fair tribe to take up the sword and put an end to this reign of terror!

ELIZABETH: Oh, very well! The sword is underneath my bed.

JEMMA: (To Lily.) Ain't that fittin'.

CEDRIC: Ladies, I do hereby bid you adieu!

LILY: But, Daddy…

CEDRIC: No tears! No tears! If this bandit's to be caught, then it will be by the good men of Beaufort County, South Carolina!

JEMMA: Elizabeth! Give the poor man a token!

ELIZABETH: A what?

JEMMA: Give Cedric your handkerchief! To carry. For luck!

ELIZABETH: You want a good luck token? *(She reaches into her pocket and pulls out a piece of paper.)* Here!

CEDRIC: What the…?

ELIZABETH: It's last month's feed bill, husband. Note the amount I have circled.

CEDRIC: Fifty dollars?

ELIZABETH: That's right. Fifty dollars to feed Jupiter last month. Fifty dollars a month to feed an animal you ride a handful of times a year. Enjoy your ride with the Beaufort County Gentlemen's Posse! *(Elizabeth exits.)*

JEMMA: She's a hard woman.

CEDRIC: Give me a kiss daughter!

LILY: Oh, Daddy, be careful!

CEDRIC: Run and get Jupiter, Mr. Seely. Bring him on up to the house.

MR. SEELY: *(Angrily.)* Yes sir. *(Mr. Seely exits.)*

JEMMA: What on earth is Daddy's sword doin' underneath her bed, Cedric?

CEDRIC: Oh, hell…I guess I nicked her with it on our so-called weddin' night and she's been havin' fits about the damn thing ever since.

JEMMA: Yes sir: a hard woman.

CEDRIC: I want the two of you to go back to the house and stay there until this "Kissing Bandit" is apprehended and strung up, do you hear?

LILY: Yes, Daddy.

JEMMA: Be careful, Cedric, dear.

CEDRIC: *(With a bow.)* Ladies, I shall return! *(Cedric exits.)*

LILY: *(To Siegfried.)* Count, I do hope you will be safe out here in the elements!

(Siegfried smiles and indicates that he has no jewels to steal.)

LILY: Then I wish you good day, sir.

JEMMA: Come, Lily! Let us gather all our jewels together in one safe place.

LILY: May I see the black pearls, Auntie Jemmaline?

JEMMA: *(As they exit.)* Of course, dear. Did you know that at one time the black pearls belonged to the di Medici family? Or was it the Borgias? I believe they're supposed to be cursed or something to that effect, but you know my memory…

(Siegfried waits until the ladies are out of sight and then he collapses on the bench, his head reeling with everything he's just heard. After a moment, Elizabeth cautiously reenters. Siegfried senses her immediately and leaps to his feet.)

ELIZABETH: Well, well. Nicely done, Rivermede Hermit.

(Siegfried indicates confusion.)

ELIZABETH: I see it has taken you little time to set about your work here in Beaufort County. A Kissing Bandit indeed.

(Siegfried indicates with great passion that he is not the Kissing Bandit.)

ELIZABETH: Stop! I am not some foolish romantic young girl like Lily. I'm a married woman. I know that romance is a figment of some man's imagination.

(Siegfried's eyebrows raise.)

ELIZABETH: Do you remember that I promised you that I would rid myself of you at the first opportunity? Well, thanks to your nocturnal escapades with the MacGregor girls, opportunity has come a knocking. *(Elizabeth sweeps off.)*

(Joe suddenly appears from the ruins. He and Siegfried watch Elizabeth leave.)

JOE: *(After a moment.)* That woman need a man…bad.

(Siegfried starts and turns to see Joe. He then bursts into surprised laughter. Clapping Joe companionably on the shoulder. Joe stiffens at Siegfried's touch.)

JOE: I come to give you friendly advice. I know white folk all my life and you ain't no Count. I'll tell you what I do think you is: I think you one big fool. This country going to war, sir. Soon. I suggest you take them black pearls and get going to wherever it is you goin' to. As long as you stay here, you puttin' yourself in danger. You think about that, sir.

(Joe stares at Siegfried until the Hermit bows low, an indication that he has heard and understood.)

JOE: You get goin', sir. And watch your back. *(Joe exits.)*

(Siegfried thoughtfully watches Joe exit. He mulls over Joe's warning for a moment, but is clearly tantalized by the thought of the black pearls. He starts to reluctantly leave in the direction in which Joe has gone, but stops.)

SIEGFRIED: *(Clearly tortured.)* Black pearls…black! *(With a rueful grin, He turns and exits in the direction of the house.)*

(Blackout. Change to: The ruins, that night. Jemmaline appears in the moonlight on tip toe. She peers cautiously into the ruins.)

JEMMA: *(Whispering.)* Count? *(She listens.)* Hoo-hoo, Count! Count Von Poobah? *(She listens.)* Anyone there? Anyone? *(Satisfied that she is alone, Jemma settles comfortably on the marble bench and produces a silver flask from which she takes a long satisfying draw. She starts when she thinks she hears a noise and hides the flask.)* Hoo-hoo? Hello? *(Satisfied that she is really alone, she produces the flask yet again and takes another swig. Meaning the hooch.)* Hoo-hoo. *(She takes another swig.)* Hoo-hoo…hoo.

Oh, yes. That's the stuff. *(Another swig.)* Yassuh. *(She drains the flask. Examining the flask's emptiness by peering into the mouth.)*

Awww…shoulda had Ol' Mars filch some more of ol' Cedric's most exquisitely delightful bourbon. Ah, well. *(She rises but is unsteady.)* Whoa, there! *(She laughs but immediately suppresses it. She then takes another unsteady step, which is a disaster. She keeps herself from falling by holding on to a piece of the ruins, but her feet seem to have a life of their own. In a moment, they're doing a soft shoe. Singing.)*

Way Over in the Westfalian Alps,

Far, Far away.

That's where Mama got treatments on her scalp

While Otto and his monkey did play!

All day…

(She stops dancing.) Why was Herr Schlagger at that spa, anyway? Oh! the monkey. Dear, dear little Pippo in his darling little Fez. Of course. Come to think of it, his fur did look a bit mottled about the eyes…

(Voices off. Jemma starts and looks for a place to hide. As the voices draw nearer, she retreats into the darkness of the ruins. Jemma will slowly sink to the ground and fall fast asleep during the following scene. Joe enters dragging an unhappy Mehitable.)

MEHITABLE: I will not listen to you anymore, Joe!

JOE: You have to! Tonight's the night, Delilah. It's now or never. Come with me. Leave this place!

MEHITABLE: And go where? There ain't no place else!

JOE: You crazy, girl? There's a whole world of someplace else!

MEHITABLE: And we'll be killed tryin' to get there!

JOE: We won't!

MEHITABLE: Joe! Last month four slaves from Green Hill was caught tryin' to run and they…

JOE: I know what happened!

MEHITABLE: Then why do you want to run, Joe?

JOE: Because I am a man! I need to…why am I explainin' this to you? Why don't you want to run? Don't you want to be free of all this? Live like a person with a life worth livin'?

MEHITABLE: Because my life ain't worth nothin' if I'm swingin' from a rope!

JOE: You ain't gonna swing from no rope. We got it planned…

MEHITABLE: We? We, Joe? Who's we?

JOE: I can't talk about that.

MEHITABLE: Who you draggin' with you, Joe?

JOE: No one! We already…

LILY: *(Off.)* Mehitable!

MEHITABLE: It's Lily. Joe, promise me…

JOE: *(Savagely.)* This is good bye. *(Joe pulls her into an embrace, kisses her and then disappears into the night.)*

MEHITABLE: Joe!

LILY: *(Entering.)* There you are! Good Lord, Mehitable, I've been looking for you everywhere…Mehitable?

MEHITABLE: *(Looking off after Joe in a tearful whisper.)* Joe.

LILY: What ever is the matter? Mehitable! Why are you cryin'? Has someone done something to you? That Joe…

MEHITABLE: No! No. It's nothin', Miss Lily. Nothin'. Just some blue, that's all.

LILY: Should I believe you? Your face is tellin' me I shouldn't.

MEHITABLE: It's nothin'! Mammy Pam's chitlins…

LILY: I've told you time and time again not to eat Mammy Pam's chitlins, Mehitable. No wonder you're white as a ghost.

MEHITABLE: *(Faintly.)* Lucky ghost.

LILY: Why?

MEHITABLE: To be white.

LILY: Yes…well, goodness! Where is the count?

MEHITABLE: I don't know, Miss Lily. I only just got here from the kitchen.

LILY: *(Calling.)* Count? Count Von Zohar?

(Lily takes a few steps and stumbles over Jemmaline whom she doesn't recognize in the darkness.)

LILY: Mehitable! There's a body! Help! Run and get help!

MEHITABLE: A body!

LILY: Go! Find Mr. Seely!

(Mehitable rushes off as Lily disentangles herself from the comatose Jemmaline. Siegfried appears out of the darkness. He takes Lily's arm and she shrieks.)

LILY: Oh! Count! Thank goodness it's you! There's a body…

(Siegfried sweeps Lily into his arms and carries her to the safety of the bench.)

LILY: Oh! Thank you, sir!

(Siegfried goes to check the body.)

LILY: Be careful, I beg you!

(He leans over Jemmaline, who groans and rolls over.)

JEMMA: *Güten abend, Herr Schlagger! Was ein schönes monkey du hast!*

LILY: Jemmaline!

JEMMA: *Güten nacht meine schatze.*

LILY: Oh, for the love of…

(Siegfried produces the silver flask with an apologetic grin.)

LILY: The old souse! I can not believe this! With a dangerous bandit on the loose and a house full of jewels! Jemmaline! Wake up!

JEMMA: Not now, mother, the rods won't set.

LILY: Jemmaline!

(Jemma struggles to sit up and then collapses.)

LILY: Mr. Seely is going to have to have some poor soul carry the foolish woman all the way back to the house. Although if you ask me she should be left out here until she's regained her sensibilities. *(She looks up at Siegfried.)* I suppose I should wait here until help arrives.

(Lily notices that Siegfried is staring intently at her.)

LILY: What is it? Why are you lookin' at me like that?

(He continues to regard her with great intensity while beginning to slowly advance.)

LILY: *(Suddenly nervous.)* Sir, you are embarrassing me. I pray you, stop.

(But he continues.)

LILY: Count Von Zohar! What is your intention, sir?

(It now becomes clear that he is focused on the black pearls that Lily is wearing.)

LILY: Oh! The pearls! Aren't they lovely? Of course they aren't really black, are they? They're really more gray…like a stormy sky.

(Siegfried can't help himself. He reaches out to touch them but then catches himself.)

LILY: You may examine them if you desire, your grace. *(Lily tilts her head back, exposing her neck.)* Jemmaline insists this necklace is priceless…one of a kind.

(Siegfried reaches out with great reverence and lifts a strand gently from Lily's neck. He is clearly transfixed and quite oblivious to the fact that he and Lily are close enough to kiss.)

LILY: I suppose pearls of this color are really quite rare. And they match so perfectly, don't you agree?

(Siegfried lifts another strand, caressing Lily's neck as he does so.)

LILY: Oh! It would be a crime for these lovely pearls to fall into the hands of that Kissing Bandit… *(Lily closes her eyes, expecting to be kissed. When a kiss is not forthcoming, she opens her eyes.)* You have my leave to kiss me, Count Von Zohar.

(This gets Siegfried's attention.)

LILY: Unless you prefer not to…

(Siegfried is clearly torn. He cannot bring himself to drop the pearls. He and Lily stare at one another. She is perplexed by the impasse.)

LILY: Count?

(Siegfried opens his mouth as if to say something.)

ELIZABETH: *(Off.)* Lily! Jemmaline!

LILY: Oh, fie on that woman! I swear she has the timin' of a bird of prey! *(Elizabeth enters with a lantern. She stops and assesses the situation while Lily sits defiantly on the bench. Siegfried drops the pearls and rises.)*

LILY: 'Evenin', Elizabeth. I see you have left your bloodhounds back at the house.

ELIZABETH: I was worried about you, Lily, and Jemmaline as well. Where is she?

LILY: Well, I came out here lookin' for her myself...

ELIZABETH: She isn't here? But I've looked everywhere in the house...

LILY: Oh, she's here, Elizabeth. You'll find her just over there by the column, sleeping it off. *(Elizabeth strides to Jemmaline and holds the lantern so she can see the other woman.)*

ELIZABETH: Jemmaline! Jemmaline! Can you hear me?

(Jemmaline groans and mumbles something incoherent.)

ELIZABETH: Oh, for the love of...how long has she been like this?

LILY: I have no idea.

ELIZABETH: Well, we can't just leave her there...

LILY: I have already sent Mehitable to bring Mr. Seely.

ELIZABETH: If she can find him.

LILY: Well, of course she can find him, Elizabeth. That man is always underfoot.

ELIZABETH: Not tonight, he isn't. I've had Cordelia searching for him for an hour or more.

LILY: Oh, he's probably in the quarters. You know how much that ridiculous man likes to spend time with the...

ELIZABETH: Not tonight! Cordelia has already been to the quarters and he wasn't there. No one was there...

LILY: No one?

ELIZABETH: Evidently there is a bush meeting tonight.

LILY: Well, we won't find Mr. Seely there, will we?

ELIZABETH: One would tend to think not. *(Peering at Lily in the lantern light.)* It's strange, though...Lily, what are you wearing?

LILY: This? Why it's just an old dress from last summer.

ELIZABETH: *(Stepping closer.)* No! Not your dress… *(She snatches up the pearls.)* these!

(Siegfried tenses.)

LILY: *(Stepping back.)* These are Jemmaline's pearls as you very well know. Kindly refrain from touchin' them!

ELIZABETH: You fool!

LILY: I do believe you are jealous, Elizabeth!

ELIZABETH: Don't be ridiculous.

LILY: You are! This is the one piece of the Montfleurry family that you can't buy with all your Yankee money!

ELIZABETH: Lily!

LILY: You bought Rivermede, Elizabeth, but you cannot buy these!

ELIZABETH: Do you ever think? About anything? Sashaying around in front of this man in those pearls is like dangling a rabbit in front of a fox!

LILY: Oh, Elizabeth, this poor man is not the Kissing Bandit!

ELIZABETH: Of course he is!

LILY: He is not! Why, he could have kissed me just a minute ago, Elizabeth, before you came trompin' in, but he did not! He just…he only… *(Lily falters, remembering Siegfried's obvious interest in the pearls. Her hand flies to her neck as she turns to give Siegfried a searching look.)*

ELIZABETH: Go back to the house Lily.

LILY: Count Von Zohar?

ELIZABETH: *(Softly.)* Go now. Send Mr. Seely here to help with Jemmaline. *(Lily gathers her skirts and rushes off.)*

ELIZABETH: You are beneath contempt, sir. I demand that you leave this plantation at once!

SIEGFRIED: No.

ELIZABETH: Well, so much for your vow of silence. Tell me, how long did you think you could manage to get by without speaking?

SIEGFRIED: You should give it a try.

ELIZABETH: What?!?

SIEGFRIED: *(Moving closer.)* There are more important things.

ELIZABETH: Such as a foolish young girl with a small fortune hanging around her neck?

SIEGFRIED: *(Moving closer still.)* Far more important.

ELIZABETH: You insolent creature; are you trying to seduce *me?*

SIEGFRIED: *(With sincere intensity.)* Absolutely. Is it working?

ELIZABETH: *(The hardest thing she's ever had to say in her life.)* Yes! *(Siegfried and Elizabeth fall into a massively passionate embrace. After allowing herself to be swept up in a brief moment of illicit pleasure, Elizabeth pushes away.)*

ELIZABETH: *(Trying to catch her breath.)* I've already told you that such foolishness won't work with…

(Siegfried kisses her again and she returns his kiss with reluctant abandon.)

SIEGFRIED: *(Holding her.)* Is it so terrible to be foolish?

ELIZABETH: *(Gently breaking away.)* At this particular moment, yes. *(Elizabeth begins checking her ears hands and throat.)*

SIEGFRIED: What are you doing?

ELIZABETH: Looking to see what you stole while you kissed me.

SIEGFRIED: *(Spinning her around to face him.)* Listen to me, Elizabeth: I am not the…

(There is a sudden commotion from the direction of the house. We hear horses, shouting men and barking dogs.)

ELIZABETH: My god will this night ever end?!?

(Siegfried leaps up onto the ruins and peers into the night.)

SIEGFRIED: There are many men at the house on horses.

ELIZABETH: It's Cedric and the MacGregor brothers!

SIEGFRIED: Ah, the Gentleman's Brigade.

ELIZABETH: You've got to run!

SIEGFRIED: *(Climbing down.)* Why? I have done nothing. Except to kiss my good Lord Cedric's beautiful wife.

ELIZABETH: Please go…don't let them catch you!

SIEGFRIED: But my dearest Elizabeth, I am not the…

(Lily runs on stage.)

LILY: Oh my goodness! I ran all the way from the house.

ELIZABETH: Lily!

LILY: I told Daddy that I saw a suspicious-looking man runnin' off through the orchards…

ELIZABETH: There was a man at the house?

LILY: No, Elizabeth! *(To Siegfried.)* That should give you enough time to make your escape.

SIEGFRIED: *(Amused.)* My escape?

LILY: They've chased you back here!

SIEGFRIED: Chased me? From where?

CEDRIC: *(Off.)* Lily! Lily Marvelle!

LILY: Oh my good Lord it's Daddy! Quickly, you must hide!

SIEGFRIED: *(Laughing.)* Why?

LILY: Please!

SIEGFRIED: Very well, if it pleases you. *(Siegfried disappears behind the ruins.)*

LILY: Don't you dare say anything, Elizabeth!

(Cedric enters with Mehitable in tow.)

CEDRIC: Aha!

LILY: Daddy!

CEDRIC: Don't "Daddy" me, gal! Why the Sam Hill did you hightail it out here to the gardens after sendin' the Gentlemen's Posse over to the orchards?

LILY: Well, I…

ELIZABETH: *(Stepping forward to take command.)* Lily was frantic about Jemmaline…

CEDRIC: Who?

ELIZABETH: Jemmaline, your sister?

CEDRIC: Oh. That Jemmaline. I thought you might have been talking' about Jemmaline Wiggins from over to Sebastian Hall…

ELIZABETH: No, Cedric! I meant that Jemmaline! *(Elizabeth points to the supine Jemmaline.)*

CEDRIC: Hell Bells! Is she dead or drunk?

ELIZABETH: The latter!

LILY: That's right, Daddy. I was so worried about her when I saw that horrible strange man run across the front yard and into the orchards that I thought I better come out here and help Elizabeth keep watch over her until Mr. Seely is found…

CEDRIC: Where's Mr. Seely?

ELIZABETH: No one knows.

CEDRIC: No one knows?

LILY: There's a big bush meetin' tonight…

CEDRIC: A bush meetin' you say?

LILY: Yes, Daddy. A bush meetin'.

CEDRIC: Hold on there, gal…what's that you got strung 'round your neck?

LILY: Oh my good lord I forgot to take them off!

ELIZABETH: Cedric, I'm sure they're far more safe on Lily than back in the empty house.

CEDRIC: I suppose you're right, 'Lizbeth.

ELIZABETH: Shouldn't you go back to the posse?

CEDRIC: Oh, hell yes! *(Laughing.)* Malcolm Braintree's got his bloodhounds with him and it's the damnedest thing you ever did see! *(He bays like a hound and laughs.)* They'll have that Kissing Bandit up a tree toot sweet. *(Cedric turns to leave.)*

LILY: Daddy, how did you know that the…bandit was here at Rivermede?

CEDRIC: Hell, gal! We've been hot on the fella's heels all the way from Brayley where we almost caught him red-handed stealin' a diamond broach from Prissy Liscombe. She is not agin' with grace, daughter, not at all. Well, those hounds picked up the bandit's thievin' scent at Brayley and we rode like hell itself to Rivermede. Thanks to you, my darlin' daughter, those hounds undoubtedly have the felon up a high tree by now. You stay here with your aunt and your step-mother.

LILY: Yes, Daddy.

CEDRIC: I shall return, ladies...Delilah. *(Cedric exits.)*

LILY: Brayley!

(Siegfried emerges.)

MEHITABLE: That's almost the other side of the county.

LILY: But, he's been here in the gardens with me for the last half hour or so...

ELIZABETH: *(To Siegfried.)* Then you couldn't be the...but you have to be!

SIEGFRIED: Why does it have to be me?

ELIZABETH: *(Sputtering.)* Because! Because it just has to be that way!

SIEGFRIED: Is your world that orderly, Elizabeth?

ELIZABETH: *(Staring to break.)* You don't know anything about my world!

SIEGFRIED: I know that in your world I am this Kissing Bandit but in my world I am not.

LILY: Then who is the Kissing Bandit?

(At that moment, a cloaked figure leaps over the brick wall and lands in the ruins.)

SIEGFRIED: *(Protectively, to the frightened women.)* Stand back.

(The man stands up, revealing his face, which is half-covered, bandit-style. Mehitable is not fooled for a moment. She strides to the man and rips off his bandanna.)

ELIZABETH: Joe?

LILY: Joe, whatever are you doin' in that costume?

SIEGFRIED: *(Laughing.)* Good women of Rivermede, I believe you are at last in the presence of your Kissing Bandit.

LILY: Who? Joe? Don't be silly!

MEHITABLE: Joe, what have you done?

JOE: *(Ragged and out of breath—he's been chased a long way.)* I ain't got time ' for this...

ELIZABETH: Is this true, Joe?

JOE: *(Trying to pull away from Mehitable.)* I got to go...

MEHITABLE: *(Furious.)* Oh, that's right, Joe, you gotta go. Gonna run north, get your freedom. We got it all planned. And to think I wasted myself bein' scared for you when all you was doin' was runnin' around the county thievin'!

JOE: You don't understand…

MEHITABLE: What's to understand, Joe? You're nothin' but a common thief. And this is what you wanted for me?

LILY: What are you speakin' about, Mehitable?

JOE: I got to go…

MEHITABLE: Go, then!

(Just then, another caped figure climbs over the wall and leaps into the ruins. The women shriek.)

SIEGFRIED: *(Incredibly amused.)* Unbelievably, it seems that there are two kissing bandits!

(The second man pulls his bandanna down.)

LILY: Mr. Seely!

MR. SEELY: *(To Joe.)* You made it! Thank god.

(Joe and Mr. Seely greet one another joyfully.)

MR. SEELY: We did it! They all got on the boat!

ELIZABETH: What boat?

LILY: Who did?

MR. SEELY: Your slaves, *Miss* Lily.

LILY: *My* slaves?

MR. SEELY: That's right, princess. Forty of your best field workers are on a boat headed for Baltimore and points north. That's forty people—human beings—whom you will no longer have the pleasure of ordering about. Forty people who will no longer cater to your every ridiculous whim. Forty people who no longer enjoy the distinct displeasure of being owned by you. Gone. Escaped. Flown the coop.

ELIZABETH: Oh, Christ you're abolitionists.

MR. SEELY: *(Proudly.)* That is correct, Mrs. Montfleurry. Abolitionists. The scourge of the south at your service.

LILY: *(Exploding in a tearful rage, attacking Mr. Seely.)* You…you horrible stupid man!

MEHITABLE: *(Trying to restrain Lily.)* Miss Lily…

LILY: *(Landing a solid blow on Mr. Seely.)* Why didn't you take Mehitable!

MR. SEELY: *(Shocked.)* What?

LILY: Why didn't you take her, too?!

MEHITABLE: Miss Lily…

LILY: She could have had a life of her own! Why didn't you take her?!?

MR. SEELY: Because…

LILY: What kind of abolitionist leaves the best behind?

MEHITABLE: But, Miss Lily…

LILY: *(Sobbing.)* Mehitable should have been on that boat!

JOE: *(Gently leading Lily away from a shocked Mr. Seely.)* She didn't want to go, Miss.

LILY: What?

JOE: I begged her to go…

MEHITABLE: It's true, Miss Lily. Joe's been after me for weeks to run.

LILY: Then why didn't you go?

MEHITABLE: It's you, Miss Lily…

LILY: Me??

MEHITABLE: I couldn't leave you.

LILY: But to be free, Mehitable! Livin' free is so much more…I'd give anything to be free of this place. Knowing that you were free would be such a wonderful gift…please, Joe, say it isn't too late. Say that Mehitable can still go!

JOE: She can come with Mr. Seely and me.

MEHITABLE: I told you I won't go, Joe. This is my home! I won't leave Rivermede!

MR. SEELY: We've got to go…

JOE: Come with me, Delilah. Just thinking of you staying here, in this place is killin' me.

MEHITABLE: I told you…

JOE: No, I'm tellin' you, Delilah! War is comin'. Sure as I'm standin' here it's gonna come! Why you want to be here for that? Come north with us. I swear to you here and now that you'll be safe. You ain't gonna swing from no rope. I'll protect you with my life, woman! Listen, I got me a place up in Massachusetts. It's mine, Delilah. I bought it with money that I made sailin' ships out of Boston and haulin' cargo on the docks. Honest work, Delilah. Day in and day out, right alongside this man here. *(He indicates Mr. Seely.)* Long and hard enough to buy my own place. My brother's workin' it for me until I get back. 'Course, it ain't much now, just a house and a couple of barns, but the pasture's good, Delilah. Lord how I'd love to give you that sweet earth, woman! Come with me, Delilah. Come north, I'm beggin' you.

ELIZABETH: Go with him.

LILY: Please, Mehitable! Go!

MEHITABLE: *(Starting to cry.)* I can't! I'm too scared!

JOE: Listen to me, Delilah. I'll wait for you in the old cotton shed off the road to Charleston until midnight.

LILY: She'll be there!

MEHITABLE: I won't!

JOE: After that, I'm leavin' the Carolinas for good. Our luck's run out here.

ELIZABETH: But thanks to the Kissing Bandit, your cause will be well-funded until war comes.

MR. SEELY: It's never enough.

ELIZABETH: *(Slipping off her engagement ring and holding it out to Joe.)* Here, this should help.

JOE: Oh, no…we couldn't…

ELIZABETH: Take it, take it. Cedric picked it out but I paid for the damn thing.

JOE: *(Accepting the ring.)* God bless you, Mrs. Montfleurry.

MR. SEELY: We can fool that posse forever, but those bloodhounds will be on to us any moment!

JOE: I'll be waitin', Delilah, until midnight!

(Joe and Mr. Seely turn to leave.)

LILY: Mr. Seely, wait! I wish to apologize, sir, for all the horrible things that I've…

MR. SEELY: You don't have to…

LILY: I do! I am so sorry, Mr. Seely. I will never forget the wonderful wonderful thing you have done here in the Carolinas.

MR. SEELY: I'm sorry, too, Lily. I had no idea you felt the way you do…

JOE: The dogs!

MR. SEELY: Good-bye.

LILY: Good-bye.

(Mr. Seely turns again to leave.)

LILY: Mr. Seely, wait!

MR. SEELY: What is it, Lily?

LILY: Take me with you!

(Everyone reacts to this.)

MR. SEELY: But, why would you…

MEHITABLE: Miss Lily! What are you thinkin'?

LILY: If you won't leave because of me, then I suppose I'll just have to go.

MEHITABLE: You can't leave Rivermede!

LILY: Why not? Forty other people just did.

MEHITABLE: But, where will you go?

LILY: To Boston, I suppose.

MEHITABLE: *(Increasingly alarmed.)* What will you do when you get there?

LILY: *(Realizing it's true.)* Anything I want!

MEHITABLE: But you ain't fit for work, Miss Lily!

LILY: I'll make myself fit! In Boston I'll be free, and a free person can do anything!

ELIZABETH: Lily, I fear you have romanticized the North. Women are no more free in Boston than they are here in the South. Do you think I actually wanted to marry Cedric?

LILY: The fact remains, Elizabeth, that if I go, Mehitable will have to go!

MEHITABLE: But, Miss Lily…

LILY: She and I can live together as free women in Boston! We could do anything! Mehitable could be a lady's maid and get paid for it, just like a white woman. She could walk the city streets just the same as anyone. In Boston I would have no domineering father to force me to marry someone I don't love, Elizabeth. I would be free to…teach school…design temples for ladies' gardens or whatever it is that I would like to do! Why, I could even marry that absurd Mr. Seely if I wanted to!

MEHITABLE: Miss Lily!

LILY: If he wanted me to, naturally. Isn't that right, Mr. Seely?

MR. SEELY: (Absolutely stunned.) Isn't what right?

LILY: Isn't it right that I could marry you if I wanted to?

MR. SEELY: (Sputtering and flustered.) Well, I…I suppose that it is…right.

LILY: (Whirling to face Mehitable.) You see?

MEHITABLE: I see, but you don't.

LILY: What don't I see?

MEHITABLE: (Picking up Lily's hands and holding them in her own.) Look. What do you see?

LILY: I see our hands.

MEHITABLE: I know that's what you see. Just hands. That ain't what the rest of the world sees. The rest of the world sees black…and white hands.

LILY: But, it's just our hands…

MEHITABLE: No! It's black hands and white hands. If I run with you and I get caught, all they'll see is a black slave who needs to be taught a lesson.

LILY: I wouldn't let them!

MR. SEELY: You wouldn't be able to stop them.

MEHITABLE: You go, Miss Lily. You found your Benjamin Strong. Take him and go.

MR. SEELY: Who is Benjamin Strong?

LILY: No one. Just an old dream.

(The hounds are getting closer.)

JOE: Let's get goin'!

MR. SEELY: Lily, are you certain that this is what you want?

LILY: Mr. Seely, I have never been more certain of anything in my life.

MR. SEELY: You don't have to…marry me…if you don't…

(Lily takes Mr. Seely and kisses him soundly.)

LILY: Aha! At last I have discovered the secret to hushin' you up, Mr. Seely.

(Mr. Seely kisses Lily.)

MR. SEELY: I see that it works both ways, Lily.

LILY: *(With great affection.)* You horrible man. Good-bye, Elizabeth! Best of luck with Daddy!

ELIZABETH: Be careful, Lily.

LILY: Good bye, Count!

SIEGFRIED: Farewell, princess.

LILY: Mehitable. *(Crying.)* If you aren't in that shed at midnight, I will switch you myself!

MEHITABLE: You go and be happy.

LILY: I love you, Mehitable.

MEHITABLE: I love you, too, Miss Lily.

LILY: Just Lily.

MEHITABLE: *(A tearful whisper.)* I know.

LILY: *(Kissing her.)* Good-bye, Delilah.

(Lily and Mr. Seely exit.)

JOE: Until midnight, Delilah. *(Joe exits.)*

(The hounds are closer. Mehitable exits tearfully.)

ELIZABETH: Those bloodhounds will track them down!

SIEGFRIED: No fears, lady.

ELIZABETH: You don't understand! Once they get the scent…

(Siegfried peers off stage and then quickly takes Elizabeth into an embrace which she fights. Cedric rushes on with sword drawn.)

CEDRIC: Aha! The Kissin' Bandit!

(In one smooth move, Siegfried spins a sputtering Elizabeth around and holds her in front of him with a knife pressed against her throat.)

SIEGFRIED: *(In a flawless Irish accent.)* That's right, you big stuffed sausage! You've found me, but you'll never take me!

CEDRIC: But…you!

SIEGFRIED: It's meself to be sure.

CEDRIC: But that's impossible! You're from the Prussian Alps…

SIEGFRIED: I'm from Cork, you jackass!

CEDRIC: *(Remembering he has the sword.)* I believe you are the jackass, sir! When Angus and the rest of the men get here…

SIEGFRIED: I'll slit your meal ticket's throat before that can happen!

ELIZABETH: Cedric!

CEDRIC: *(Realizing.)* You mean you would actually…?

SIEGFRIED: Just give me a try, boy-o. You call for those men and I'll do her sure as I'm holdin' this here knife to her throat!

CEDRIC: *(Considering.)* I'd have a duce of a time tryin' to explain such a violent demise to her father up in New York…

ELIZABETH: Cedric, you gutless worm!

CEDRIC: Now, now. Give me time to think this through, 'Lizbeth!

SIEGFRIED: You got no time, Cedric Montfleurry! Go back to those men and tell them that them hounds got the wrong scent! Tell 'em the kissin' bandit's been here and gone off to the *south!* D'you hear me? The south! Say them exact words, or I'll spill your rich wife's blood all over these stones leavin' you a pauper until the next colleen comes along with a pocketful of money and a nearsided gaze!

CEDRIC: All right! All right, you Irish jackanapes! *(Without much enthusiasm.)* 'Lizbeth, I shall return. *(Cedric rushes off.)*

(Siegfried releases Elizabeth who is madder than a wet dog.)

ELIZABETH: Who are you??

SIEGFRIED: *(Still Irish.)* Y'ask that question quite a bit, Lizzy darlin'.

ELIZABETH: You're not from Eastern Europe!

SIEGFRIED: *(As the Count.)* I am if you want me to be, dear lady.

ELIZABETH: But…

SIEGFRIED: *(In a new, Yorkshire accent; this is his real accent.)* Your husband will be back any moment, Elizabeth. The time has come to make your decision.

ELIZABETH: What decision??

SIEGFRIED: To stay here or to come with me.

ELIZABETH: But…but where are you going?

SIEGFRIED: San Francisco…

ELIZABETH: San Francisco!!

SIEGFRIED: I have friends there who will help me buy a ship…

ELIZABETH: *(This is crazy.)* A ship?? Who are you??

SIEGFRIED: *(Ignoring the question.)* After we get the ship and a crew it's off to the South Seas for trade. There's money to be made runnin' goods and… other things in the South Pacific, good solid money. With your head for finance and my initiative, we could have our own plantation on Bali or Tahiti in no time. What do you think, Elizabeth? Are you game? You don't have anything here, come with me.

ELIZABETH: BUT WHO ARE YOU???

SIEGFRIED: *(Irish.)* I'm whoever you want me to be, Lizzy darlin'.

ELIZABETH: That's not an answer! You're asking me to give up everything I've worked for and everything I know…

SIEGFRIED: *(Yorkshire.)* Everything you've worked for will be lost when the states go to war and I respectfully submit that what you know represents a minuscule portion of the world. Come with me and see the rest of it!

ELIZABETH: But it's crazy! I just can't pick up and go west with someone whose name I don't even know to sail around the South Pacific! You can't expect me to…

(Siegfried silences her with a kiss.)

ELIZABETH: Please, I need to know who you are.

SIEGFRIED: *(Yorkshire.)* It seems to me, Elizabeth, that you need to spend less time wondering who other people are and more time trying to discover who you might be.

ELIZABETH: Who I might be.

SIEGFRIED: *(Yorkshire.)* Come with me and find out. I've got two horses waiting at the slave quarters. If we ride all night we could be out of the state by morning.

ELIZABETH: But, what will we do for…

(Siegfried pulls the black pearls out of his pocket and hands them to Elizabeth.)

ELIZABETH: The black pearls! But how…?

SIEGFRIED: *(Irish.)* Ask me no questions, I'll tell you no lies.

ELIZABETH: These will buy a fleet of ships!

SIEGFRIED: *(Yorkshire.)* That's my Elizabeth! I can see you, my darling, standing by the ship's wheel with the wind in your hair…free of this life and these people…

ELIZABETH: *(Quietly.)* I'll go.

SIEGFRIED: You'll…

ELIZABETH: However! I will hold these *(She holds up the pearls.)* and you will tell me your name! I refuse to make love to a man named "Siegfried."

SIEGFRIED: *(After a moment.)* My name is Strong. Benjamin Strong.

ELIZABETH: Benjamin Strong…why is that familiar…?

SIEGFRIED: It doesn't matter.

ELIZABETH: It does…Mehitable said that name to Lily! Who are you, why did you come here?

SIEGFRIED: My name is Benjamin Strong and I came here chasing an old dream.

ELIZABETH: Did you find it?

SIEGFRIED: I found something much better.

JEMMA: *(Struggling to sit up.)* You two better go if you're goin'.

ELIZABETH: Jemmaline!

JEMMA: My head!

SIEGFRIED: She's right, we must go.

JEMMA: Just let me...see those pearls one more time.

ELIZABETH: *(Holding them out.)* We can't take your pearls, Jemmaline!

JEMMA: Of course you can! *(She strokes them lovingly.)* I only hope that they bring you better luck than they have me. They're cursed, you know. Italians. They're always cursing one another over the most petty little things...

ELIZABETH: Thank you, Jemmaline...

JEMMA: I once knew an Italian woman in Milan, when Cedric and I were there with Father and Mother, who spent every morning wishin' bad luck on her enemies...

SIEGFRIED: *(Taking her hand and kissing it.)* Thank you, dear lady. You have given us good luck.

JEMMA: You're welcome, Benjemin Strong. A letter, from time to time, Elizabeth? To give me somethin' new to dream about?

ELIZABETH: Of course, Jemmaline.

SIEGFRIED: Good-bye. Come, Elizabeth.

ELIZABETH: Good-bye, Jemmaline.

   (They exit.)

JEMMA: Farewell! Best of luck in the South Seas, Elizabeth. Mind the cannibals and the treacherous tsetse fly! *(She collapses on the bench, rubbing her head.)*

   (Cedric rushes back on.)

CEDRIC: I've done it! I've sent the men and the dogs south to Hanesport... where is everyone?

JEMMA: The Kissin' Bandit has absconded with your wife, Cedric.

CEDRIC: With my wife!!! Oh, you mean 'Lizbeth?

JEMMA: I do.

CEDRIC: What in hell does he want with that old harridan?

JEMMA: I believe he means to keep her as a hostage...

CEDRIC: A hostage, you say?

JEMMA: Yes, Cedric, a hostage, until he has made good his escape from Beaufort County and the Carolinas.

CEDRIC: *(Sitting down next to her.)* Well, don't that beat all.

JEMMA: Cedric, you've got to give some thought to how you're going to handle this.

CEDRIC: Handle what?

JEMMA: With Elizabeth's father.

CEDRIC: Oh, that. I spose I'll just have to tell that northern devil the truth, that his daughter up and left with a Kissin' Bandit!

JEMMA: Do you think that's wise, Cedric?

CEDRIC: Wise? *(Seeing Mehitable.)* Delilah! Get on over here, girl!
(Mehitable enters.)

JEMMA: After all, what Elizabeth's father doesn't know won't hurt us.

CEDRIC: Fetch us a couple of mint juleps, Delilah. And tell Mars to make mine a double!

MEHITABLE: Yes, Mister Cedric. *(She begins to exit but pauses.)* Mr. Cedric?

CEDRIC: What's that, Delilah?

MEHITABLE: Beggin' your pardon, but what time is it?

CEDRIC: What? Oh… *(He checks his pocket watch.)* It's gettin' up on 11:30… we keepin' you from your beauty sleep gal? *(To Jemma.)* So you're sayin' that if we keep quiet about Elizabeth leavin' with that Kissin' Bandit, that our cash flow will continue…unabated?

JEMMA: That's the ticket.
(Mehitable has stopped in her tracks.)

CEDRIC: Ain't you goin', Delilah?

MEHITABLE: *(With a new smile.)* Yes Sir, Mr. Cedric, I'm goin'!
(As Cedric and Jemmaline babble, She takes one last look around the garden and exits in the direction of freedom.)

CEDRIC: I suppose we could come up with some kind of "emergency" that would get us set for when he finds out…

JEMMA: All the cotton bales burned up in a tragic fire!

CEDRIC: Oh, I like that one, sister. I do! We could put that money away…

JEMMA: Or use it to leave this place.

CEDRIC: And go where?

JEMMA: Anywhere! To live with Cousin Melville at Drummond Hall…or maybe we could find that little spa in Switzerland…

CEDRIC: Liechtenstein.

JEMMA: What? Are you certain?

CEDRIC: It was in Liechtenstein.

JEMMA: Oh, yes! I remember now. The city of Vaduz, with that lovely castle high on that mountain…do you remember it, Cedric?

CEDRIC: I do, sister. I do.

(The two sit for a moment in silence, contemplating the sky.)

CEDRIC: Storm's comin'.

JEMMA: You think so?

CEDRIC: Look at the sky, sister. Big one. Comin' from the north.

JEMMA: From the north, you say?

CEDRIC: From the north. Can't you feel it? It's suckin' all the air out.

JEMMA: We better get inside, then.

CEDRIC: I spose we better.

(But they continue to sit and stare at the sky.)

JEMMA: Liechtenstein, are you certain?

(The lights begin to fade.)

CEDRIC: *(Firmly.)* Liechtenstein. And that Pippo wasn't no monkey, sister, he was a weasel or a marmot or somethin' to that effect.

JEMMA: A weasel!!

CEDRIC: Or a marmot.

JEMMA: My! A weasel in Liechtenstein. Now I am going to have to rethink everything…

(Blackout.)

END OF PLAY

JODIE'S BODY

by Aviva Jane Carlin

To my Mother,
Margery Fairless Carlin,
and to the mothers next door,
Dr. Grace Bennett and Anne Sage Saxton

THE AUTHOR

Aviva Jane Carlin's family comes from South Africa and moved from there to Uganda, where Aviva was raised, while her father taught English Literature at the University of East Africa, and her mother worked in the Department of Preventive Medicine at Mulago Hospital. She was educated at Kenya High School For Girls, and later at London University.

She did a post-graduate acting course at The Drama Studio, London and from there was invited to join Theatre Impact, Maggi Law's award-winning ensemble company, in which she spent two very happy years, acting, writing and touring.

She came to The United States in 1989, to work with her brother, Seattle film-maker Alec Carlin. She stayed on in Seattle, acting, writing and teaching until March 1996, when she moved to New York.

She has written and performed four one-woman shows: *Almost Grown Up, What Does The Devil Look Like?; Nanny In The Park;* and *Jodie's Body;* as well as one two-hander, *Finn & Roxy's Christmas.* She is at present writing a full-length play, *The Mother Teresa Girl,* for the Joseph Papp Public Theatre.

ORIGINAL PRODUCTION

Jodie's Body, written and performed by Aviva Jane Carlin, began performances Off Broadway at the Gene Frankel Theatre on January 5, 1998. It was produced by The New Mercury Players, William Repicci and Michael Minichiello in association with Michael Stoller, Joel O. Thayer and Rare Gem Productions. The production was directed by Kenneth Elliott with set design by B. T. Whitehill and lighting design by Viveon Leone. Aviva Jane Carlin played Jodie. On February 18, 1999 the production was transferred to the ArcLight Theatre where it was produced by Julian Schlossberg, Gloria Steinem, William Repicci, Chris Groenewold and Meyer Ackerman. On June 27, 1999 *Jodie's Body* closed after its 400th performance.

Lights up on an artists' studio. There is a block, draped with fabric, stage left and an armchair stage right, with a kikoi—an African body-wrap—lying over it. Upstage is a still life arrangement which includes a bowl of fruit. Jodie, an artists' model, is alone on stage, posing naked. She stands, facing the audience, her weight on one supporting leg, her hands clasped against the back of her head. Supposedly there are three art students drawing her. She regards each of them in turn.

JODIE: Look at them all, fidgeting around. You'd think they'd get organized before I start, wouldn't you? When I first began this job, I decided, after I'd been doing it for a few weeks, that I was not going to take the robe off until people had got all their stuff arranged. Because I felt a bit weird, you know, standing there, posed, with everyone busily sharpening pencils and squeezing out blobs of paint and completely ignoring me. Sometimes I'd get this panicky feeling that I had totally misunderstood the whole concept and they were all just too embarrassed to ask me why I had taken my clothes off. So I'd wait until they were all quite ready and looking at me expectantly and then I'd take off the robe and get into the pose and then they'd all immediately find something else to mess around with. So after a while I realized, it's no good, they just have to, they just have to do a bit of fiddling around, before they get going. Creative process kind of thing. Or maybe it's just the plain old work evasion tactics that accompany beginning every human endeavor. Or sometimes, specially with first timers, you know, evening institute or something, it's a way of, kind of…dissipating the tension of suddenly finding yourself in a room with a naked person. Because not everybody realizes what life drawing is, you know, when they sign up. So I get some wonderful looks sometimes, when I take off the robe. Almost always immediately suppressed, of course. *"Naked.* Hey, well, don't worry about me, I'm sophisticated. In fact I'm bored. Naked woman in the middle of the room, I mean, *what* could be more boring?"…There. Now they're settling down. Well, too late, time's up, I'm changing the pose.
(She changes to a pose with one foot resting on the heel. Pause.)
…Here's an interesting thing that can sometimes happen. You can be quite experienced at this and then one day, for some reason, you take up a pose and within seconds you realize you've made a huge mistake. See this foot? This is a huge mistake…Shooting pains up the calf already…No, it's no good, I'll have to adjust. *(The foot comes down. Then, to one of the students.)* Oh, don't give me that little sigh, you. You

haven't drawn a single stroke yet. *(To the audience.)* That's Sherman. He thinks he's in charge of the class while George is away. But actually, I am. *(Back to Sherman.)* So. Tough luck, hard cheese, this is the pose, get on with it.

When I began I always did these really complicated poses. I was very earnest about it. Now I just make bloody sure I'm comfortable… Actually that's not true. I just had a little vision of my mother, there. Giving me the raised eyebrow. By which she meant, "Jodie. You have a tendency to sacrifice veracity for style. You like to say things that aren't quite so, just because they sound rather dashing. Well kindly remember, please, that however striking the packaging, it is what is contained within that counts." Sorry, Ma. *(Back to the audience.)* It's true, I do do that. And I don't want you to think I don't care about this, because I do. I want them to be…you know…to love the life class. The attitude of the model makes a big difference, you know. You have to want people to be inspired. That's what separates the good model from the one who's just okay. It looks as if it's only about your body, but it isn't. In fact, you know, people can actually find it quite difficult to draw you, if you don't…if only your body is in the room and not you. It sounds odd, but it's quite true. You have to care. You have to want them to look over and see the shape you make, and the lines of the pose, and the way the light hits you, and think, "Oh God I must draw that, I must paint that." On the other hand, you can learn to combine comfort with commitment. If you're doing a forty-five minute pose, ja nee, man, you'd better learn it… Ag, listen to that, I'm going all South African. I've been like this for the last three days. Ever since Tuesday…The miracle day.

(Changing the pose.) I decided we'd do a short poses class today. Which basically means me changing whenever I get bored or uncomfortable and them just bloody well putting up with it…Ag, there I go again! Okay, no, it doesn't mean that, sorry, Ma, it means…this is what George says, it means them disciplining themselves to draw quickly and surely and to look at the body as a whole, not get stuck on detail… and…what else? To relax! Just be happy with whatever they get done in the time and then move on. George thinks that's very good for them and so do I. This is, in fact, the favourite kind of class for many models. Apart from the kind where you're lying down on a velvet sofa with heaters all around you, reading a book.

It really changes your perspective you know, modeling. I mean about art. Well, not all art, obviously. Sunflowers make you feel whatever they did before, but if there's a figure in the work, your foremost consideration becomes…Was that person comfortable? And if they couldn't possibly have been, well…you develop a certain resentment towards that particular artist. Now take Gauguin. We all love Gauguin. Women just sitting around, in the sunshine, barefoot, eating mangoes, chatting to each other. That's what good painting is.

(Changing the pose to one with arms clasped at elbows on top of her head. Then looking at Sherman.) If George were here you would not be getting away with those impatient little noises over there. *(To the audience.)* …Of course they're all painting themselves, you know. That's one of those things people say about artists, isn't it? But it's amazing how often it actually happens. And fascinating to see, too. I mean how do they do it? I mean look at Sherman, right? Short, pale, freckled man, little bit weedy, bald. And when you look at the drawing he's doing, which is of me, tall, dark woman, not remotely weedy, or bald, you're going to see him in there. In the drawing. Somewhere in my face, he will be peering through. It's just the strangest thing.

(Nodding at another of the students.) And her over there. In the nice clean painting smock and the French beret. That's Estelle. She's going to paint me thin, like she is. She's sorry for me, 'cause I'm a fat girl, so she's going to paint me thin so as not to embarrass me. And I think so as not to have a horrid picture in her portfolio. She's very shy, but whenever she catches my eye she gives me this terrifically supportive smile. She kind of breaks my heart actually. Although I admire her, too, I do. I think she's brave. Because I think she's rather lonely. But look, see? She's not home by herself, watching television, is she? She's out at evening classes. And she's bought special clothes, so she'll look right for them. And she thinks about other people, she worries about poor fat models who have to expose their huge bums to rude buggers like him. *(Nodding towards Sherman.)*

She has to absolutely force herself to speak to people. She's only spoken to me once or twice. That time he *(Indicating Sherman.)* didn't want to paint me, she came up to me on the break and she offered me some lemon verbena tea out of her thermos and she said, "Well, um, I…I don't think that, um, being an *artist* is…is any *excuse* for…ungentlemanly behaviour, do you?" I said, "I think it's very kind of you to call him an artist." I said, "Your work's ten times better than his." Which wasn't actually true because their work is equally dire. But I didn't want to add to her emotion by saying, "You know what, Estelle? I just love you." Somehow I didn't think that would help her to relax around me…Well, this probably looks comfortable enough to you, doesn't it? In fact, I am slowly crushing my head into my neck.

(Changing the pose. Then, looking over at Sherman.) Fucker… *(Laughing.)* Actually it was pretty funny that day. There were two of us, two models, we didn't know each other. We started off with standing poses, as usual. And the class was absolutely full, easels crammed in everywhere. Then he *(Sherman.)* suddenly announces he has to move to a different spot. George says, "Oh, Sherman! Jesus ordered pizza! You can't disturb the whole room now! Just paint whatever you can see from there." And Sherman says, "No. I can hardly see the pretty one at all. I can only see the other one." Horrified silence, as you can imagine. The other model and I are, like, checking his angle of vision out of the corners of our eyes. We're studiously avoiding checking each other. 'Cause we both know we're each wondering which is which. George gave him hell, you'll be glad to know. He's very volatile, George is, he's lovely. He's a terrific artist. And he has a most original set of expletives, based around the idea of Jesus being engaged in various rather mundane activities. Estelle gets a bit flustered by that. Anyway, Sherman was not at all fazed by George hitting the roof. He just folded his arms and closed his eyes and waited, pointedly not painting, till the next pose was set. And then he says, he says, "Um. George, I'm going to paint this one's face…" that was me, "…on the other one's body. Just so you'll know, when you come round." George says, "What the bloody hell are you talking about now? What d'you mean, just so I'll know? You think you could paint a total mutilation of what you see before you and I might not notice if you don't tell me? Jesus put some shelves up!" He says, "What do you think this class is, anyway, bloody tabloid trick photography? If you paint Jodie's face, you'll paint Jodie's body. And if you're too stupid to appreciate it, then just paint the wall behind her! And shut up! Jesus defrosted the fridge!"

(Changing the pose. Nodding at the third student.) She's fun this one. With the gravity-resistant hair. Look at her, slapping the oil paint on. She always makes the most spectacular mess of herself. When she does charcoal, I mean, with that hair, she ends up looking like someone in a cartoon who's just suffered an explosion. She always wears those long scarves. And her name, so she claims, is Isadora. Which would seem like a rather bad luck combination to me. But she drives a VW bug and the scarves are always well weighted down with dried paint, so she's proba-

bly safe enough…She set me up as Isadora, once. She brought in all this lovely, flowing, Greek-style drapery for me to wear, and she put the fan in front of me so the drapery all went billowing out behind and she posed me in a walking forward position, very simple. Only I was doing it a bit too, sort of, prettily, I think, at first. She said, "No. No, dear. No. Not like that." And she told me how Isadora would always start her performance standing quite still, at the back of the stage, and then, after a moment, ("A moment of deathly hush, dear," she said to me), she would walk forward to the footlights. "And that was all she had to do, dear, for the audience to leap to its feet, applauding wildly. Weeping, dear, moved to a sense of glory by the power and presence of Isadora Duncan, *just walking.*"

Well, I may say, I was a little intimidated, and I think it showed. Because she assured me, hastily, that she'd been waiting a very long time to do this drawing and I was the model she'd been waiting for. I said, "Me?" I said, "But…I'm not exactly dancer-shaped, am I?" She said, "Well, no, you're not like today's dancers, are you dear? No. You're not some wispy little chain-smoking birdy-legs, are you? Well, nor was Isadora. That's the point. She had some proper flesh on her, like you and me. Look!" she says, thrusting this rather blurry old photograph at me, "Look at the thighs on that woman! Magnificent!" George comes to look over my shoulder. "Abso-bloody-lutely! Stupendous pair of thighs. Safe harbour for any man." *(She shares a look of amused exasperation with the audience.)* She says, "There's a male mind at work for you, eh? Isadora's thighs only mean one thing to him." George says, "Well? Well? If we're talking magnificence. What's the most magnificent thing God gave us, eh?" Sherman says, "Art!" George says, "He didn't give us that, you fool, Jesus rented Star Wars!" He says, "We invented art. To make up for the loss of everything else! Which in your case probably includes the ability to worship at the sacred shrine of Isadora's thighs." Of course poor old Sherman's not the only one who's lost the ability to love fat thighs, is he?

(She crosses to the block and takes the first in a series of sitting poses.) I wonder why thighs, particularly. I mean I would say thighs come top, wouldn't you? On the loathing and despair list. First thighs, then stomach, then bum. What a bloody waste of energy, eh?…Do you ever do that Martian trick?…You know, where you pretend you're a Martian and try and look at things anew? My mother likes doing that. And suggesting it to other people, she likes doing that, too. There was this woman on the beach, at Plettenburg Bay, once. I was happily disporting myself,

naked, in the waves and this woman wanted me to wear a swimsuit. I was four, I should say. Ma said, "Oh now wait a minute, here, wait a minute! Let us pretend, just for a moment, that we are *Martians,* all right? Now. Let us look at this scene anew. Because, you see, I think, as Martians, we really don't see any immodesty here. Or even any nudity, come to that. All we actually *see,* as Martians, is a small life form, splashing…Don't you think?"

So, Estelle. I want you to pretend for a moment that you're a Martian, all right? Now. How does getting all upset and embarrassed about thigh-wobble look to you as a Martian? Bearing in mind, Estelle, that thigh-wobble accompanies motion. In every single post-pubescent female that gets enough to eat, on the planet. H'm?

(Changing the pose.) Ooh, yes, I think veracity *and style* rather superbly married, there, Ma, wouldn't you agree?

I wrote my first book when I was six. It was about a little girl who caught a star with a fishing-rod. And she kept it in a shoe-box with holes punched in the lid. But it went all dim and lost its shine, so she tries all different ways of making the shine come back, but nothing works, so, eventually, she throws it back in the sky. And then, of course, it shines. Ma thought it was pretty good. She had a few suggestions, you know, for tightening it up and grounding the structure of the through line. But on the whole, for a first novel, she thought it was pretty well done…She called Golden in and had me read it to him. He was polishing the silver on the back lawn, I remember. Came rather reluctantly I thought. Ma said, "You' going to like this, Golden." So he did. *(Laughs.)* No, I think he really did, actually. And without any constructive criticism, either, which was nice and relaxing for me. And then Ma and Lally discussed it at length. Lally is Ma's best friend. She's a doctor. She never doesn't have a cigarette in her mouth. Ma said the book was about South Africa. She said that was the only thing South African authors could write about. She challenged Lally to mention a South African author who wrote about anything else. And Lally said, Patience Heartland, who wrote romantic novels and who inspired in my mother the most withering scorn. *"Authors,* Lally! I said *Authors!* Are we going to discuss this seriously or not?" Question she asked quite frequently of Lally, actually. Which Lally always enjoyed enormously.

(She changes the pose.) Every time I move, he gives me this exasperated sigh. *(To Sherman.)* Draw faster. *(She looks at each of the students in turn.)* These three never miss a class. There are some who just drop in

intermittently, and others who never miss…And there's no correlation between attendance and talent, which you might expect. There's a couple of casual droppers-in who are just brilliant. And then here's our core group. Three-quarters of it, anyway. And two of them are brilliant. And two of them are really beyond help.

Barry is the other brilliant one, he and Isadora. He's not here because he has to work some nights, to get money for materials. But he comes to as many classes as he can. 'Cause he goes to the local tech and their art department is not all that hot. He looks like this sort of rough, tough kid, you know, punk clothes, spiky haircut, cockney accent and everything. At the end of his first class, George told him that he *must* get himself into a good art school. He told him he could get a scholarship anywhere. He told him, "Don't even mess around, start at the top, apply to The Royal College of Art." Well. Sherman heard him. He was putting his things away and he started banging around, slamming the easel up against the rack. And George turned and looked at him and I was afraid he was going to start yelling, 'cause he hates the easels being slung around, but then I saw this look of…compassion, really, on George's face, and I suddenly felt just…so sorry for Sherman. I mean can you imagine? Having all that desire, and no talent? George said, "All right, there, Sherman?…'Ere, good work tonight. Yeah. Good work, mate." Sherman just gave him a dirty look and marched off in a huff. I suppose, "Good work, mate," hardly compares with, "You should get a full scholarship to The Royal College of Art."… Anyway Barry was saying something about opposition. I wasn't really listening, I was focused on Sherman, but I assumed he meant, you know…opposition at home. And I imagined him in this cockney home in the East End, with his dockworker father saying, "No son of mine is going to ponce about with *art!* That's for *fairies,* that is, *art!*" And his housewife mother saying, "Ooh, disgusting! All that nakedness. Dear me! What kind of woman strips off in front of strangers, I'd like to know! Disgusting!" And I made up this whole life for him. Furious, uncomprehending family, him struggling on, in the middle of them, going on making art against all resistance.

(Changing the pose.) Sculpture is Barry's real thing. I was doing this eight week pose, once. Most people were painting with oils, but three of them were sculpting, he among them. And they were set up directly opposite me, so I could watch them, working. And they were all doing torsos, so they looked sort of similar at first, but then…Barry's began to

be a woman and the other two's didn't. I don't mean they were totally incompetent, these other two, I mean their pieces looked like women… anatomically. But they also looked sort of thick and dense all the way through, you know? Whereas with Barry's…you had a sense of the sinews inside, holding the twist of the back…I got completely entranced, watching. I was trying to actually *see* where the talent came in. I mean how could it be that two of these sculptures had the weight of clay and the third had the weight of a woman's body?…Even the stillness of them had a…a different quality, you know? Two of them were still because they were objects. But the other one breathed. The other one was still because the woman had paused for a second…And with Barry's, you know, you got this feeling in your hand…you wanted to put your hand out and round it over the shoulder and the hip. And the other two did-n't do that to you. And why not? This was the thing. What was Barry actually *doing* that was different from what the others were doing? It was taking place right in front of my eyes, day after day, week after week… and yet, you know…There was no way to actually see it.

God, I loved that piece with such a passion. I got quite desperate, thinking of how his ignorant parents would dismiss it as pointless, if not pornographic. *(Changing the pose.)* So anyway…at the end of the session we had a little exhibition, you know, just for family and friends, and Barry came in with this older couple. Who could they be, I wondered? Kindly counselors from the tech, I bet. So he saw me staring and he brought them over to introduce them. And while I was still mouthing like a fish, his mother says to me, "Oh, we reckernize you, dear, 'course we do. You are all over our house, now do they keep you warm enough, dear?" And his father says, "Course we think Barry is another Leonardo, we do. 'E's been at it since 'e were a nipper. I've always found 'is work exceptional, meself, an' all 'is teachers all agree. I been putting money aside for 'im, ever since 'e drew 'is first drawring. If I 'ave anythink to do with it, 'e's 'eaded for The Royal College of Art!" So I was completely disoriented. And what had he been saying to George, then, about oppo-sition? I found out later, this was just artist talk, all about structure on the page and so on. This was when I was wailing and squirming all over George's flat, wringing my hands at my own awfulness. George says, "Oh, relax. You just fell prey to a bit of class prejudice. Happens to everyone." I said, "Don't even say that word while I'm in the building if you don't mind."…'Cause when South Africans hear the word prejudice they have to talk for about twelve hours.

(She returns centre-stage.) I'll do one more and then I'm going to take a break. *(Stretching her arms above her head.)* Let's see, what shall we have? *(Laughs. Indicates Sherman.)* Oh, *now* the enthusiastic sounds of approval. This is not a pose, you twit, I can't hold this, I'm stretching! *(She drops her arms.)* Oh!…okay, well, just for that little noise, we' going to do…vanilla. *(She simply stands, arms by her sides, weight slightly on one foot.)* …There are general rules about how long you're supposed to pose before you take a break, but we don't often stick to them in this class. Although Sherman always thinks we should. He does a lot of puzzled staring at his watch, if I break before I'm supposed to. Once he even shook it and held it to his ear. George said, "Oh, Sherman, Jesus paid his lib'ry fines, we're painting the human body, here! That means we need a human model! She'll take a break according to her human body's needs, is that clear?" *(Laughs.)* It's odd to do the class without George striding about, ranting. He's exhibiting in The Manchester Festival at the moment. Told you he was good. Many, many paintings of me are being gazed at by people from all over the world, as we speak…There's a South African dance troupe there…they've only just arrived, because of course they waited, for the day of days…I have this fantasy that Toujie is with them. That's Toujie Lungiswa, Golden's eldest daughter. She always wanted to be a dancer and I have this fantasy, that she's there, in Manchester. And she sees the paintings. And she goes, "God, man,* it's Jodie." And then she finds George, and she says, "How can I get hold of this model of yours, eh? She's my friend, from home." *(A moment of grief. Then she recovers.)* …Not very likely, though. Ma still keeps in touch with Golden. If Toujie were coming to England, he would certainly tell her, he knows I'm here. He sent me congratulations, through Ma, when my play was put on. He told her to ask me, are there any stars in it? I wrote back, no, no, no, it's as fringe as it could be. But I thought, later, ag, maybe he meant the plot, not the actors, maybe he was remembering the story. I wonder what he thought about, on Tuesday, eh? Golden…I wonder if he was remembering those…those thugs. Yeah, well, we won, thugs, we won. Golden and Jane and Ma and Lally and Toujie and me. And several million other people. We won.

Twice over, really, if you think about it. I mean, first because it happened. And then again because it happened the way it did, by means of the use of reason and language. And by means, finally, ultimately, even after all that killing, by means of the use of the process of law. And this

---

* God, man" with Afrikaans pronunciation.

is a miracle. I'm not just bandying the word around. If you'd grown up in South Africa, you would know this. What happened on Tuesday is a real, actual miracle…And now I really am going to take a break.

(She puts on the kikoi while watching the students exiting, and then performs various stretches throughout the next paragraph.) This is when George and I usually have some good chats. When they've all sped off to the coffee shop. Or we walk around and look at their work together. Barry's and Isadora's first, of course. George with a fierce, critical glare and me with cries of pleasure and admiration. Toujie used to teach me these tribal dances when we were little girls, you know, and it was the same thing there…I mean about talent. 'Cause I could do them, the dances, I had the rhythm, I had the movement, I wasn't particularly… restrained or anything about it, but when we did these little shows, for our families, everyone watched her. They couldn't help it. I did not command any attention. I was this little white blur at her side. I didn't mind, though. I didn't even mind when Ma would say, "Now! Let's see Toujie on her own! Eh?" *(Laughing.)* No, no, that was the right thing. She was the dancing girl, I was the word girl. *(She eats some grapes from the bowl of fruit.)* I leave it to you to determine whether Sherman likes it when I eat the still life. "'Scuse me! I was drawing that grape!" I love modeling. Perfect job for a starving writer, I mean look at the material I get! And I never have to worry about what to wear for work.

I learned to read by being read to. My Ma was a tireless reader aloud. I used to get six or seven stories, every night. She would never stop to explain anything, but when she came across a word that she thought I might not know, she would put a kind of thrilling, magical emphasis on it, as if she could somehow just *push* the meaning into my mind. "She gazed at him, *inscrutably*"…"launching out bravely, into the *perilous* seas"…"lost and *forlorn*"…"through a tiny, leaded, *casement* window"… "dancing *exuberantly* round and round the *clavichord*" Oh! It was *so exciting!* I mean, she might as well have given me a bloody great cup of black coffee before she put me to bed…And then the other way I learned to read was by copying words out of magazines and asking people what they said. "Ma, what does this say?" "That says, sparkle!" "Golden, what does this say?" "That says Kimberley." "Lally, what does this say?" "That says go away, Jodie, I'm busy. Oh, don't flounce! I'm having a joke with you! Come here!"

I longed to go to school. I waited and waited and *waited. Finally* the day arrived. I had a new green and white checked dress, school uniform.

And a satchel on my back, with lunch in it. And a hat. And...*shoes!* A good four sizes too big, so I could wear them for several years. And my first pair ever. English people never believe this, that I had no shoes till I was five. It's a sign, to me, of the fact that they don't really *get* that I come from another country. I am not an English person who just sort of happened to grow up in South Africa. I am a South African person. The only reason I'm in England is because *we travel.* We are like Australians. We look around one day and we say…"H-m…Yes, I have to go now." Anyway. My first day at school. I said goodbye to Ma, and went inside, vibrating with anticipation. And I saw all the children hanging up their hats and their satchels, on little hooks, in the hall. I thought, "Ah, yes, good, I see what to do, new things go on those little hooks, 'kay, good, I see." And I hung up my hat and my satchel and my shoes, with my new socks tucked neatly inside, and went on into class. I was ready, let the learning begin! And then all the children began to giggle, and all of them were looking at me. And I stood there, barefoot, between the little coloured tables, and for the first time in my life, I doubted myself. *(Becoming the teacher, bending over kindly.)* "Where are your shoes, little girl? Didn't your mother buy you any shoes for school?" *(As herself, looks at the other children's feet. Surprised.)* All the other children were wearing their shoes! Inside! Whatever for? This was curious. I said, "Well, I didn't know children wore shoes inside." *(Teacher.)* "Well, p'aps not at home, but you' in school now. School is where we learn to be grown up. Grown ups wear shoes inside, don't they? Ask your mother to buy you some shoes for school, eh? And make sure and wear them tomorrow. Okay?…All right?…Lovely." I didn't tell her they were hanging on the hook outside, just didn't want to complicate the matter any further, I think. So I did have one day where I wasn't flapping around in those bloody huge shoes all day long.

The work was a great disappointment, though, colouring in shapes and stringing beads and then, inexplicably, she puts on this scratchy old record and we all have to run about the room on tiptoe. Swooping occasionally. This is not what I came to school for…swooping! But that didn't last, thank God. Because by the end of that afternoon they had discovered that I could read and the next day I was transferred. To Miss Boshoff's class. Where there was a blackboard, with the alphabet most beautifully inscribed upon it. All the straight lines so nobly, so implacably straight, and the curves so lusciously curvy. Each big letter standing protectively over its little sibling. And Miss Boshoff launched the class into reading without any nonsense at all. Pointing out to us, that by mastering a mere twenty-six letters, we could have the world of language, "Which is, as a matter of fact…the whole world," she said to us, "At our feet for ever"…This is beginning to sound like a story about how clever I was, isn't it? It's not supposed to be. It's about how I was the word girl. Because…I understood Miss Boshoff. And when she said that, about the whole world, something like a pair of heavy wings started beating in my chest, and I stood up, out of my little blue chair…I said, "Oh, Miss Boshoff… *(Hands clasped, bowing passionately.)* …*Yes!*"

She got me off to a very good start, Miss Boshoff. I was lucky to have her, you know. None of my other English teachers was ever quite so inspiring again. However, I had Ma. When I went to university I was the only person in English Literature who could diagram a sentence. Ma was torn between mourning the loss of education, and triumph at my acknowledgement, finally, that I was glad she had worked me so hard. Because all my friends thought she was such a dragon, keeping me in every other night, studying. And I pretended to think so too, but secretly…I was extremely interested. I was such a swotbag, ever since Miss Boshoff. In high school, all the girls used to pretend to read Jane Austen on the desk, like this, but they would *really* be reading Patience Heartland, *under* the desk, you see. So I had Patience under the desk as well, so that nobody would know what a brainbox I was. And I was pretending to pretend to read Jane while I was really reading Patience, but in fact I really *was* reading Jane. And I was terrified that the girls would find out about Jane, and Ma would find out about Patience. I mean not that I was reading her, she bored me to death, but…well, just the fact that I wasn't open about who I was, that I cared what the other girls thought. That was a bit of a crime to her. Lally was more sympathetic. "Ag, man, Margaret, the child doesn't want to be teased, that's all there is to it, it's no more sinister than that." Ma thought you should have the courage of your convictions and take a chance on being teased, and then *flout* your tormentors with *intelligence* and *argument*.

She said this to Michaela Van Der Byl, who was my friend when I was nine. Although why she was my friend, I will never know. I think it was her dullness that attracted me. She was teased for being extremely thin and pale…and sort of wavy…she was a wafty sort of girl…In fact now I come to think of it she was really rather an odd little creature…There might even have been something a little bit wrong with her. She was given to making these slightly un-called-for remarks, out of the blue. Like, "Your Ma is as fat as a hippo. She's nice. But she's fat as a hippo." I mean. Supposed to be my friend. I don't call that very polite, do you? I said, *(Much offended.)* "Oh, is she?... Really?...Well...Well... *(Sudden thought.)* Hippos aren't fat! They' just the perfect size for hippos!" To which of course Ma or Lally, or I would have replied, "True, but they' pretty fat for people, aren't they?" I counted on Michaela not being advanced enough to think of this. Counted quite correctly, thank you. Later on, I asked Golden if he thought Ma was too fat. First of all he said it was not for him to say, but when I *insisted,* that I *must* have his opinion, he said no, he thought she was just right for a woman. Then I asked Lally. She said, "Oh. Well. She is...solid, isn't she? But I always think of her as big and strong, you see, not fat." I said, "So, then, um, not...anything like, um, as fat as...for instance...oh I don't know, let's think of an example...well...say, um...a hippo, for instance. Nothing like that, eh?" Lally said, *(Derisive laugh, as Lally.)* "Who told you that, eh? Your friend the noodle? Vermicelli girl?"

Now. A couple of weeks after Michaela made this remark, my mother saved her from drowning. We were all standing on the end of the pier, gazing down into the deep dark water, twelve feet below, and all of a sudden there was this pathetic little splash and Michaela had just wafted over the edge and dropped in. Well. Ma went in after her before she hit the water. Perfect dive. Straight as a submarine. Hands together, head down, toes pointed. Royal blue dress streamlined against her. Cleaving the water like a diving whale...And listen, in my memory, she comes up out of the water, holding Michaela in one hand, above her head, like this. Don't think that's a real memory, do you?

Anyway Michaela's parents came over later, to thank her, and they were all sitting on the stoop, having a drink and a chat...I was swinging on the swing, in the garden, watching them, thinking how beautiful Ma looked. Sitting up straight, feet planted, her hair in its usual squashed bun. And then Lally drove up and went and joined them and I saw Ma give Lally a sort of warning look, so I stopped swinging and went and sat on the steps to listen, because this looked interesting. Mrs. Van Der Byl was telling about a present she had given her maid, a very smart little beach dress, with a matching bag and scarf. Mr. Van Der Byl was nodding approvingly. Lally said, "Well, now. There's an encouraging move towards a new South Africa. That should hold off any complaints from her. Eh?" Mr. Van Der Byl narrowed his eyes thoughtfully. Mrs. Van Der Byl said "Yes, you' so right...My own outfit, you know, from last year. Nice bright colours. I don't give her the pastels. I think they look rather odd in the pastels, don't you? Of course she'd wear them, they'll wear anything, won't they, these girls, but I think the bright colours suit them best, don't you?" Ma and Lally exchanged what might be described as a richly textured look. Mr. Van Der Byl stood up and said, *(Hearty, agreeable.)* "I think we'd better be rolling along. Come on, Butterfly, time to go home."

Next day, Ma told me, quite straightforwardly, that she didn't want me to go to the Van Der Byls' house any more. She said it would be dishonest to have Michaela come to my house without telling her that I wasn't going to her house any more, and, well, the best thing would be to just…detach myself from the friendship. As gracefully as possible. She said, "You don't really care for her, all that much, do you, Jodie?" Lally said, "I can't think what you ever saw in the child. She looks like a tapeworm with a face." I didn't particularly care. I did a bit of token whining, for form's sake. But I did want to know why Michaela should be blamed for her parents' shortcomings, whatever they were. I said, "What? Are they boring, too?" Lally hooted. Ma said, "I don't want you to be exposed to the way they talk, Jodie. The things that they believe to be true, are lies. The sorts of lies that make people's souls get sick and they' brains stop working. Now if you were a little older, you see, it wouldn't matter so much, but at your age, your mind has no…sort of…*shell* on it, yet, you see. It's part of my job, to make a sort of *shell* for your mind. Not to close it off! God forbid! But to protect it, you see, until it's stronger. So that it can still live and breathe and *grow,* but so that no-one can *poison* it, or twist it into a shape that stops it thinking or…" Here Lally interrupted, "Ag, man, Margaret, the child doesn't know what the hell you' talking about! Jodie. The reason your mother does not want you to play with the tapeworm is that her father is a stupid bloody rugger-playing racialist banker and her mother is a stupid bloody bowls-playing racialist bimbo. Okay?" And then Ma and Lally had a big fight. All about language and the ability of children to comprehend metaphor. But only initially. They soon got round to the real business. And they worked their way right back to nineteen-forty-eight, Cape Town University, when the Minister of Interior Affairs came to address the students, and Ma was all ready to *flout,* with *intelligence* and *argument,* but *Lally* kept *heckling* him, with *ribald remarks,* until in the end, *he left!* "Yes, with his tail between his legs, Margaret!" "And his thought processes untouched, Lally!" *(She laughs.)* …Passion and reason, that was them. Sense and sensibility, South Africa style. Wonderful women.

I wonder if Ma's ever thought she was too fat. Can't think so, somehow. I remember when I was about thirteen, I remarked, tentatively, once or twice, that I thought I might…go on a diet. First time she said, "M-m", she was reading an article about pulsars. She said, "M-m. We are not our bodies, Jodie. We merely live in them." Second time she said, "Ag, Jodie. Do you think Jane worries about her weight?" Jane is Golden's wife. I said I didn't know. Maybe. She said, "I don't think so, Jodie. Of course we can ask her, when she comes here, next week, but I think you will find, that she has other worries to concentrate on. Of a rather more serious and compelling nature." I said everyone's worries were serious and compelling to themselves. She said that was a good point. And a true one, too. *(Sudden thought.)* Which ought, of course, always, to be exactly the same thing. Would it be possible even, to have a good point that was not at the same time a true…worries! Worries! The worries of a safe, privileged, well-nourished, properly-educated, intelligent and beautiful little white girl, living in the suburbs were not to be compared, from an objective point of view, say that of a Martian, for instance, with the worries of an African woman with five children, forcibly separated from her husband for most of the year, and living under a government that did not consider her a responsible adult!…So. You know what I picked up on? Out of all that? The word beautiful. Just thrown in there, without any weight attached to it, just because that's what I was, to her. It made my heart do a little wriggle of love for her. But I was thirteen, I would far rather go on arguing than tell her I loved her. I said, well, even if Jane did have other worries, how did we *know*, that she didn't *also*…worry about her *weight?…In secret?* Ma pointed out to me that Jane had been the same size ever since I had known her, which was my whole life. I said, "Well, maybe she just doesn't do anything about it, eh? Because Golden likes her that way." And I did a bit of a smirk, here, and she gave me a very dry look. "You are perfectly clever enough, Jodie, to follow my argument and respond to it. Without all these red herrings. We are discussing comparative concerns in South African society. Not Jane's and Golden's attractions for each other. Which are none of your business, Missy"…Well, all the same, I thought, I would ask Jane, when she came, if she'd ever thought she was too fat, and if she cared. *(Realization.)* But in fact, you know…I never got round to it before the…before everything happened.

Anyway. They came. Toujie and I made friends again. We liked each other such a lot, you know…really…such a lot. But we only saw each other every now and then and somehow…it was like we always had to start all over again. Although not when we were little…then we just used to pick up where we'd left off last time. Racing across the back lawn to our house in the hibiscus hedge…But as we got older, as we found out our country…a certain…shyness…was born between us…and we'd have to make a small effort, every time, to get back to being easy with each other. Someone…someone was building a little wall across the landscape that we knew, and we kept accidentally finding ourselves on opposite sides of it. So one of us would climb over, with the other one's help…and every time we did it…we thought…we thought we'd done it forever…and we'd be so relieved…And then the next time, there it was again, a brick or two higher…just kept on growing up…

Anyway. They came. Golden took a few days off, as usual, and we all had a happy time for a while.

You know I think the pass laws were the bedrock of Apartheid. It wasn't so much the separation of races that…kind of…shored that structure up. But the separation of black men and women from their families…that was…so fundamentally demoralizing. I mean when Ma wanted Golden to sue the police, he wouldn't, because Jane and the children were out of reach of his protection. Even though his ability to protect them wasn't really…very real.

Anyway what happened to end the happy time, was this. Golden went out one evening, and Jane and Ma and Toujie and the little ones and I were all in the kitchen, drinking tea, catching up, trying to coax the little ones to talk, and about ten o'clock, we heard this big knocking on the front door. Ma said, "Is that Lally? Why doesn't she come round the back?" *(Then an uneasy thought. A look at the little ones.)* "Well, I bet the side path light is gone again! I bet that's it. She's left her silly glasses at home!" And she went into the lounge and looked through the front window. And then she came back, and she said "I'm just going to close this door." And she didn't look at anybody. And Jane stood up and said, "…Madam…" Ma said, "I'll just see what they want. Probably a mistake, Jane." And she closed the door. And then we heard her walking across the lounge floor, and we heard the front door open, and we heard men's voices. We couldn't hear any words, just a sort of rumbling sound. And Jane said, "Jodie. Put out the light." So I did, and Jane went very close to the door, and Toujie and I went too. The little ones sat quite still. They were well-trained. Well-trained little African children. You could hear their breathing, quick and light and frightened, in the dark. And Jane turned the door handle, slowly, slowly, slowly, and she eased the door open, just about an inch, and we heard Ma saying, "…'Fraid you are mistaken, Gentlemen, Mrs. Lungiswa is not my servant. She is an occasional visitor to my home." And then we heard, rumble, rumble, rumble, Golden Lungiswa, rumble, rumble, rumble. Their accents were heavy, Afrikaans accents, but their voices were muffled by the bulk of my mother, standing there, barring their way. Toujie and I were crouched and wedged, down between Jane and the wall and we could only see her outline, which was sort of blurred, there was a kind of yellow haze all around her, from the light on the stoop. But she looked so solid. She looked as if you could run full tilt against her and you'd just bounce off. She stood with one hand on the wood of the doorway and the other one just relaxed at her side, and she barred the way to Jane. With her big, solid, beautiful body.

"Well, now, Gentlemen, as to that, I'm afraid I would need to see a search warrant." Rumble, rumble, rumble, rumble "You know I don't know where, Gentlemen. Mr. Lungiswa did not confide in me. I can't help you, there." Rumble, rumble, rumble, rumble "Ah…well…as to that, you see, Mr. Lungiswa and I do not discuss…politics, as a general rule, so I would have no idea where his sympathies might lie." Rumble, rumble, rumble, rumble "Well, now, co-operation, that's a two-way matter, isn't it, Gentlemen? The word means, working *with,* as I'm sure you know, co from the Latin, meaning…" Rumble, rumble, rumble, rumble, rumble, "I'm sorry, Gentlemen, Mrs. Lungiswa is not available at the moment." Rumble, rumble, rumble, rumble "Oh, m-m, that's odd. I thought I had just said. Not without a search warrant." Rumble, rumble, rumble, rumble, rumble "Dear me, you having some trouble understanding me, Gentlemen. Let me be plain. The answer is…No. You may not come in." *(She takes a deep breath, revisited for a moment by the intensity of this event.)*

…Well. Anyway. They went away in the end. Ma came back in the kitchen and we sat in the dark and talked. Ma thought Jane and the children should leave straight away, in case they got a search warrant and came back, and took Jane in for questioning. They were looking for Golden of course. They had broken up a meeting and he had got away. Ma knew of several places they could go to. The Chancellor of the University, for instance, could get them to a farm belonging to some relatives of his, up country. With five children to conceal that seemed like the best place. It was a big farm with a lot of families. So Ma phoned the Chancellor and he said he would come over right away. Jane and Toujie went to pack and Ma started making some food, for the journey. I took the little ones to the bathroom and made sure they went. I chatted heartily the whole time, but they just gazed up at me, holding on to the seat, so as not to fall in. When the Chancellor arrived he said there were no cars at the end of the road or anything, but still, best not to hang around, eh? So we turned off the outside lights and went out to his car. Which was right up close to the side path, with the doors already open. And then…for the first time, I'm sure, in their long, respectful history…Jane and Ma embraced. They stood by the open car door, with their arms wrapped around each other, just…holding on, holding on. In the warm South African night.

Now…um…Toujie and I hadn't hugged for about a year at this point and I thought this would be a good moment to get past that. Of course she was in a hurry, and probably a little bit frightened, everyone was a little bit frightened, and she was bundling the little ones into the back, and I don't think she saw me…at least not, you know, that I was, sort of…standing there, all ready to hug, because she…she actually sort of pushed past me, to get in. And I lost my balance a bit, which was, you know…tiny bit…embarrassing. But…I recovered…and I thought… "Okay…well, um… I…I could…I could still do it. I could, um…lean in the car, I could do it like that." So I bent down to look in. *(She bends, looks.)* And she was sitting with her back hard against the seat and her hands jammed in between her knees, like that…And in the end I just…sort of…well, I just…patted her on the shoulder. I said, "Cheers, eh, Toujie…I s'pose I'll see you next time, eh?" *(She recreates herself hesitating and then awkwardly patting Toujie on the shoulder.)* And she said, *(Becoming Toujie leaning away.)* "Yes…yes…I s'pose so…goodbye."… And then the Chancellor said they really should get going and Jane got in the front seat and they drove away.

So…Golden did not come back that night…So Ma went to the police station the next morning to see if he'd been arrested. But they said they'd never heard of him. Which turned out to be a clerical error, because he came home three days later and he had, in fact, been arrested that same night. He wasn't very important, Golden, he wasn't a leader of anything, they hadn't actually broken any bones. They had mainly… well, you can imagine…slammed their fists into him really hard. Kicked him with those great big boots they wear. Smashed him with nightsticks. *(Sudden memory.)* Here's something interesting, Lally told me this once. She said that there is a fracture of the forearms which is actually *called* a nightstick fracture. You get it across here, and across here, *(Indicating the underside of each forearm in turn.)* from going like this. *(Arms crossed protectively over her head with forearms exposed.)* She checked Golden for that but he didn't have it, luckily. He was mainly just really horribly bruised. And *really* swollen up. And his skin was split, it was like it was just burst open, all over the place. Had a lot of dried…blood on him. I kept thinking about it actually happening. All these beefy, cruel men crowding over, beating and beating, as hard as they could…and Golden underneath them sort of…rolling and scrabbling around on this dirty floor smeared with blood. And after a while I went and stood on the stoop. And Lally fixed him up, as well as possible, and then she came outside and she went and sat in her car and had a cigarette. And she saw a little smudge of dirt on the inside of the windscreen and she licked her finger and leaned forward to rub it off…and I saw that she was crying. And I went back inside. Golden was sitting at the kitchen table, drinking tea through a straw. I said to Ma, "Ma…Lally's crying. In the car." She said, *(Tired, irritated.)* "Oh, shut up, Jodie." I said to Golden, "Um…Are you all right, Golden?" And he nodded. He even smiled at me a little bit. Round the straw.

Ma wanted him to sue the police. They talked about it two nights later. He was feeling a tiny bit better, and we had heard from the Chancellor that Jane and the children were all right, no-one had come looking for them, or anything, so Ma thought Golden could concentrate, now, on what to do. Which was, use the law and sue the police. Golden didn't want to. They talked till late. They sat on either side of the kitchen table, with just that one light on above them. I sat in the window seat, in the lounge, in the dark, and listened, and looked at Golden's bashed up face…We are not our bodies, we merely live in them…

Ma said she understood his reluctance, of course she did, but this was the way forward, the best way, for him, for the country, for all of us. "Look at Mr. Mandela, Golden," she said. "There he is, locked up in prison, but every time, Golden, every single time, the guards do not obey the rules, he writes a letter to the prison governor. And he keeps on writing until something is done." Golden said he was not Mr. Mandela, Madam, he did not have Mr. Mandela's mental powers. "Oh, of course you do, Golden, of course you do!" Golden said no, he did not, he was not a lawyer, like Mr. Mandela, he was a servant. Ma said that a man's profession was no indication of his intellectual ability, not in this country, "And anyway, Golden, it doesn't make any difference, you are just as important, as a man." Golden said it did make a difference, Madam, he did not have Mr. Mandela's education, to write a letter to anybody, and he did not have any powerful organization behind him. He had been to meetings. They could not protect everyone who went to meetings. Ma said, "But you have me, and Dr. Lally and the Chancellor, and many other friends, who have something to say about this and who will say it, in court." Golden looked down at the table. Ma said, "We must behave... *as if the law worked.* This is a powerful stance to take, Golden. People have sued the police and won. You know this, Golden. We must use the law. As Mr. Mandela recommends. We must do as he asks us to do... while we wait for him. Surely we must, Golden...Surely we must."

(Pause. She shakes her head.) Golden wouldn't do it. Jane and the children were too vulnerable, for one thing...and for another, he just didn't believe that any of *us* could save *him* from another beating up... Brute thugs... Yeah, well...their sun is set. *(Pause.)* I wonder what they thought about on Tuesday, eh? I wonder how they felt? On election day! I bet they spat blood!...There's an appropriate metaphor, eh? Considering how many other people they made spit blood.

(She puts her hands over her face for a moment, then sighs and leans back in the armchair. Pause. She hears something and looks in the direction the students exited.) Is that them?...No, good...They will be back soon, though...

I think I'll do sitting in the armchair poses next...Promise to keep them up for at least half an hour. I feel like sitting still, thinking. I do usually try and use this time, you know, modeling time. I write in my head, or I make lists of things I have to do, or I plan out letters I owe people. But just this last three days, I have not been able to concentrate on anything. I just keep on filling up with feeling.

Oh! Hey! *(Jumps up, returns centre-stage.)* On the day itself, on Tuesday, right? I was walking along, I was on my way to George's for a final sitting before he left for Manchester. I was going to help him load the van up afterwards, with paintings, and then he was going to drop me off at the embassy to vote. So I was walking along and I was thinking, "Back home. They all standing in line, waiting, right now. If you could go up in the sky and look down on the country, you could probably actually see them, thousands of people, in thousands of winding lines... like veins, carrying the country's blood. And every sign that says *Vote*

Here, is pointing to a piece of its beating heart and it's beating stronger and stronger all day long. By midnight tonight it's going to be pounding like a great drum. So I'm walking along, thinking this, and all of a sudden everything around me suddenly went...into, like, sharp focus kind of thing. It's hard to describe... *(Sudden thought.)* It was a bit like when you're in a foreign country, you know? And the light is all different. And it makes everything look...intriguing, doesn't it? And everything has its own life, and its own force, and its own beauty, whatever it is...It was a bit like that...There was the street, and the trees and the buildings and the sky...looking just like they had, you know, a moment before, but...different. Everything was the same, and everything was different.

I was trying to explain it to George, and he said, "O-oh! You should phone your Ma. That was probably the exact moment she dropped her ballot in the box, eh?" And then I just burst into tears. George said, "Hello?...Jodie...compose yourself, please...'Ere I got two hours to finish this painting, you know. Jesus took a spider out the bath, eh? What is there to cry about may I ask? People vote every day." Every day. So then I stopped crying and started laughing. A bit wildly, I think. In the end George just gave up on finishing the painting. *(She crosses to sit on the block.)* And he went into the kitchen, and he came out with his election day surprise for me. Which was several bottles of South African beer and a great big slab of billtong, which I never eat. And George started off sitting on the bed, with me, but then he just had to jump up and draw me, drinking to South Africa, in the nude.

And George said to me, "You know what? You are the best fat model I've ever had." He said, "How is it you don't buy into all the nonsense, eh?" I said, "Well, partly because I really do come from another country. Partly because Ma saved Michaela Van Der Byl from drowning. And didn't let the cops in the house. Partly because Golden loved Jane. And partly because I just don't give a shit." Which is true. I mean it's only flesh, isn't it? There's just a bit more of it than somebody I don't even know decided was okay.

(She unwraps the kikoi.) I would really recommend this job, you know, to anyone who doesn't like their body. You hear yourself described in the most glowing terms all the time, by the tutors. Because they're all artists, obviously. They live in a whole different world from people who think fashion models are more beautiful than my Ma. And you see people gazing at you intently, but without any judgement at all. Just trying to capture you as a work of art. And after a while, you start gazing your-

self. Anew. Like a Martian. And I bet that if you started off with a little tendency to be frightened of the thighs, you would end up thinking, "Ag, you know…Those girls are not that scary…in fact basically just a couple of fat old thighs, spreading out, relaxing…few little veins, here and there…dimples…nice little wiggly stretch marks in there…not all that repulsive, really, actually…*(She pats and wobbles her thighs, fondly.)* Hello girls! Hello!

Now I recognize, of course, that there is a structure in place, that maintains this notion, that we should all look a particular way. But… well…it's all made up, isn't it? It's a house of air…There's nobody guarding it, with a real army. With real men. With real guns…And fists and clubs and boots and chains and nightsticks…And twenty-seven years in prison if you say you won't live like that. I mean, my God!…If Apartheid could come down!…If *Apartheid* could be dismantled…there is nothing on earth that couldn't be…Apartheid was like this unbelievably huge steel eagle. Whose wing span blotted out the whole sky and whose eagle eye saw everything and whose razor beak stabbed out at anyone who defied it and whose talons went into the land, through the earth, through the rock, through the diamond mines. Holding on. Biting into the country. Holding on, holding on, holding on. And I'm telling you… the people…who maintained that structure…thought nothing ever… would dislodge it…But you see what happened…Three days ago, over there…Golden voted.

And over here…Jenny Craig banked another million.

Oh, here they come, all pepped up with ginger biscuits and English coffee…which I'm sure you will agree, has to be distinguished from every other coffee in the world. *(She rises and returns center stage.)* So. Is it time to dismantle that other structure now, girls? Eh? The good body, bad body one? Shall we do that? Use the energy for something else, shall we? Of a rather more serious and compelling nature? *(She takes up her final pose, an echo of the first one.)* How's this? *(She looks at the students, one by one.)* Oh, fidget time first, of course, I forgot. Go on then, fidget away…I'll be here when you're ready…Okay, things I have to do… Write The Great South African Novel…I'll call it, Golden Voted… Use the money from this week's classes to go up to Manchester and surprise George…Take him to see the South African dance troupe performing…Write a letter to my fat Ma…

Dear Ma, it was wonderful to talk to you on Tuesday…Your voice was all shaky…Oh, Ma.

(Lights down.)

END OF PLAY

REFUGE

by Jessica Goldberg

For my family

THE AUTHOR

Jessica Goldberg's play *Refuge* was was developed at The Juilliard School and subsequently won the Susan Smith Blackburn Prize in 1999. The play premiered off-Broadway at Playwrights' Horizons in November 1999. The play will be produced at Stages Rep. in Houston, Texas in February 2000.

Her other plays include: *Stuck,* which was presented at Rattlestick last season; *The Hunger Education* developed at The Mark Taper Forum's New Work Festival, Hartford Stage, The Eugene O'Neill Theater Center, and The Royal Court in London. Her play *The Hologram Theory* will have it's New York Debut at The Blue Light Theater Co. in March 2000. Among the theaters where her work has been performed are Soho Rep., Primary Stages, New Georges, Montana Rep., The Access Theater, and The Juilliard School.

Jessica is a graduate of NYU's Tisch School of the Arts Dramatic Writing Program and The Juilliard School's Playwrighting Fellowship under the direction of Marsha Norman and Christopher Durang. She is the recipient of the 1997 and 1998 Le Compte de Nuoy stipend, and the 1999 Helen Merrill Award. She has been a writer-in-residence at New York Stage and Film, a Fellow at The Sewanee Writers' Conference, and a Tennessee Williams Fellow in Residence at the University of the South. She is currently a member of The Primary Stages New American Writers' Group.

ACKNOWLEDGMENTS

There are a few people I need to thank who were crucial in the life of this play: Neil Pepe, Playwrights' Horizons, Richard Feldman, The Juilliard School, Charmaine Ferenczi, Soho Rep, and all the actors who helped to develop these characters.

ORIGINAL PRODUCTION

Refuge, winner of the 1999 Susan Smith Blackburn Prize, was originally pro-
duced at Playwrights' Horizons in its New Theater Wing in 1999. Tim
Sanford, Artistic Director; Lynn Landis, General Manager; Leslie Marcus,
Managing Director. It was directed by Neil Pepe, the scenic design was by
Scott Pask, the costume design was by Sarah Edwards, the lighting design was
by Tyler Micoleau, the sound design was by David Arbonara, the Production
Manager was Peter Waxdal and the Stage Manager was Karen Shepherd. The
cast was as follows:

Amy. . . . . Catherine Kellner
Nat . . . . Chris Messina
Sam . . . . Chris Bauer
Becca. . . . . Mandy Siegfried

CHARACTERS

AMY: mid twenties. The caretaker. No nonsense.
NAT: Amy's brother, twenty. The survivor of two massive brain tumors. He is
     handicapped.
BECCA: Amy's sister, sixteen. A raver.
SAM: A guy, late twenties to early thirties.

SETTING

The play takes place in a run-down lower middle-class home. The house
looks like it has been lived in for years.

TIME

The present

SCENE I

A small bedroom—books, a dresser, a bed, not much decoration, clothes strewn about. Amy sits on the bed smoking. She holds a ton of stuff inside. She looks worn but is dressed sexy. Sam moves about the room looking at things.

SAM: Nice room.

AMY: You think?

SAM: Yeah. Lots of books.

AMY: Yeah.

SAM: Reading feeds the mind, huh?

AMY: Supposed to.

SAM: Yeah, small.

AMY: The room?

SAM: Yeah.

AMY: Big enough.

SAM: Sure.

(He approaches her, looks at her cigarette.)

SAM: You gonna put that out?

AMY: Sure.

SAM: You're pretty.

AMY: Nah, I got hips.

SAM: That s a good thing.

AMY: A butt.

SAM: That's good too. *(He kisses her.)* Taste nice.

AMY: Thanks.

(He kisses her again, longer now.)

SAM: You wanna turn the lights off?

AMY: How do you want 'em?

SAM: Most ladies don't like it with the lights on.

AMY: I don't care.

(He kisses her hard, real, she pulls his belt.)

SAM: Ow! You're a wild thing, aren't you?

AMY: Nah.

SAM: Its okay. Don't mind.

(She undoes his belt, they fall on the bed kissing.)

SAM: You got a bag?

AMY: What?

SAM: A safe?

AMY: Rubber?

SAM: Yeah.

AMY: No.

SAM: Shit. Let me check. *(He goes to his wallet, looks in.)* Got one.

AMY: Great.

(He comes back to Amy, puts the condom on the bed, begins to kiss her. They get into it, they begin rolling around on the bed.)

SAM: Can we turn a light off?

AMY: Sure.

SAM: Got a candle?

AMY: Doubt it.

SAM: It's romantic.

AMY: I don't have one.

SAM: Okay. *(He gets up, turns the light off.)* You do this a lot?

AMY: What?

SAM: This.

AMY: No.

SAM: Shouldn't, it's not healthy.

AMY: I don't.

(He kisses her more and more... They get into it, they are into it. A sound in the house, unheard, then, outside the door, then, a knock, a voice.)

NAT: Ames, Amy, Ames.

SAM: Who's that?

AMY: Shh... What?

NAT: *(Unseen, behind the door.)* I can't sleep.

AMY: Lay on your side.

NAT: Hurts.

AMY: Try your back.

NAT: It hurts everything. C'I come in?

AMY: C'mon.

NAT: Someone in there?

AMY: Go to bed.

NAT: You okay?

AMY: Fine, go to bed.

NAT: *(Whining in pain.)* Everything hurts, my head, my back, havin' nightmares.

AMY: *(To Sam.)* Shit. *(To the door.)* Go in your room, I'll be in in a sec.

NAT: I could come in.

AMY: I'll be right there, please.
(Quiet. They wait, then, the sound of Nat shuffling away.)
AMY: Sorry. My brother.
SAM: Oh.
AMY: He's been sick.
SAM: Yeah.
AMY: Gotta go, I'll be back.
SAM: Right.
AMY: You don't have to wait.
SAM: It's okay.
AMY: You sure?
SAM: How long?
AMY: Quick, I'll be quick.
(She goes. Sam sits on the bed, smokes, looks around the room, moves around, turns things over, takes off his shoes, gets up, moves, uneasy. Amy returns.)
AMY: Sorry.
SAM: He okay?
AMY: Yeah. He gets nightmares, had an operation, doesn't have a bone back there.
SAM: That's gotta be hard.
AMY: Yeah.
SAM: You take care of him?
AMY: Yeah.
SAM: Must be hard.
AMY: You took your shoes off?
SAM: Just him and you?
AMY: And my sis.
SAM: Where's your parents?
AMY: That mean you're staying?
SAM: Yeah. Did they die?
AMY: No.
SAM: My brother died, few years back, car accident, family you can't replace 'em, hardest thing to lose ya' know? People are full of sorry's, think they understand, they don't. We were close, real close, after he died—
AMY: I'm tired.
SAM: What?
(She approaches him.)
AMY: I'd just like that, if you stayed.
(Blackout.)

SCENE II

Lights up in the kitchen the next afternoon. Becca dances around the kitchen. She wears huge headphones and bops her head to the music. She is sixteen, pretty, dressed to club. Amy enters, she is reading.

BECCA: Wanna hear about my dream?

AMY: What?

BECCA: My dream, wanna hear about it?

AMY: Sure. *(Amy reluctantly closes the book.)*

BECCA: Dreamt I was a baby again, in one of those baby things, you know, on moms back, right? And anyway thing is, it was stuck, you know, she couldn't get it off, right? She was freaking, but I was just happy shaking my rattle.

AMY: Wonder what it means?

(Becca makes a face as if to say: duh. She snorts.)

BECCA: Where's Nat?

AMY: McDonald's.

BECCA: By himself?

AMY: We're on a plan.

BECCA: Oh yeah, what kind of plan?

AMY: It's on the fridge.

(Becca gets up, looks at the fridge, reads the plan.)

BECCA: One: get up have coffee, Two: walk to McDonald's for an Egg McMuffin—try to talk to someone, Three: watch TV, Four: Read a half hour, Five: Walk with Amy, twice around the house, Six: More TV—eat a vegetable, Seven: write in journal before dinner. He writes in a journal?

AMY: Think it will be good for him.

BECCA: Yeah, right. *(Becca pulls out a bag of heroin. She cuts a line on the kitchen table.)* Have some of this shit left over from a few days ago, just want to get rid of it you know? Don't like to keep it around, you never know you could get searched or something so it's probably better to do it, 'cause you never know, right?

AMY: Nat'll be home soon, it'll freak him out.

(Becca snorts.)

BECCA: Want some?

AMY: I don't do that shit. You got any coke? I'll do some coke.

BECCA: Nah. I'm quittin' soon anyway, all the shit.

(Becca puts the heroin away, lights a cigarette. Amy takes one, lights up as well.)

BECCA: You love me, so I don't touch the needle. If you want me to stop just tell me, you can tell me to stop.

AMY: As long as you don't shoot up—Nat's here, lets not talk about this anymore.

(Nat enters, twenty, he is heavy, stiff, awkward. He carries his McDonald's bag. He stands in the doorway a little lost, like a sleepwalker.)

BECCA: Sit Nat, right here, c'mon.

NAT: Hey.

AMY: How was the walk?

NAT: All right.

AMY: Talk to anyone?

NAT: C'mon.

AMY: Gotta try.

NAT: I ordered the McMuffin.

AMY: Gotta try, only way.

NAT: *(Sits at the table, opens his Egg McMuffin.)* You don't understand.

BECCA: Its not like you're mute, you know.

AMY: Can we not—

NAT: I hate her, she doesn't get it, not at all, selfish—

BECCA: I'm so sick of you complaining.

NAT: Maybe people look at me, but they don't care, they don't give a shit—

BECCA: Like they give a shit about me, but I don't care.

AMY: Let's be nice.

NAT: Drug addict.

AMY: Stop, please stop.

(Nat eats.)

NAT: I could be a fly, I am a fly.

AMY: You're not a fly Nat.

BECCA: Could be.

AMY: You stop it.

NAT: She's so selfish, you don't spend every day alone, you don't have to know that no one will ever want you, that you'll never have a girlfriend, that you'll be alone, always alone, and your body will ache when you get up, and sometimes you can't even piss—if the piss comes that'll be your friend for one second, then it's in the toilet, gone.

BECCA: Amy's a fly.

NAT: No she isn't.

BECCA: I'm a fly too, even in a club or at a rave with hundreds of people around me. I'm dancing, and dancing, so hard, but still, it's just me, you know, only me. My arms, my legs, my head, movin, up and down, up and down, up and down. *(Becca closes her eyes, the heroin has hit.)*

NAT: Ame?

AMY: Yeah?

NAT: I got those shooting pains again, through my hand.

AMY: I'll get your pills.

BECCA: C'I borrow some cash, money Amy?

NAT: And lie down with me, rub it.

AMY: Its not time yet, wanna finish this book, days just begun, why don't you watch some tv, relax and I'll be in soon. No Bec we're broke.

NAT: Wish you could feel the pain.

AMY: Me too—

BECCA: I feel the pain.

AMY: —sometimes I wish it was me.

NAT: No you don't, you're too good, gotta take care of us.

BECCA: Please Amy.

AMY: How much?

BECCA: Ten, twenty, thirty bucks?

AMY: I don't know.

(Amy lights a cigarette, Nat eats slowly, Bec just stares off into space, the doorbell rings.)

AMY: Who's that?

BECCA: I don't know, could you get it?

(Amy goes to the door, she opens it. Sam stands in the doorway. Nat and Becca stare at him.)

SAM: Hi, I was wondering if you wanted to go out?

AMY: Now?

SAM: Yeah, it's a nice day.

(Amy looks out.)

AMY: I'm kinda busy. Where?

SAM: I don't know, Can I come in?

AMY: I guess. *(She lets him in.)*

SAM: How many rooms in this house?

AMY: What?

SAM: How many bedrooms?

AMY: Three.

SAM: Any extra space?

AMY: Why?

SAM: Lost my job.

AMY: So?

SAM: Need to rent, cheap, thought maybe the extra cash would do you good.

AMY: You wanna move in?

SAM: Sort of.

BECCA: Who's he Amy? What's he say he wants?

(Amy looks at Sam.)

AMY: What do you want?

SAM: A place to stay, that's all.

NAT: No space here.

AMY: The living room.

NAT: The living room? That's my room.

AMY: You have a room.

NAT: What about the tv?

AMY: We'll put it in here.

NAT: In the kitchen?

AMY: Why not?

NAT: He can't live here. Who is he?

AMY: Who?

NAT: Him, who is he?

AMY: Who are you?

SAM: I'm just Sam, need a place, lost my job, I do carpentry stuff, odd jobs.
Met you, you seemed nice. Its a calm house, I like a calm house, thought
I'd ask, give it a shot.

BECCA: Amy, can you get me a glass of water.

NAT: Nope sorry, no room here. *(Nat closes the door in Sam's face.)*

BECCA: Water, Amy, water.

NAT: What kinda shit person thinks he can live here, no room here.

(Amy opens the door, Sam is still standing there.)

BECCA: How much he gonna pay?

SAM: What do you think?

BECCA: Fifty a week.

SAM: Sounds good, sounds do-able, I could do that, if it's cool with you.

AMY: I guess, couldn't hurt, the money.

SAM: I like you.

(Blackout.)

SCENE III

The next day. Nat is watching WWF Wrestling on TV in the kitchen. Sam enters, gets a six-pack from the fridge. He sits, starts to watch the television. Nat looks at Sam and looks away, Sam tries to smile. Silence. Sam clears his throat.

SAM: What's up?

NAT: Nothin'.

(Nat watches the TV again. Silence. Sam tries again.)

SAM: Huh, this is great, funny.

NAT: Scum of the earth.

SAM: Yeah, lowest of the low.

NAT: Got a problem with scum?

SAM: Nah.

NAT: Cause you are?

SAM: What?

NAT: Scum.

SAM: You think I'm scum?

NAT: Didn't say that, you did.

SAM: When?

NAT: Said you were scum.

SAM: Who?

NAT: Forget it.

(Quiet. Sam tries again.)

SAM: Wanna beer?

NAT: I don't drink.

SAM: No?

NAT: What? That bothers you? Huh? Can't stand a guy who doesn't drink, not cool, huh?

SAM: I don't care.

NAT: Course you don't care. Nobody does. I don't need drinks, I don't need drugs, they're stupid. Never did, even before this, you're outcast if you don't do that stuff, you know? I went to college one-year and I was like this, this outcast cause I never took a sip of beer. People like you making me a outcast. I can't move my neck.

SAM: I didn't go to college.

NAT: So? Do what you want. Drink, drink eighty beers, I don't care.

(Silence.)

SAM: What happened to your parents?

NAT: I drove them crazy.

SAM: Huh...really?

NAT: Yeah.

SAM: Okay.

(They watch the tv.)

NAT: So, you're a bum, huh?

SAM: Sort of.

NAT: She doesn't need another bum.

SAM: Amy?

NAT: You staying in her room? At night?

SAM: I've only been here one night.

NAT: Did you stay with her?

SAM: Yeah, uh, yes.

NAT: I'll never be with a girl, never, I want to, but I won't.

SAM: I can get you a girl.

NAT: I don't want a girl. I want a wife.

SAM: Right.

NAT: *(Calling.)* Ame, Amy Ammmyyy!!!

(Amy comes.)

AMY: What?

NAT: Can you get me a green apple and a glass of water?

SAM: I coulda got it.

AMY: I'll get it. *(Amy gets the water and apple, puts them on the table. She leaves.)*

SAM: I coulda got it.

NAT: Nah, that's her job.

SAM: Can't get your own.

NAT: I get dizzy when I stand up. How are you gonna pay the rent without a job?

SAM: I'll get a job, tomorrow.

NAT: Nothin' I hate more than freeloaders. People just don't know what they've got.

(Amy comes back into the kitchen.)

AMY: *(To Sam.)* Are you gonna be around for supper?

SAM: I don't think so.

AMY: Okay. *(She leaves.)*

NAT: I used to play sports you know. Run, all that, I mean mentally I was off, but physically I was okay, look at my body now.

SAM: Can't you work on it?

NAT: What good would that do? It hurts too much anyway.

SAM: You could go to one of those places, you know, like a gym with doctors.

NAT: Yeah. I got the back of my head cut open twice, and all I got was one month of that therapy shit, only enough to get me off the couch. Gotta have money to be normal in this shit country, America, the rich get richer and the poor get drunk.

SAM: I think I'm gonna go out.

NAT: Am I driving you crazy?

SAM: No.

NAT: Sure.

SAM: I just gotta go. *(He gets up, moves out of the room.)*

NAT: I drive everyone crazy.

SCENE IV

Amy and Sam in bed, afterwards.

SAM: C'I ask you a question?

AMY: Depends.

SAM: You have an orgasm?

AMY: What?

SAM: You cum?

AMY: Why?

SAM: Just wondering.

AMY: Didn't I act like I did?

SAM: I was just wondering if maybe you don't feel, like the way you walk through this house, not feeling, not yelling, like that's what makes you safe. So I was wondering if you feel me, you know, in there.

AMY: What?

SAM: Am I gettin' to you?

AMY: You really think you'd be here if I didn't feel anything?

SAM: You using me?

AMY: No. Just talking back.

SAM: Hey, I'm no one's gigolo.

AMY: C'mon.

SAM: Then, talk to me.

AMY: What about?

SAM: Normal things, you ask questions, learn stuff about the person, you know.

AMY: Fine. You start. Go ahead, ask a question.

SAM: Okay, your brother really drive your parents crazy?

AMY: No. Where you from?

SAM: C'mon, gotta give a better answer than that. He really drive your parents crazy?

AMY: Nah, they retired to Florida, that's all I know, didn't leave an address, just a note: "Can't take it anymore, gone to Florida to retire, so little time left, please try to understand, love, mom and dad."

SAM: I'm from Cleveland.

AMY: What are you doing here?

SAM: Like to move around, never felt tied to anything.

AMY: That's lucky, I guess.

SAM: I guess. Hey, you ever want to get out of here?

AMY: Nah.

SAM: What were you doing before they left?

AMY: Was gonna go to school, I don't really like talkin' about this.

SAM: Maybe I was tied to my brother before he died, he used to get beat up and shit on the playground, I was in the car when it crashed—

AMY: Please. I'm not good at, I can't hear about…it makes me nauseous.

SAM: Hell Amy, you're like a…a…shook up beer, it's unhealthy.

(Amy turns away from him, on her side, and stares at the wall.)

SCENE V

Becca dressed to go out, and Nat playing checkers in the kitchen. Amy leans against the fridge reading. She smokes, she is somewhere else.

NAT: I met a Christian.

BECCA: Cool.

NAT: They're interesting, those Christians.

BECCA: Really.

NAT: I'm in McDonald's, and this Christian says, "you're not well, something's not right, I can tell."

BECCA: Yeah.

NAT: He was sick too, that's how he knew, sick like you, going to Dead shows, doin' acid, he found Jesus—

BECCA: That's scary.

NAT: He talked to me, about things, 'bout how we suffer, that was good, I don't get to have deep conversations much. Amy?

BECCA: I have lots of deep conversations.

(Sam enters with a black eye, he gets a beer.)

AMY: What happened to your eye?

SAM: Job interview.

BECCA: Really?

SAM: This fuck, he's taking me round the site, we're shooting the shit, everything's going great, I'm the man for the job, then, pow, $6.50 an hour for fucking construction. Construction! I told him to suck my ass-hole.

NAT: $6.50's better than freeloading.

BECCA: It's good to stand up for your rights.

AMY: You need some ice?

SAM: Punches me, pow, in the eye. Six fucking fifty an hour, my ass, my fucking ass-hole—you know? I smashed out all the lights on his car, front window too.

(Amy comes to Sam, touches his eye.)

AMY: Doesn't look so good.

(Sam holds her hand there, she tries to retract it.)

BECCA: It's walk time, isn't it?

NAT: What's that supposed to mean?

BECCA: It's time for you and Amy to take your walk.

AMY: That's right, lets go, once around the house.

NAT: "It's walk time, it's reading time, it's talking time," I just friggin'… yuhh… *(A guttural noise.)*

AMY: I know. I know.

BECCA: Better walk, or you'll get fat.

NAT: Fuck off.

BECCA: Hey Sam, Nat's getting brainwashed by the Christians.

NAT: What?

BECCA: He was in McDonald's and some Christian starts talkin' to him and he's so weak he starts talkin back, now he's getting brainwashed. They like people like him you know, fuckin' scary those Christians, always tryin' to save you, making life all serious.

SAM: Hey, I'm a Christian!

BECCA: Life is fun.

NAT: We talked about suffering. I like talking about suffering.

AMY: We'll walk, you'll tell me about it.

(Nat and Amy leave. Becca pulls a couple of pills out of her purse, pops them, drinks water.)

SAM: What's that?

BECCA: Ex. Slow hit, figure a couple of hours, by the time I get to Baltimore.

SAM: You're going to Baltimore?

BECCA: Rave.

SAM: What d'ya do there?

BECCA: Dance, get high. Wanna come?

SAM: Maybe.

BECCA: You should.

SAM: Amy go?

BECCA: Yeah right.

SAM: C'I get one of those?

BECCA: Ex?

SAM: Yeah.

BECCA: It'll cost you.

SAM: How much?

BECCA: Thirty bucks.

SAM: Isn't there a family discount?

BECCA: What? You?

SAM: Sure.

BECCA: 'Cause you're fucking Amy?

SAM: Hey.

BECCA: What? You like her?

SAM: Sure. Why? What do you think?

BECCA: Think you need a place to stay.

SAM: I'll give you ten now, twenty when I get a job.

BECCA: You coming to Baltimore?

SAM: Maybe.

BECCA: Okay.

SAM: You shouldn't do all those drugs.

BECCA: I'm only sixteen.

SAM: So.

BECCA: Got plenty of time to straighten out.

(Amy is back, comes in the kitchen for water for her and Nat.)

BECCA: Sam's coming to Baltimore, he thinks he's family.

AMY: Are you?

SAM: I don't know.

BECCA: He wants to.

SAM: That okay with you?

AMY: What do I care?

BECCA: *(Hands Sam a pill.)* Here, you better take it now.

SAM: Thanks.

AMY: You gonna take that?

SAM: Maybe. Wanna do it together.

AMY: No.

SAM: You be mad if I do it?

AMY: I said I don't care.

BECCA: She cares, wow.

AMY: No I don't. Do what you want, whatever you want.

SAM: Okay. *(He puts the pill in his pocket.)*

SAM: Wanna go to Baltimore?

AMY: No. No, I don't, okay.

SAM: Sorry.

BECCA: Did I piss you off Ame?

AMY: No.

BECCA: 'Cause I feel like I did.

AMY: You didn't.

BECCA: *(To Sam.)* Give it back.

SAM: What?

BECCA: The Ex, give it back.

SAM: Why?

AMY: You didn't piss me off, okay.

SAM: I'll give it back.

AMY: Look I don't care, both of you do what you want, okay.

BECCA: Fuck, see what you did.

AMY: He didn't do anything, nothing happened.

BECCA: It did Amy, I don't have to go, if you don't want, or I could come home, like with a curfew.

AMY: Its fine Bec fine, everything is fine.

BECCA: Really?

AMY: Yes, go.

BECCA: Amy?

AMY: What?

BECCA: I got bruises.

AMY: What?

BECCA: I got bruises on my arms and legs, big black and purple hard ones, wanna see?

AMY: What d'ya mean?

BECCA: See. *(Becca pulls up her sleeves, there are large purple and blue bruises covering her arms.)*

AMY: Oh my god.

(Sam gets up look at the bruises.)

SAM: You been shooting up?

BECCA: No.

AMY: Have you? Have you? I'll kill you.

BECCA: No, I swear, got 'em on my legs too.

AMY: Oh my god, has she been shooting up?

(Sam examines Bec's arms.)

SAM: I don't see any marks.

AMY: Well why does she have bruises?

BECCA: I don't know why. They come, they go, you know.

AMY: Maybe you're sick, are you sick?

BECCA: No.

SAM: She's gotta go to a doctor.

AMY: Why didn't you tell me, huh? Why?

SAM: Hey, just relax, probably from all that dancing, right? She'll go to the doctor, don't get worried till then, okay? Fuck, acting all crazy about a few bruises, hey. Okay Amy? Okay?

AMY: Right.

BECCA: I didn't want to tell you, didn't want you to get upset. Hug me.

AMY: Okay. *(Amy hugs her.)* We'll go to the doctor.

BECCA: Ow Amy, you're squashing me.

(Amy lets go.)

SAM: See everything's all right, right?

(The sound of a car horn.)

BECCA: That's my ride to Baltimore. *(Becca looks to Amy, waits.)*

AMY: Have fun Bec.

BECCA: If you don't want I don't have to go, you could make me go to bed early, sleep in the bed with me if you need to.

AMY: It's okay, have a great night.

BECCA: Yeah, bye.

(Becca leaves. Amy sits.)

AMY: What is it?

SAM: Don't worry about it, you'll go to the doctor.

AMY: I hate the doctor.

(Sam throws the hit of Ex in the garbage like he is making a basket.)

AMY: Didn't have to do that for me.

SAM: Wasn't gonna do that shit anyway.

(Nat shuffles in.)

AMY: Can't talk about it in front of him, everything's fine.

NAT: What? What?

AMY: Nothing, time to cook.

(Amy gets up to cook, Nat sits at the table, Sam and Amy act particularly okay.)

NAT: Get me a carrot Amy?

SAM: I'll get it.

AMY: Wouldya.

SAM: Yeah. (He gets up to get the carrot, he brushes by Amy at the stove making sauce, on his way back to the table, he bites her neck.) Look at us, like a family, me getting Nat a carrot.

(He kisses her again, Amy smiles.)

NAT: I can get my own carrot.

SAM: Look at that, Amy smiling. You see that Nat?

NAT: What?

(Sam brings the carrot to Nat, holds it out in front of him.)

SAM: Its good having me here, isn't it Amy?

(She doesn't answer.)

NAT: Amy?

SAM: It's good right?

NAT: Is it? Amy?

SAM: Is it?

AMY: I'm not saying it's not good, okay.

SAM: Yessss…

(Nat snatches the carrot out of his hand, eats.)

SAM: We could rent a movie or something later.

AMY: That would be nice.

SAM: Yeah…would be. Amy cares…

AMY: Please.

SAM: Tell you how I really got this black eye.

AMY: I thought you had a job interview?

SAM: Didn't make it, went to a bar, this guy asks me where I'm living, I say here, with you. This motherfucker says this family's crazy, bad luck, messed up, called you a slut.

AMY: What?

SAM: Said you were a wild teenager—

NAT: Amy's not a slut.

SAM: Always goin' to bars taking guys home.

AMY: It's not true. God people they've got no…it's not true.

SAM: Look, doesn't matter, long as you're my slut.

AMY: Shut up. I'm nobody's nothing, okay-nobody's nothing!

NAT: You should get outta here.

SAM: Hey, sorry, Amy knows I'm just joking.

NAT: Nobody has to get mad, Amy's happy. Amy's good. This Christian right, he said, that God or Jesus, or someone is gonna come back, come down, and you know, he's gonna judge who's been good, who's been bad, and the good go to Paradise, the bad go to hell, right? Amy'd go to Paradise, where would you go? Huh? She'll go to Paradise.

AMY: What'd he say it was 'sposed to be like, paradise?

NAT: Didn't say, I'll ask him tomorrow.

SAM: This is Paradise. Right here baby. This is it.

AMY: Yeah. Yes it is, this is paradise. Hallelujah! *(Amy turns back to the stove, she begins to stir her sauce furiously.)*
(Blackout.)

SCENE VI

A Rave in Baltimore. Becca moves through flashing lights. The music throbs. Becca dances, alone, wild…

Amy and Sam in the bedroom. Sam tries to turn Amy on.

SAM: What?

AMY: Not in the mood.

SAM: Why?

AMY: Pissed at you.

SAM: Why?

AMY: I hate going to the doctor.

SAM: What'd I do?

AMY: Called me that word.

SAM: What?

AMY: You know, that word, 'bout me sleeping with people, it's not true. You know I left one year, before all the shit came down and mom and dad motored…got back here and god…it was so…quiet.

SAM: Nobody really called you that.

AMY: What?

SAM: Just wanted to know why you picked me up that night in the bar?

AMY: 'Cause I'm a slut. Duh. You're an asshole, why'd you come home with me?

SAM: Nice hips.

AMY: Already know you're a liar. Fuck, you're probably not even from Cleveland.

SAM: Cleveland, Ohio, my brother died, went to Mexico.

AMY: Read, reading all the time, started this book about this woman who gets lost in Morocco, got sick of reading, couldn't turn another page of a goddamn book. You went to Mexico?

SAM: Yeah, drove. Long ride you know, specially from Cleveland. Broke down in Kansas. Big fucking country, lots a' states, some of 'em fuck bigger than others. Lots of road, lots a' color, lots of rest stops, lots of cigarettes. Drank too much, listened to the Stones "I can't get no, no satisfaction." Met a girl even, Nomie from Israel, she was wild, we had fun…turned out she was a bitch. Anyway, kept driving just had to get there—

AMY: And?

SAM: Couldn't find a place though. Kept driving. Days of driving, days and days. Nothing…more of fucking nothing, and no one. Too many nights sleeping in the car. Kept driving, came through here, first steady bed I've had in years.

AMY: What was it like?

(Sam tries to kiss her.)

AMY: Tell me what Mexico was like.

SAM: It wasn't like anything.

AMY: It was. It was beautiful and warm and you were really far away, tell me, tell me, c'mon pleeeze. See, I was reading this book about Morocco and there's sand, warm sand on your feet, and sometimes there's thunder, only it's not scary, and there's this woman, this woman who gets lost, well, once she gets lost she can't get back you know.

SAM: But you can, see, I think you can get back, that's what happened to me, here, meeting you. A secret, Amy?

AMY: About Mexico?

SAM: I want a safe place.

AMY: Tell me more about Mexico.

SAM: Your eyes look funny, I'm gettin' hard. C'mhere.

AMY: Tell me about the states you drove through.

SAM: C'mhere, kiss me, maybe you'll taste 'em.

AMY: Yeah?

SAM: Its all there inside, you can smell 'em.

(She comes to him inhales deeply, smells.)

AMY: Oh God.

(They begin to make love.)

SCENE VIII

The kitchen, the next evening. Nat writes in his journal. Becca, back from Baltimore, pours herself a glass of water.

BECCA: Watcha' writin' about?

NAT: Myself.

BECCA: What?

NAT: Personal.

BECCA: I'm starved.

NAT: You look sick.

BECCA: Feel great, I need food, where's Amy?

NAT: At the store. I could tell you about what I'm writing about, how I'm trying to change myself, if you want.

BECCA: Sure.

NAT: You have a soul Bec?

BECCA: Amy say something about me last night?

NAT: No.

BECCA: She didn't?

NAT: No.

(*Amy enters with the groceries, she's pretty flustered.*)

AMY: Where's Sam, you seen Sam?

NAT: Not today.

AMY: He wasn't here, when I woke up—

BECCA: I'm feeling much better today Amy.

AMY: You think he's gone?

BECCA: Who?

AMY: Sam.

NAT: He's got nowhere else to go.

BECCA: I took an aspirin, and they're going away.

AMY: I think maybe I scared him, last night.

BECCA: How?

AMY: I, oh, nevermind.

BECCA: But I'll go to the doctor if you want me to.

NAT: He'll be back.

AMY: Why? You think he likes me?

BECCA: He gives me the eye.

AMY: Really?

NAT: She's full of shit.

AMY: Where is he? Oh, what do I care right?

NAT: Exactly.

AMY: I don't care he was just a pain in the ass.

NAT: Exactly. You could do better.

AMY: I could find a rich man.

BECCA: A rich man.

AMY: You think? Really?

BECCA: I don't know.

NAT: I'm hungry.

BECCA: Yeah me too, Amy. (*Becca puts her arms around Amy.*)

NAT: I'm gonna put my journal away Amy, less you want me to read it to you.

AMY: Not now.

NAT: I'm writing about Cleveland, and Mexico.

(Amy looks at him.)

BECCA: I felt sad today, this morning, you weren't here.

NAT: You're like a lesbian Bec, you don't have to always be touching her.

AMY: (Confidential.) C'I ask you a question Bec?

NAT: You could ask me.

BECCA: I had the coolest night, there was this—

AMY: You think it would scare someone off if you made their back bleed with your nails?

BECCA: Huh?

AMY: You know, while doing it, you know.

BECCA: Thing is I don't want to go to the doctor.

NAT: Why she have to go to the doctor?

AMY: He can move, see states, I probably wouldn't even like him anymore if he came back. He coulda asked if I wanted to go, I wouldn't of, but he coulda asked.

NAT: What Amy?

BECCA: Remember Aunt A.?

(Amy falls into a chair.)

BECCA: Remember we went to visit her, right, she had all those bruises, so mom is like you gotta go to the hospital, you gotta go, so she goes, then she's dead, you know?

AMY: Yeah.

NAT: What's she talking about Amy? Amy?

BECCA: Then there was Nat, and he was just having a little trouble walking before he went to the doctor.

AMY: Right.

BECCA: Then mom, she wouldn't have freaked out if she didn't start going to that group. And Grandma, and Grandpa, and Uncle Freddy—

NAT: She's so crazy, yuhhh, (A guttural noise.) I'm gettin' a friggin' headache, tell her to shut up—

(Amy covers her ears.)

BECCA: You don't want me to be sick, do you Ame? Amy? Amy? AMY!!!

(Amy stands, she begins to move slowly out of the kitchen.)

NAT: Amy?

BECCA: I'm hungry.

AMY: I have to go to the bathroom, I'll cook in a bit.

BECCA: I could cook, don't know how to make anything, but I could cook.

AMY: That would be good maybe.

NAT: You okay Amy, you look weird.

AMY: Oh I'm fine, just fine, I just need to pee, to pee, to pee.

(Amy is out of the room, Bec sits at the table with Nat. The sound of a door slamming, then a sound, muffled, the sound of steady sobbing, gasping...far away. Nat and Bec sit in silence. Sam comes in the kitchen, he carries a shoebox, his shoes are filled with sand, his shirt is unbuttoned and there is sand in his nails and hair, he looks tired and excited.)

SAM: Hey!

NAT AND BECCA: Hey.

SAM: What's going on? Isn't it dinner time? Where's Amy?

(No one answers, he hears the sound.)

SAM: Sounds like a horse is dying, what's the noise?

NAT: Amy.

SAM: What's she doing?

BECCA: I think she's crying.

SAM: She is?

NAT: Amy never cries.

SAM: Why's she crying?

BECCA: I don't know. Maybe one of us should go in there?

NAT: *(To Sam.)* Probably you.

SAM: She's in the bathroom?

NAT: Yeah.

BECCA: Shit, what if we have to pee?

SAM: Oh, I was gonna...why's she crying?

BECCA: I don't know. I'm not going in there.

NAT: Me either.

SAM: Okay. I was gonna... *(Sam sits at the table.)*

NAT: Amy never cries.

(They all remain seated, not moving, silent, listening to the sound of Amy broken open, as the lights fade. Pause. The rhythms of techno fill the house as the night moves on, and morning comes.)

SCENE IX

Morning in the kitchen. Becca and Nat are asleep with their heads on the kitchen table. Becca's headphones lie on the table, techno drifts out of them. Sam just sits stares forward, plays with his shoebox. Nat wakes up, looks around, remembers slowly, looks at Sam, Sam looks away. Nat stands, he's stiff, he tries to stretch, he aches, he mumbles, he goes to the cabinet to attempt to make coffee. Sam watches him. Nat fumbles with the coffee can, drops it on the floor.

SAM: I can do that.

NAT: I got it.

(Nat drops the can again, Sam gets up, picks it up, begins to make the coffee.)

NAT: Didn't go in there, huh?

(Sam ignores him, makes coffee.)

NAT: I said, you couldn't go in there, huh?

SAM: I was gonna…

NAT: Yeah.

SAM: Look.

NAT: What?

SAM: Nothing. You want milk?

NAT: Yeah.

(Becca wakes up looks around, puts her headphones on, bops to the music for a few seconds, looks at Nat and Sam, remembers, pulls the headphones around her neck.)

BECCA: No Amy?

NAT: No.

BECCA: What'd she say when you went in?

NAT: He didn't.

BECCA: He didn't go in?

SAM: No.

BECCA: Shit. Someone should, 'specially if she doesn't come out. *(She notices the box.)* What's in the box?

(Sam grabs the box.)

SAM: Hey, nothing.

BECCA: What is it?

SAM: A present, for Amy.

BECCA: You should go give it to her.

SAM: Yeah, after breakfast, I'll cook, what do you guys eat?

BECCA: Huh?

SAM: Like if I made breakfast what would I make?

BECCA: You could make eggs, or just cereal.

NAT: You don't have to make us anything.

SAM: That sounds good, cereal.

(Amy enters quietly. She sees Sam first.)

AMY: Sam?

SAM: Morning.

AMY: Thought you left?!

SAM: No.

NAT: You okay Amy?

AMY: Fine. When did you come back?

SAM: Last night.

AMY: Oh.

SAM: I'm making the coffee.

AMY: So?

BECCA: Think we should make that appointment with the doctor today?

AMY: Yeah. Where'd you go?

SAM: Built a roof, construction, job.

AMY: Really?

SAM: Yeah, basically.

AMY: When'd you get back?

SAM: Get back?

AMY: Yeah, when'd you get back here?

SAM: Oh, around, dinner time.

AMY: Dinner time, huh? Sure you left. I would've.

NAT: What?

SAM: Disappointed?

AMY: Whatever.

BECCA: Maybe we could go out for a sundae or something, after the doctor.

NAT: Why's she have to go to the doctor?

BECCA: Might be sick.

NAT: You're not sick.

BECCA: Might be.

AMY: What'd you do when you got back?

SAM: Hung out.

AMY: Where?

SAM: Here.

AMY: In the kitchen?

BECCA: We should have pancakes today.

AMY: Did you hear me?

SAM: What?

AMY: Nothing. If youd've left, where would you of gone?

SAM: Nowhere, wanna stay here.

AMY: Please.

SAM: Wanna help you out.

AMY: Make yourself a doctor's appointment Bec.

BECCA: Okay. *(Becca leaves to call the doctor.)*

AMY: I'm not in the mood for pancakes, who wanted pancakes?

NAT: Bec did.

AMY: Wish I had a car.

SAM: You could use mine.

AMY: I'm just so sick of having nothing I've been wearing the same clothes for five years, I want new clothes.

SAM: I'll buy you clothes.

NAT: You look good.

AMY: No one heard.

SAM: Heard what Amy?

AMY: Forget it, just fucking forget it.

SAM: I'd a come if I heard.

AMY: You hear Nat?

NAT: What?

AMY: You hear me?

NAT: Uhmmm…

AMY: Did he? Did he hear?

(Nat looks at his feet.)

AMY: Bec!! BECCA!

BECCA: Got us a doctors appointment, tomorrow, three o'clock.

AMY: You hear anything wierd last night?

BECCA: Heard something, didn't know what it was.

AMY: Fuck. I just need to get out of here.

BECCA: We got an appointment, did you hear me? Three o'clock tomorrow.

NAT: What d'ya mean Amy? What?

AMY: I don't want to go to the doctor, I don't have anything to wear to the doctor, my shoes got holes—

SAM: I told you I'll take her to the doctor.

BECCA: I'm only going to the doctor with Amy.

AMY: Nothing to read.

NAT: I don't know what's going on here, what's going on? *(To Sam.)* You shoulda gone in, yughhh…I told you.

AMY: Great, fucking great, great!

SAM: Look Amy, got a gift for you—

AMY: What? Not "safe" enough?

SAM: Hey.

AMY: I'm not feeling very "safe" right now. Pussy.

NAT: What's safe?

AMY: This is safe, right here, me, I'm safe. Right Sam? Right? Safer than fucking Mexico, right Sam? Right?

SAM: Hey.

BECCA: You're acting like mom Amy.

SAM: Calm down Amy, c'mhere, I'm gonna take you out tonight, special you and me.
(Silence.)

NAT: Amy?

AMY: You are?

SAM: Yeah, want to talk…

AMY: You're gonna take me out later?

SAM: Yeah.

AMY: Out?

SAM: Yeah.

AMY: Now?

SAM: Not now. *(He comes to her, puts his hands on her shoulders, rubs.)* First you gotta finish cooking, then you gotta take Nat for his walk, then I'll take you for a ride, got some things I wanna talk over with you.

NAT: Where you gonna take her?

SAM: Want some privacy, want to talk to Amy.

NAT: You'll bring her back?

BECCA: Duh, course he will, we got to go to the doctor tomorrow, me and Amy, it'll be fun.

AMY: Will you?

SAM: Hell, of course I will, you'll see, you'll see what I wanna talk to you about
(Amy cooks.)

AMY: I'd like to go out.

SAM: Yeah, you'll like this. *(He kisses her at the stove.)* Like to watch you make breakfast, like man of the house, hell, get me a beer Bec.

(Becca gets him a beer.)

BECCA: You could come to the doctor too, but only if Amy comes, three of us.

NAT: Why's she going to the doctor?

SAM: I'll take you both to the doctor, pick up some ice cream, we'll celebrate, paradise, Morocco.

AMY: I'd like to go out.

(Blackout.)

SCENE X

Sam and Amy outside. They walk.

AMY: Where we going?

SAM: Up this hill, nice spot, we'll talk.

AMY: I know this hill.

(Amy stands and looks out. There is a view. She breathes deep.)

AMY: Smell that? That tree?

SAM: I smell something.

AMY: That's sumac, smells like sperm, we used to park under it, in high school, just to smell, in amazement.

SAM: That's weird.

AMY: Yeah. We were teenagers, it made us laugh. So nice out here.

SAM: Yeah.

AMY: So?

SAM: Amy.

AMY: Yeah Sam.

SAM: You look real good.

AMY: Really?

SAM: I'm gonna buy you new shoes.

AMY: It's okay, so nice out here.

SAM: Yeah.

AMY: So?

SAM: What?

AMY: My nerves are all jumpy.

SAM: Me too.

AMY: Got scared 'bout what I did to your back.

SAM: Fuckin' hurt.

AMY: I can be crazy huh?

SAM: Yeah, but that's okay, now.

AMY: Now?

SAM: Yeah.

AMY: Why?

SAM: Because, because…I wanna do something, you and me.

AMY: Oh.

SAM: Yeah.

AMY: I don't know.

SAM: You don't.

AMY: Shit, my heart's going so fast. The other night when I smelt you Sam, smelt all that—

SAM: Mine too.

AMY: What about them?

SAM: I think they'll like it.

AMY: No, no they won't, they might die without me.

SAM: Without you?

AMY: You think I'd be able to stop thinking about them, I don't know, I don't know if I could live with that but maybe you could help me? I'd have to forget everything. Maybe you could make me forget.

SAM: They'll have both of us, I'll be good to them, I want it, a family, a fucking family. If it's something bad with Bec we'll take care of it together. *(Silence, as Amy tries to figure out what he has said.)*

AMY: A fam…what?

SAM: C'mon don't make me say it.

AMY: Say what? Say what?

SAM: Wait. *(He goes off to the car, comes back with the shoebox.)* Here, for you. *(Amy opens the box, it is full of sand, she reaches her hand in, scoops up handfulls of sand, elated.)*

AMY: Oh Sam!

SAM: I woke up, other morning, and I knew before, but now I really knew, went out, built that roof, bought it, no big deal, small, but hey, it's in there somewhere. *(Amy picks up a handful of sand, it falls through her fingers till she's left with a ring, she stares at the ring.)*

SAM: So, wanna marry me?

AMY: *(Just staring at the ring.)* Oh.

SAM: We could even have our own kid, you know, I'll get a job. I'll buy you clothes. Clothes and shoes.

AMY: *(Still staring at the ring.)* Oh.

SAM: What do you think?

AMY: Well, I was starting to get ideas, in my head, ideas, I was starting to... *(Amy is having trouble breathing.)*

SAM: All those books, all those ideas, something I really like about you Amy.

AMY: *(Hyperventilating a bit.)* Oh well, it's very, well, what do you mean get married?

SAM: I mean you put on a nice white dress and I put a ring on you, and we make something together, you know with our lives, something with a lot of meaning, you know.

AMY: Where will we live?

SAM: 208 Flat Lane, your house, our house.

AMY: Right.

SAM: Yeah. I figured, you know, it's time, why the hell not, we could get married on the weekend.

AMY: This weekend?

SAM: Look Amy, we'll have this house right, an it'll be a lot realer than I ever been. You'll have a lot more time to you know, do what you like, you know, read and stuff, and it'll be like it's sposed to, you know. Tomorrow we'll take Bec to the doctor. *(Amy starts to laugh.)*

SAM: What? What? Why you laughing? That mean yes?

AMY: How could I ever of thought...they need me so bad, you know, our parents when they left, shit, shit, shit. *(Amy's body limpens, Sam holds her in his arms.)*

SAM: Amy, Amy, this is life, real life, see I got an idea in my head too.

AMY: Yeah.

SAM: Sounds good doesn't it, you and me, right?

AMY: Sure, sure it does.

SAM: C'mon, let's go home. *(Amy pushes him away.)*

AMY: I don't know Sam, I don't know if I can do that, I don't know.

SAM: Fuck Amy, here I go putting myself out there, shit.

AMY: I didn't say no, I just said I don't know.

SAM: All right, all right, you'll think about it. Hey, I know, I know it's right, you'll know it too, I got no doubt of that, so I'm fine, see? *(He holds his arms out, smiles at her.)* You like me Amy, don't you?

AMY: Yeah.
SAM: I like you.
(*Blackout.*)

SCENE XI

The kitchen the next day, late afternoon, early evening. Nat sits at the table. Amy enters in a slightly misfitted wedding gown that she wears over her day clothes, she stands behind Nat, her hands on his shoulders staring out.

NAT: Sometimes, sometimes when I'm alone in this house I can't find things, like I forget where things are, then I think maybe something, something happened, like a UFO came and took me away for ten years and I had this whole other life, and they brought me back here, and I'm having trouble remembering this life, even though I can't remember that life at all. I wonder what it was like. Maybe I looked different, maybe I had a family, maybe I was the mayor or something, maybe it was easy to move, to get out of bed. Then you come in Amy, and I know where things are cause you show me.
(*Amy strokes his shoulders and arms.*)
NAT: Wish I could feel that, but my body is numb.
(*Amy moves so she is facing Nat.*)
AMY: Whadd'ya think?
NAT: Why you wearing that?
AMY: Sam asked me to marry him.
NAT: Oh.
AMY: What do you think?
NAT: It looks good, pretty.
AMY: 'Bout me getting married?
NAT: He gonna take you away?
AMY: No, he wants to live here, all of us, a big happy family.
NAT: You want to?
AMY: Maybe. Its pretty weird, you know, never would of thought—
NAT: If he promises never to take you away from us.
AMY: This dress was mom's.
NAT: Yeah.
(*Beat, as if Nat and Amy have traveled somewhere else.*)

NAT: What's she look like again?

AMY: Who?

NAT: Mom, what's mom look like again?

AMY: Brown hair.

NAT: Eyes?

AMY: Brown.

NAT: Skin?

AMY: Just skin.

NAT: Small.

AMY: Yeah.

NAT: And Dad?

AMY: Do you hate them?

NAT: Try not to.

AMY: Think you could forget what I look like?

NAT: Nah. Would you have a baby?

AMY: God, I don't know.

NAT: I wouldn't mind a baby.

AMY: I'd like to go on a honeymoon.

NAT: Why?

AMY: Gotta celebrate, specially if you get married, you know?

NAT: Where you go?

AMY: Some beach or something, I don't know.

NAT: What are we gonna do?

AMY: You can take care of yourselves for a few days can't you?

NAT: How long does it take to starve?

AMY: You won't starve.

NAT: Sure we will.

AMY: Only if the car crashes on the way.

NAT: Oh no, that wouldn't happen.

AMY: Or if I got kidnapped or something.

NAT: That wouldn't happen to you.

AMY: But if it did, you wouldn't starve.

NAT: Course we would.

AMY: It's just sometimes, I miss something...

NAT: What?

AMY: I don't know. I don't know. *(She does a quick turn in the dress.)* C'mon really, m'I a sight for sore eyes?

NAT: It's a little big.

AMY: Too big to wear?

NAT: Nah, you look beautiful.

AMY: I do.

NAT: Yes Amy.

(Beat.)

AMY: Think I'll take it off now, before they get home. (She takes the dress off, folds it carefully, returning it to a big beat up box.)

NAT: Amy?

AMY: Yeah?

NAT: What's love like?

AMY: What?

NAT: What's it like, to be in love?

AMY: Oh. It's great.

NAT: Wish I could feel it.

AMY: You're in love with me, aren't you?

NAT: But that's different.

AMY: No it isn't, it's exactly the same.

(Sam and Bec enter with a Friendly's ice cream cake.)

SAM: Hey guys. Celebration time!

NAT: That Christian, you know, he talks about how people are put on the world for a reason, and you're lucky 'cause you've got this reason that makes sense. The Christian, he wants to come over and meet you, he thinks you sound great.

BECCA: (Getting plates and forks.) How come he doesn't want to meet me?

NAT: Not ready.

BECCA: I could be sick.

NAT: Yeah right.

BECCA: I've got blood clots, isn't that right? Amy? Sam? We went to the doctor.

SAM: That's right.

AMY: Thanks for takin' us.

SAM: Amy was so scared she couldn't get out of the car.

AMY: I told you, I hate the friggin' doctor.

NAT: She's not sick, no way.

BECCA: I'm gonna have a test, maybe I got a virus.

NAT: Unh-uh.

BECCA: My blood is thin.

NAT: Nah.

BECCA: It's true, it's true, lah di, dah dah dah.

(Amy plays with her cake.)

AMY: I prayed in the car.

(Sam comes to her, kisses her.)

NAT: I'll talk to the Christian.

BECCA: I can have tests, and whatever happens, you can take care of me, and it's probably nothing.

SAM: I know all about that, prayin' in the car.

AMY: *(To Sam.)* What'd you think life was gonna be like when you were a kid?

SAM: I don't know.

AMY: I mean when you were little and you imagined yourself now?

SAM: Thought it would be better, there'd be a girl like you.

AMY: *(Smiling.)* C'mon.

BECCA: Awww, sweet.

SAM: What'd you think?

AMY: Oh, I don't know, some kinda movie or something, no one got sick and no one dissappeared, you did things 'cause you wanted to, not because you had to. Stupid. Now I don't kow. People, they get sick, they disappear, they die, and the thing to do, the only thing that won't kill your insides is to do this.

BECCA: I'll bet mom's insides are like a real heavy bowling bowl.

AMY: Sam?

SAM: Yeah baby?

(Amy gets up, she begins to move out of the kitchen.)

AMY: Guess I'll marry you.

(Everyone stops eating, looks up, Amy leaves the room.)

SAM: What?

(He follows her out of the room, Nat and Bec sit there.)

BECCA: Wow. *(Becca pulls a joint out of her pocket, lights it.)*

BECCA: I can't wait to get married.

NAT: You have to smoke that?

BECCA: It's just a special cigarette.

NAT: C'mon. You know Amy talked this whole thing over with me, asked me what I thought, when you guys were out.

BECCA: Sam talked it over with me. Makes sense though you know, I've always been sort of psychic right? The other night I had a dream the four of us lived on a seashell floating in the ocean, it was such a nice dream.

NAT: I never dream when I'm sleeping.

BECCA: Fucking beautiful.

NAT: You're on drugs.

BECCA: Duh.

NAT: Maybe Amy will have a baby?

BECCA: No. At the end of my dream the shell got really heavy and started to sink, but I forgot that part.

(Blackout.)

SCENE XII

Colored lights flash. A rave, another night, another city...Becca dances, Moby "I'm feeling so real..." The dance is slow at first. It grows, and grows until Becca is dancing wildly, punching her arms and legs with her fists, beating herself. The music fades and Becca falls in a heap on the dance floor.

SCENE XIII

Amy and Sam in the bedroom, the eve of their wedding.

SAM: Tomorrow you're gonna be Mrs. Sam.

AMY: I could be dead tomorrow.

SAM: What?

AMY: Just kidding.

SAM: You make stupid jokes Amy.

AMY: You ever been in love Sam?

SAM: What kinda question is that?

AMY: What's it feel like?

SAM: I'm in love with you.

AMY: What's it feel like?

SAM: You feel it don't you?

AMY: Sure. Just want to know what it's like for you.

SAM: It's like...I don't know. It's like paradise.

AMY: What's paradise like?

SAM: Like, like being a little buzzed all the time.

AMY: What's that like?

SAM: I don't know Amy.

AMY: Aren't you gonna miss driving, goin' places.

SAM: No.

AMY: We'll go on a honeymoon, won't we?

SAM: Course, after we settle down, get the kids used to us, get some money together.

AMY: Not right away?

SAM: Its hard to just take off, I like it here.

AMY: We could go to Florida.

SAM: Yeah.

AMY: Bump into mom and dad.

SAM: That would be a hoot.

AMY: Not gonna happen though, is it?

SAM: We could go to Florida, couple months, or so.

AMY: Danger is, we could have a car accident on the way.

SAM: Not with me behind the wheel.

AMY: I could get shot.

SAM: Relax Amy we're just getting married, you're a nervous wreck.

AMY: Yeah I'm nervous.

SAM: C'mhere.

   (She comes.)

SAM: Mrs. Sam.

AMY: Tell me about Mexico.

SAM: No. *(He kisses her.)* Fucking husband and wife, hell, say it.

AMY: Husband and wife.

   (He laughs, he kisses her.)

AMY: Sam?

SAM: Yeah baby.

AMY: That night when I cried, and you heard, you couldn't come in right?

SAM: You won't cry anymore.

AMY: You couldn't come in, you can't take me away. You want a family.

SAM: We've got a family.

AMY: Fuck you Sam.

SAM: Hey, I'll learn, I'll learn what to do if you cry.

AMY: Fuck you Sam.

SAM: What?

AMY: Just said fuck you.

SAM: I'll take care of you, I'll keep you safe, and me, you'll do that for me, 'cause you don't know about the road Amy, you don't know.

AMY: Did you ever get to Mexico Sam?

   (He doesn't answer.)

AMY: Sam?

   (He doesn't answer.)

AMY: Where's the keys to your car?

SAM: On the drawers.

(Amy goes to the dresser, picks up the keys, holds them.)

SAM: Amy.

AMY: I could take 'em and I could go, I could go to Florida, I could drive to Florida, right now.

SAM: Amy?

AMY: —'Cause it all fucking sucks, all of it, I'm totally sick of it, I'm gonna leave you behind, with all this, huh, see, how'd you like that? You, you totally stupid person! Shit I don't know how to get to Florida!

SAM: You could buy a map.

AMY: I could buy a map. A map, yes.

SAM: Go ahead!

AMY: Yeah I'll buy a fucking map! 'Cause you ever think about it Sam, who I'd be without all this shit, who else I'd be?

SAM: You wouldn't be anyone.

(Beat.)

AMY: I hate you, I hate all of you.

(Blackout.)

SCENE XIV

The kitchen, Nat and Becca playing checkers.

NAT: Couldn't sleep.

BECCA: Dreamt our house was on fire, but it was okay there was a new house waiting down the street.

NAT: Afraid I won't make the walk down the aisle.

BECCA: I could do it for you.

NAT: I'm gonna give her to him, if anyone is.

(Sam enters.)

SAM: Morning family.

NAT AND BECCA: Morning.

SAM: I'm cooking this morning. *(He puts on Amy's apron.)*

BECCA: Feel like eggs.

SAM: Eggs, huh. *(He goes to the fridge, takes out eggs, he proceeds to crack and scramble, making a mess.)*

NAT: I'm still writing, writing about my life on the UFO.

  (*Becca takes out a joint, lights it.*)

NAT: Not again.

BECCA: Gonna celebrate tonight, celebrate for you guys Pennsylvania, Amish country if it's okay Sam.

SAM: You could call me Dad.

BECCA: (*Winks at him.*) I can't call you dad.

SAM: Why not?

NAT: What's in Amish country?

BECCA: Rave.

NAT: In Amish country?

BECCA: Yeah, cool.

NAT: Nothin', nothing goes untouched, disgusting. C'I have a glass of water?

SAM: Sure.

BECCA: Me too. Any munchies?

SAM: Not before breakfast, gotta start the day right, you know, eggs, bacon, toast. Can I have a hit of that.

  (*Becca passes Sam the joint.*)

NAT: Where's Amy?

SAM: Shower.

BECCA: Nervous?

SAM: Yeah.

  (*Amy enters, in the wedding gown, in all it's glory.*)

AMY: Morning.

SAM: Morning baby.

AMY: How do I look?

NAT: You look beautiful.

SAM: You do.

AMY: Really?

NAT: Wish I was marrying you.

BECCA: Ewww…

AMY: (*Reaches out her hands to Nat and Bec.*) Mom and Dad had some great kids.

BECCA: Now they're yours isn't that funny.

AMY: Yeah. (*She smiles, a slow, slow smile, and turns to Sam.*) You cooking?

SAM: That's right.

AMY: Making a mess.

SAM: I'll get better at it.

AMY: I'll do it.

SAM: You sure?

AMY: Yeah.

(Sam takes off the apron, hands it to Amy, she puts it on very slowly, they watch her, Sam sits at the table takes another hit of Bec's joint, Amy moves to the stove.)

NAT: What's it gonna be like now that you guys are married?

(No one answers.)

NAT: Ame, Amy, Ames, what's it gonna be like?

AMY: It'll be the same, 'cept there'll be two of us. We'll take you for your walk. We'll eat. You'll watch tv. Becca will dance. I'll read. Sam will have a beer, we'll see the doctor again and again if we have to, we'll deal, we'll go on, we'll keep going, and we'll do it together, keep going, together, because we are a family. We are a family. Maybe some day, when we die, we'll go to Paradise and we'll look back on this, we'll watch everything we did here, and we'll smile. 'Cause this is life, real life, this, doing this, keeping each other safe, that's what we'll do, it's all we can do. *(Amy cooks, turns to the table.)* Breakfast is ready.

(Amy serves the breakfast, she watches as Sam, Nat, and Becca salt their eggs, reach for the ketchup, etc. Finally Amy joins them.)

END OF PLAY

THE WATER CHILDREN

by Wendy MacLeod

To Foss and Avery

ORIGINAL PRODUCTION

The Water Children was produced by Playwrights Horizons (Tim Sanford, Artistic Director; Leslie Marcus, Managing Director) and Women's Project & Productions, (Julia Miles, Artistic Director; Patricia Taylor, Managing Director) in New York City, in October, 1997. It was directed by David Petrarca; the set and lighting designs were by Michael Philippi; the costume design was by Therese Bruck; the sound design was by Edward Cosla; and the production stage manager was Cat Domiano. The cast was as follows:

Kit/Mom/Cat	Joyce Reehling
Megan	Wendy Makkena
Liz	Deirdre Lovejoy
Chance	Kevin Isola
Dad/Roger/Jim/Buddhist Priest	Michael Mastro
Randall	Jonathan Walker
Tony Dinardi	Robert Sella
Crystal	Elizabeth Bunch

The Water Children received its West Coast premiere at the Matrix Theatre Company (Joseph Stern, Producing Artistic Director; Mareli Mitchel, Managing Director; Amanda Spain, Assistant Director) in Los Angeles, California, on April 7, 1998. It was directed by Lisa James; the set design was by Deborah Raymond and Dorian Vernacchio; the costume design was by Naomi Yoshido Rodriguez; the lighting design was by Keith Endo; the sound design was by Matthew C. Beville; and the stage manager was Becky Smith. The cast was as follows:

Kit, an Agent/Mom/A Cat	Marilyn McIntyre, Claudette Nevins
Megan	Pam Dawber, Wendy Makkena
Liz	Cindy Katz, Sarah Zinsser
Chance	Christopher Collet, Christopher Gorham
The Father/Hairstylist/ Jim/Buddhist Priest	Dave Higgins, Time Winters
Randall	Gregg Henry, Don McManus
Tony Dinardi	JD Cullum, Billie Worley
Crystal	Sarah Bibb, Sara Rue

AUTHOR'S NOTE

I remember critiques in grad school where there were earnest discussions about what was and wasn't a "large play." As far as I could tell a large play was anything having to do with war, politics, and men. "Small plays" involved love, family, and women. I suppose *The Water Children* is a medium-sized play because it deals with a political issue—abortion—but it is also about love, family and a woman making peace with her past.

After I had my own children, I was unable to see abortion as matter-of-factly as I did before. I realized that in the event of an unplanned pregnancy now, I would probably choose to have the child. At the same time, I realized an accidental pregnancy in your thirties when you're married and employed is very different from an accidental pregnancy when you're sixteen, alone or poor. So my emotional self was at war with my rational, feminist self.

I had been thinking about writing a play about an actress who appeared in a pro-life commercial. At about this time I read an excerpt in *Harper's* about Japanese abortion rituals from a book called *Liquid Life*. It seems that in Japan there is no stigma against abortion, in fact, in many cases, it is considered the height of family values to do what's best for the child and not invite it into difficult circumstances. But temples were springing up where women could go and apologize to their aborted children, who were called the *mizuko* or "the water children." Somehow the Japanese culture was acknowledging women's ambivalent feelings about abortion without threatening to take away their legal right to do it. A light bulb went off in my own head, and I was pretty sure that this would be the ending of my heroine's journey as well. Suddenly there was a third point of view, which acknowledged the life of the fetus at the same time it acknowledged circumstances where abortion was necessary. Coincidentally, the man who wrote the book, William LaFleur, came to speak at the college where I teach and I went to hear him. And coincidentally, I ran into him the next day and had, what was for me, a profound conversation.

I felt that the only way to say something new about the issue of abortion was to challenge the presumptions of the predominantly liberal theater-going audience. Instead of making the Randall Terry figure a cartoon, I wanted to make him an intelligent, sympathetic pro-lifer. There is, at least, a consistency, an integrity, to his position. He started out as an anti-Vietnam War protester and, because he opposed all killing, found his way into the pro-life movement. Randall is not a villain and should not be played as one. We have to believe that Megan would consider marrying him, at least until she discovers that, when push comes to shove, he might literally try to control her body.

Megan is a savvy, ironic New Yorker—she doesn't reveal her pain, she covers it, at least until it's no longer possible to do so. While she finds the forgiveness she's craved in the temple scene with Chance, Megan's return to her mother is also important. The play is about children searching for parents as much as it is about parents searching for lost children. Crystal is hoping Megan will be a mother to her, and Dinardi has found a surrogate father in Randall. I want to avoid a fairy-tale single mother happy ending. I want to acknowledge that Megan is going to need some help with that baby. Chance should be played as a regular kid, and a regular twenty-year-old, not as some sort of angel-boy. Lastly, there is a danger of the Liz character becoming one-note and didactic—her struggle with Randall has to be as much about wanting Megan for herself as it is about her politics.

David Petrarca, who directed the premiere at Playwrights Horizons, did a masterful job of keeping the play moving, so that we fluidly moved in and out of Megan's head and in and out of the many locations. I would like to thank David, the designers, the brilliant original cast, and especially the producers Tim Sanford and Julia Miles for creating my best experience in the theater to date.

CHARACTERS

MEGAN: an actress, mid-thirties
RANDALL: late thirties, executive director of Life Force, a pro-life organization
LIZ: mid-thirties, a lesbian, Megan's friend and roommate
TONY DINARDI: early twenties, a pro-life zealot
CHANCE: twenty, the soul of Megan's unborn son
CRYSTAL: teens, pro-life volunteer
KIT/MOM/CAT: Megan's agent/her mother/her cat
DAD/ROGER/JIM/BUDDHIST PRIEST: thirties, Chance's father/a hairdresser/a television commercial director/a Buddhist priest

SETTING
New York City and points East, agent's office, Megan's apartment, Randall's office, a hair salon, television studio, a park bench, restaurant, Randall's apartment, Randall's car, a Buddhist temple

TIME
Now

Agent's office. Megan sits in front of Kit's desk. Kit, her agent, hangs up the phone.

KIT: You didn't get it.

MEGAN: Why not?

KIT: They went with somebody else.

MEGAN: Who was it?

KIT: They couldn't tell me that, the offer's still out.

MEGAN: Who did they offer it to?

KIT: What difference does it make? Janet Carlton.

MEGAN: She's ten years younger.

KIT: She's another type.

MEGAN: She's not another type. She's the same type but she's ten years younger.

KIT: So they went younger. Sometimes they go older.

MEGAN: When?

KIT: When they want a mom.

MEGAN: So this is it. I've entered the mom era.

KIT: It's an option that's opening up to you.

MEGAN: Great.

KIT: What's wrong with playing a mom? I'm a mom.

MEGAN: Plays are never about moms. They're about the misunderstood artist offspring.

KIT: You've had your artist offspring roles. I should think you'd be getting tired of those.

MEGAN: But at least the play is their story.

KIT: So write a play for yourself.

MEGAN: I can't write.

KIT: That doesn't stop a lot of people. Look, television commercials are another place to look. You're perfect. You're middle America.

MEGAN: Still?

KIT: Something's come in.

MEGAN: Well send me out.

KIT: Great. They saw your tape. They liked you.

MEGAN: What is it?

KIT: It's a poignant piece. About a woman who aborted a child and can't get over it.

MEGAN: What do you mean she can't get over it?

KIT: I mean she's sad. She's questioning abortion, you know, whether it's right or wrong. It's a pro-life organization.

MEGAN: Forget it.

KIT: It's a job. It's a role. It's not you. It's her. A woman who's questioning abortion.

MEGAN: I've had an abortion.

KIT: Who hasn't?

MEGAN: I got over it.

KIT: It's $15,000 plus residuals.

MEGAN: $15,000?

KIT: These people are funded. Fifteen thousand plus for three days work.

MEGAN: My friends would never speak to me again.

KIT: If you don't do it, somebody else will.

MEGAN: Would you ever speak to me again?

KIT: Look, I'm a liberal right?

MEGAN: I am too!

KIT: We have two children. We have two children in a two-bedroom apartment. We're at capacity. But if I got pregnant tomorrow I wouldn't have an abortion. I couldn't have an abortion. Not knowing what I know now. I just mean. My children grew inside me and once they're here you can't imagine your life without them. There's an overwhelming sense of meant to be. I can't look at a fetus as a cell cluster anymore. I saw an ethicist on PBS and he said that brain waves determine life and that there are no brain waves until the last trimester. All right. But what about the heartbeat? When I first heard my children's heartbeat, I wept. And I'm not, you know, I'm not some Earth mother miracle of life person, but well it is a miracle. When I see my face and Lee's face all mixed up in Brian and Conor…I think abortion is killing a child. Maybe it's a necessary evil, but on some level it is evil.

MEGAN: But you're not telling other people not to have them…

KIT: No.

MEGAN: But that's the difference between us and them.

KIT: But maybe that's because I lack the courage of my convictions. I guess what I'm trying to tell you is that I'm a them. In some sense I'm a them. Do you really believe that life, some kind of life, doesn't begin at conception?

(Megan is silent.)

KIT: Should I set up a meeting?

(Agent freezes. Liz, Megan's roommate, enters. Megan crosses stage. Agent exits.)

LIZ: Who's gonna be there? Gingrich? Buchanan? Satan?

MEGAN: The ad agency. The sponsors. I'm just going to meet with them.

LIZ: Why would you meet with them?

MEGAN: I need the money.

LIZ: Temp!

MEGAN: I do! I still need the money!

LIZ: I'm living with Leni Riefenstahl.

MEGAN: If I don't do the role, somebody else will!

LIZ: Janet Carlton, for example?

MEGAN: Yes!

LIZ: Your agent managed to suck you in when you were vulnerable…

MEGAN: She doesn't care if I take the job. She's not gonna make much off it.

LIZ: She's gonna make more than if you don't take the job.

MEGAN: She's got seventy-nine other actresses who'd do it.

LIZ: But they liked *you*. This is more than her commission. This is an alliance with the new world order. This is big business.

MEGAN: This is a *role*.

LIZ: This is propaganda.

MEGAN: If I were doing a pro-choice commercial would you be upset?

LIZ: Of course not.

MEGAN: But that's propaganda too.

LIZ: It's not propaganda, it's the truth.

MEGAN: You don't know that.

LIZ: All right let me ask you a question. If abortion is murder then how come they allow it in cases of incest or rape?

MEGAN: Well if it's incest, the baby might be deformed…

LIZ: So they let you kill babies when they're not perfect? Why is it allowed when a woman's been raped? I'll tell you why. Because the woman didn't enjoy the sex. They're only interested in punishing the woman who had desires.

MEGAN: Well do you think a woman *should* have to have a baby if she were raped?

LIZ: Of course not! I don't think a woman should have to have any baby at all! I'm just pointing out the holes in their logic.

MEGAN: This commercial is just presenting a point of view, which is what any work of art does.

LIZ: Now it's *art?*

MEGAN: The script was actually sort of moving.

LIZ: I almost threw up!

MEGAN: Don't you ever think about having a child?

LIZ: What's that got to do with it?

MEGAN: I mean, we're in our thirties, we're single, no prospects, the odds are we're never going to have a child…

LIZ: So?

MEGAN: So if I had kept the child I aborted, I wouldn't be childless today.

LIZ: You'd be on welfare.

MEGAN: You don't know that.

LIZ: You were sixteen at the time. You never would have gone to college, you never would have become an actress, you never would have left Ohio, you'd be married to some feed salesmen…

MEGAN: Every time you mention Ohio you talk about feed salesmen! There are professionals in Ohio! There are doctors and lawyers!

(Chance and Dad enter and sit at a dining room table. Chance's seat is low to make him appear to be a six year old child.)

LIZ: Your boyfriend would have been a doctor or lawyer?

MEGAN: No. *(Megan joins them.)*

BOY (CHANCE.): So then he *pushed* me.

MOM (MEGAN.): On purpose?

BOY: Yes!

MOM: Lynette told me it was an accident.

BOY: He shouldn't have been waving that rake around. Rakes should be kept on the ground.

MOM: That's true.

DAD: Which one was this?

BOY: Patrick.

MOM: Runny nose.

DAD: I tell you what, that kid's a spaz.

MOM: *Brad.*

BOY: Patrick's a spaz!

DAD: Hey.

BOY: Can I have a popsicle?

MOM: No.

BOY: Can I have a butterfly net?

MOM: There's no butterflies now.

BOY: I know. But I just want the net.

MOM: Why?

BOY: To catch things. You could get it at your K-Mart.

DAD: We don't have the money to be buying a damn butterfly net.

BOY: WHY?

MOM: They don't sell them now anyway.

BOY: I've *seen* them.

MOM: That was last summer.

BOY: No it wasn't.

DAD: You're not getting a damn butterfly net.

BOY: WHY?

DAD: I'm gonna shoot someone.

MOM: Hush now.

BOY: Who's he gonna shoot?

MOM: He's not gonna shoot anyone.

BOY: He said he was gonna shoot someone.

MOM: What he meant was he *felt* like shooting someone but he's not going to.

BOY: Why not?

DAD: *(Exiting.)* I'm watching the game.

MOM: You want your beer?

>   *(Dad returns for beer and exits.)*

BOY: Why isn't he gonna shoot someone?

MOM: Chance, you're giving me a headache.

BOY: You're giving *me* a headache. Where are you going?

MOM: Work.

BOY: What about me?

MOM: Daddy'll be here.

BOY: I don't want to be with Daddy!

DAD: *(Offstage.)* Feeling's mutual!

BOY: Can I go with you?

MOM: No.

BOY: He might shoot me.

MOM: He's just tired. Just go to your room. Read books.

BOY: Will you buy me a book?

DAD: *(Offstage.)* Ever heard of the library?

BOY: I wish I never got born!

MOM: Well it's too late, you're born.

BOY: Dad said you could have gone to college if it wasn't for me.

MOM: Well you'll have to go to college for me.

BOY: You know what I'm gonna study?

MOM: What?

BOY: Butterflies. You see my point?

>   *(Boy exits, taking the low chair. Randall sits where Dad was sitting. The table now appears to be a desk. Randall's office. Life Force.)*

RANDALL: Your agent mentioned that you had an abortion when you were sixteen.

MEGAN: What?

RANDALL: Listen, we're not looking for some Bible belt, Nazarene college goody-two shoes. We're looking for a modern woman who's on a spiritual quest.

MEGAN: Well I don't know if I'm on a spiritual quest...

RANDALL: Do you know what the sex was? Of the child you lost?

MEGAN: I'm not sure I can say that I *lost* the child, I *chose* to lose...the fetus.

RANDALL: Boy, right?

MEGAN: How did you know that?

RANDALL: I pick things up. I try not to creep people out, but I pick things up.

MEGAN: Well of course you had a fifty fifty chance of being right. They're not supposed to tell you what sex it was.

RANDALL: Of course not. That would be acknowledging its humanity. Have you read the script?

MEGAN: Yes.

RANDALL: What did you think?

MEGAN: I thought it was very moving.

RANDALL: You were moved.

MEGAN: Yes.

RANDALL: Why do you suppose that was?

MEGAN: Well I suppose it pushed the right buttons. The way good advertising should. I mean I'm childless and...

RANDALL: You're not married?

MEGAN: No.

RANDALL: Boyfriend?

MEGAN: No. But I broke up with someone about a year ago.

RANDALL: Were you seeing him a long time?

MEGAN: Yes.

RANDALL: Did you ever think about having children?

MEGAN: We were both actors and we didn't have a lot of money, and we're out of town a lot...

RANDALL: Children are...I never knew what love was until I had my children. I had never loved another human being that much. Romantic love it's... selfish, in a way. It's jealous and possessive, but your love for a child is rare, generous...

MEGAN: Not everyone should have children.

RANDALL: Of course not.

MEGAN: Some people don't have the money, or the patience, or they're too
	young...

RANDALL: That's why there's adoption. My sister tried for years to get preg-
	nant and finally adopted a beautiful little mixed-race girl. And do you
	know what? Ten months later she was pregnant!

MEGAN: I've heard those stories.

RANDALL: They think it's something in the baby's urine. Makes you fertile. So
	how old would your son be today?

MEGAN: Well it was twenty years ago...

RANDALL: He'd be in college...

MEGAN: I probably couldn't have afforded college...

RANDALL: Home for Thanksgiving all that...water?

MEGAN: Sure.

	(Randall goes offstage. Chance appears.)

MEGAN: Get your feet off the table.

CHANCE: Why?

MEGAN: There's mud and...

CHANCE: No there's not.

MEGAN: You might scratch it.

CHANCE: This is a hard finish. What's for dinner?

MEGAN: When do you go back to school?

CHANCE: Hand me the take-out menus.

MEGAN: What take-out menus?

CHANCE: The ones the Chinese men stick under doors.

MEGAN: I throw them out.

CHANCE: Why?

MEGAN: It's just trash. It's just clutter.

CHANCE: But I want to order Chinese.

MEGAN: Look in the phone book.

CHANCE: What's the restaurant on the corner?

MEGAN: I don't know.

CHANCE: Let's just go there.

MEGAN: You and me?

CHANCE: Like a date.

MEGAN: It could be a date. I mean I'm only sixteen years older.

CHANCE: You're still a fox, Mom, don't worry.

MEGAN: Still?

CHANCE: Stuart thinks you're a fox.

MEGAN: Really?

CHANCE: Don't sleep with Stuart, Mom. It would be gross.

MEGAN: I'm not gonna sleep with Stuart. I'm not Blanche du Bois.

CHANCE: You got money? I'm out of cash. What? What I say?

MEGAN: I was only sixteen. I mean I was younger than you are now. It's not that I didn't want you, I didn't know enough to want you, I didn't know you. I didn't even know you were a boy until…

CHANCE: Mom, it's cool. *(Chance exits. Turns back.)* But maybe next time I could come.

(Randall re-enters with water.)

MEGAN: I'm sorry but I have another audition scheduled this afternoon…

RANDALL: Not for another commercial?

MEGAN: No.

RANDALL: Good because you've got the job.

MEGAN: Really?

RANDALL: But Megan, if you sign on to do this project, there are some ground rules. I've discussed this with your agent, and regardless of what your views are about abortion, and those are your concern, we need to ask you to refrain from sharing those views in any public forum—marches, public service announcements, even donations—because some reporter would love to have a field day making you out to be a hypocrite and we want to protect you from that. Any problem with that?

MEGAN: Well I'd like to have my agent look over it.

RANDALL: Of course.

MEGAN: And in all honesty, I have donated money to Planned Parenthood…

RANDALL: We're not concerned about that. This commercial is about a woman who started in one place and is ending in another, and for all anybody has to know that's your story as well. People do change their minds about things as they get older…

MEGAN: Well I haven't actually changed my mind…

RANDALL: That is not my concern. My concern is making a commercial that moves people in the same way that you yourself were moved. We're just trying to tell a story here. Right? Once upon a time. And Megan, this is awkward, but the ad agency suggests…would it be possible to go blonder? *(Hair salon.)*

ROGER: So I says to him, I say, Tony, you have a girlfriend? No. A boyfriend? No. A *chia pet?* The only time I ever heard him string three words together was about abortion. I'm like, where is this guy coming from? He's Catholic, okay, but so am I. I don't plaster my truck with bumper stickers and *obsess*. I mean honest to God he scares me. On his day off, he parks across the street and stares at the salon. We'd fire him if we weren't so scared.

MEGAN: Where are his parents?

ROGER: They came to visit, they went to Christmas Eve services, he walks up the aisle and calls the priest a cunt, I swear to God, one of my customers was there. Does this fit? Does this make sense? This altar boy who's "the Pope this, the Pope that" calls a priest a cunt. He's out of his mind. He's like schizophrenic or manic-depressive or obsessive-compulsive or something and la-di-dah his folks return to Worcester tucking money in his pocket so he can go out and buy more guns.

MEGAN: So he really does have guns?

ROGER: He has an automatic, like those playground murderers. He walks in the door, I have an overwhelming urge to hit the floor. The NRA calls it a pleasure gun, hello? Am I missing something? Save the babies, save the whales! I'm just trying to save some money. I hope you know what you're getting into that's all I'm saying. Aren't there other jobs?

MEGAN: I'm trying. I had an audition this morning.

ROGER: What for? A public service announcement for the Aryan nations?

MEGAN: *No.* It's for a Japanese soap. I'd get to go to Japan.

ROGER: I saw a Japanese soap commercial on one of the funniest videos show. They showed these little babies in the tub. And there's a big water bubble and it's obvious you know, that one of them farted. And the baby has this shit-eating grin on his face. Babies are a kick. I love babies.

MEGAN: Why don't you adopt?

ROGER: Good afternoon, I'm a big 'mo hairdresser who's HIV Positive who lives in a illegal sublet with no significant other and none on the horizon. May I please be responsible for somebody else's life? Next!

MEGAN: They might give you a special needs baby.

ROGER: I don't want a broken one! Do you? Honestly, do you? I have friends with babies. A normal one nearly kills you.

(Dinardi enters.)

ROGER: Hi Tony. Where you been? You were due in at two.

DINARDI: I had a prayer vigil.

ROGER: Next time pray a little faster.

DINARDI: It's a matter of priorities. Oh the Nazis are marching into Poland? Sorry. I have to sweep up hair clumps.

ROGER: The Nazis are marching into Poland? We should really get a radio.

DINARDI: You should. Maybe you'd know what's going on in the world instead of listening to this disco crap. Pre-Term alone is killing seventy-five thousand babies a year.

ROGER: Well there still seems to be plenty of babies! Somebody's keeping Baby Gap in business.

DINARDI: Is this a joke to you?

ROGER: Of course not.

DINARDI: *(To Megan.)* Is this a joke to you?

ROGER: She's your *spokesperson*. She's about to do one of your commercials.

DINARDI: For who?

MEGAN: Life Force.

DINARDI: With Randall?

MEGAN: Yes.

ROGER: Small world!

(Dinardi stares at her. He exits.)

ROGER: If only *his* mother had had an abortion.

(Television studio. Megan pages through a thin script. Crystal enters and sits beside her.)

CRYSTAL: I was nearly an abortion. I mean I was in the *pail*. A nurse rescued me and put me in an incubator and wheeled me out of the hospital. She took me to Save the Babies and they did they saved me.

MEGAN: That's a little hard to believe. I mean the nurse would have been fired.

CRYSTAL: They never knew. She was one of us. She was undercover. If I had been a partial-birth abortion, my brains would have been sucked out. I would have been decapitated! I would have been a vegetable.

MEGAN: Well if you had been decapitated you wouldn't have been anything. You would have been dead.

CRYSTAL: Yeah. I would have been *garbage*. I would have been *incinerated*. She heard me cry. I was twenty-four weeks old.

MEGAN: I'm sorry but sixteen years ago…

CRYSTAL: Fifteen.

MEGAN: Fifteen years ago a fetus could not survive at twenty-four weeks. The lungs wouldn't have been functioning yet.

CRYSTAL: It was a miracle! My heart was beating. My arms and legs were wiggling. And I smiled up at her.

MEGAN: Newborns do *not* smile…

CRYSTAL: I like to melted her heart she said.

MEGAN: She was a nurse and she performed abortions?

CRYSTAL: Undercover.

MEGAN: But what about the ones that didn't survive? I mean she helped to kill them.

CRYSTAL: Yeah but like before the women had abortions she'd try to talk them out of it. Like she'd say "Don't you hear your baby crying? Don't you hear your baby calling Mama?"

MEGAN: But she didn't talk your mother out of it, did she?

(Beat.)

CRYSTAL: You're an actress?

MEGAN: Yes.

CRYSTAL: They have an actress playing me. There she is. They tried to find someone who looked like me. To tell my story.

MEGAN: She doesn't look like you. She's blonde.

CRYSTAL: But otherwise…You're from Ohio?

MEGAN: Yes…

CRYSTAL: I'm from West Virginia, same like Randall. That's really close to Ohio, that could practically be Ohio if there wasn't a border.

MEGAN: Did they pay you? For your story?

CRYSTAL: No, God, no, I mean they saved my life.

MEGAN: So this nurse raised you?

CRYSTAL: She couldn't cause she already had a mess of kids but the organization placed me. I was in foster care. Different families. That's why I like…This is like a family to me. This organization. And Randall. God. I love him so much. I get to ride in his mobile home when we travel. And when he does interviews he brings me in to tell them I was a fetus.

MEGAN: We were all fetuses.

CRYSTAL: Exactly! See this charm bracelet. Randall gave it to me. For my birthday. It's got babies. That's how many babies are killed in one second, less than a second, an electron.

MEGAN: That seems like an odd choice for a birthday present.

CRYSTAL: Well he bought me the chain. I bought the babies. They're life size. See that's seven weeks pregnant. To scale. That's what a lot of women are scraping away. And if they've had an abortion, I can tell. I see shadows around them like ghosts. I look for women with shadows because I want to find my mother. And when she sees me, and how I turned out, she'll be proud of me, and be sad for what she did, and she'll cry and I'll forgive her. And she'll take me home and cook for me. Make me soup. And not from a can either. I saw a shadow around you.

MEGAN: I'm not your mother.

CRYSTAL: How do you know? Maybe you are.

(Megan collects her purse, sets the script down and starts to leave.)

MEGAN: Excuse me.

(Randall enters with Jim, the commercial's director.)

RANDALL: Megan, have you met Jim yet? You probably know Jim's work from the Reebok campaign.

JIM: I loved your tape.

MEGAN: I'm sorry, I just don't think I'm the right woman for the job...

RANDALL: You're perfect.

MEGAN: You see, I don't know what that means, I don't know if that's a good thing.

CRYSTAL: I told her my story Randall, about me being in the pail.

RANDALL: Ahh. Would you excuse us Crystal?

CRYSTAL: I'm not listening.

RANDALL: Could you just make sure that Rhonda has the latest script? The November 15 version?

CRYSTAL: I could maybe give her some background.

RANDALL: I think it's important not to do that Crystal, I think at a certain point actors need to make the role their own, if you see what I mean.

CRYSTAL: But it's my story.

RANDALL: But it's a story that goes beyond you. It's awesome. It's enormous. To think that you wouldn't be here.

CRYSTAL: I'll check on the script Randall.

RANDALL: Good girl. *(To Megan.)* I've created a monster.

MEGAN: Does she believe that story?

RANDALL: Oh, her story is true. She just embellishes it thereby rendering it totally implausible. Please sit. I know this must seem like a comedown for you.

MEGAN: It's not...

RANDALL: I saw your resume. You've worked Broadway, Off-Broadway, you've done the great roles. Medea.

(Megan laughs.)

RANDALL: We were lucky to get you. Your agent should hold out for more money next time.

MEGAN: Next time?

RANDALL: We're thinking that this might be an ongoing campaign. Tell a story, like in the coffee ads. I saw you were looking at the script. Any problems? Suggestions?

MEGAN: In the ad...

RANDALL: Yes?

MEGAN: I look at the playground, my hand travels to protect my stomach. I turn away...

RANDALL: Yes.

MEGAN: So I'm looking at an empty playground?

RANDALL: Yes.

MEGAN: And I'm thinking about the pregnancy I terminated?

RANDALL: You're thinking about the child you lost.

MEGAN: It just seems like...

RANDALL: Yes? Tell me.

MEGAN: It just seems like seeing children would make her think about children.

RANDALL: Excuse me. Jim? Could you come over here? *(To Megan.)* Tell him.

MEGAN: It just seems like seeing children would make her think about children.

JIM: But if we see a full playground, we'll just assume that she's watching her children play.

RANDALL: The point is that you have no children to watch. That you feel a hollowness, an emptiness.

MEGAN: But the script says that "twenty years ago" I made a choice, so if my child would be twenty now, I'm just wondering, why would I be looking at a merry-go-round?

JIM: It's not a merry-go-round.

MEGAN: Well what do you call it?

JIM: I don't know but it's not a merry-go-round. Merry-go-rounds have horses.

RANDALL: I think you, our woman, is thinking about the years she missed with her child at the playground, and is thinking that perhaps she'll never have a child, that she'll never have those years at the playground.

MEGAN: I don't mean to be difficult, but then why does she clutch her stomach?

JIM: Well she's remembering the abortion.

MEGAN: Well is she thinking about the actual operation? I mean, the aftermath of the actual operation, the discomfort? Or is it a larger pain, a larger sense of loss...?

RANDALL: Yes, yes, I see, we're going for that sense of loss, so perhaps the stomach gesture is clouding the issue...

MEGAN: Perhaps.

RANDALL: Jim, would you excuse us a minute? Is it painful for you? To remember your own abortion?

MEGAN: It was a long time ago.

RANDALL: Was it painful then?

MEGAN: I was sixteen. All there was was relief. The only...

RANDALL: What?

MEGAN: The only pain was that I lied to my parents. That I had to lie to my parents.

RANDALL: If there wasn't anything wrong with abortion, why did you lie about it?

MEGAN: Because there was something wrong with getting pregnant. I mean there was something wrong about having sex with my boyfriend. In their eyes. My parents were Catholic.

RANDALL: Were?

MEGAN: Are.

RANDALL: I didn't know that.

MEGAN: How would you?

RANDALL: Jim, we're losing the stomach gesture. We're trying to capture that sense of having missed the playground years...any other suggestions?

MEGAN: Maybe just the sound of children...

JIM: What?

RANDALL: The sound of children?

MEGAN: I was just thinking that you'd get a greater sense of the absence of children if you heard them but didn't see them...

JIM: I'm sorry, but there is a script.

RANDALL: Like she heard them in her mind?

MEGAN: Exactly.

RANDALL: Good. Jim? You like that? Does that work for you?

JIM: Whatever.

RANDALL: Will that slow us down?

JIM: We can dub it in later.

RANDALL: Good thought, Megan...

MEGAN: I didn't mean to be difficult.

RANDALL: We're all trying to tell the same story. You made it better.
(*Park bench. Liz enters carrying a tub of movie popcorn and a soda.*)

MEGAN: I mean, they had me clutching my stomach, why would I be clutching my stomach?

LIZ: Cause you were gonna throw up?

MEGAN: I mean, I wasn't supposed to be thinking about the *procedure,* I was supposed to be thinking about the *child*...

LIZ: It wasn't a child, it was a fetus.

MEGAN: It was a potential child.

LIZ: So is a spermatozoon, but nobody blows up drug stores for selling condoms.

MEGAN: Why are you so uncomfortable saying it's a potential child?

LIZ: Because the logic is deeply flawed. I'm a potential astronaut, but that doesn't mean I *will* be an astronaut, or *should* be an astronaut.

MEGAN: They weren't being clear, about her emotional state.

LIZ: Whose emotional state?

MEGAN: The woman. In the commercial. So I told them how to make it clearer. I suggested adding the sound of children's voices playing. Laughing. You know.

LIZ: Well that's pathetic.

MEGAN: It isn't pathetic, if you *hear* the voices, and *see* the empty playground, you understand what she's thinking.

LIZ: Maybe she's thinking, thank God I never wasted years of my life on some park bench watching my children poke each other's eyes out with popsicle sticks.

MEGAN: Is that what you think? That taking care of children is wasting your life?

LIZ: I think raising children involves long stretches of tedium, yes.

MEGAN: Like we don't have long stretches of tedium.

LIZ: I didn't say that life, per se, isn't tedious, but having children is inviting tedium into your life!

MEGAN: I mean, what do we do all day? We watch t.v. and eat Lean Cuisine and go to the gym and audition for assholes and go see lousy movies that star actors we don't like. Why not have a child?

LIZ: And give all that up?

MEGAN: I want to have a child.

LIZ: That's just because you haven't worked in six months.

MEGAN: It is not.

LIZ: You want to have a child someday, fine. But that's got nothing to do with an abortion you had at age sixteen.

MEGAN: I didn't say it did.

LIZ: I mean look at those pro-life demonstrators. Who are they? Mothers with bad perms and pastel sweatsuits struggling to make a movement out of diaper pails!

MEGAN: You're underestimating the enemy. Of course there are rednecks, but there are men and women who are having a crisis of conscience, who are questioning…

LIZ: Then let them question. I mean, if they decide abortion is wrong, fine, they don't have to have one. I'm not out there blowing up delivery rooms so that they can't give birth to their babies...

MEGAN: You're right, you're right, I'm just trying to play devil's advocate.

LIZ: You got that right.

MEGAN: I mean usually when I suggest things, nobody listens to me, cause who am I? I'm just the actress, but this guy actually listened to me.

LIZ: Just...

MEGAN: What?

LIZ: Don't help him make it better.

(Liz exits. Randall enters, sits. Restaurant.)

MEGAN: You're stacking the deck, because you're showing a well-dressed thirty-six year old woman walking through a suburban playground so of course it looks selfish that she aborted the child, but if you showed her at sixteen, with her sixteen year old pimply boyfriend, working at Tastee Freeze, filling out college applications...

RANDALL: We're not saying that sixteen year old should marry the man, drop out of school, and raise that baby, we're saying that maybe she could give that baby up for adoption, maybe to be adopted by the well-dressed thirty-six year old walking through the suburban playground...

MEGAN: Well there are adoption horror stories, I mean, what if you give your child up to child abusers?

RANDALL: Is the child better off dead?

MEGAN: I think so, yes, in certain cases. And it would still interrupt that girl's life in a way that is irrevocable, she'd have to drop out of school, suffer the stigma...

RANDALL: If only there were still such a thing as a stigma...

MEGAN: You *want* the girl to suffer a stigma?

RANDALL: I just don't believe the girl would be ostracized in any way...

MEGAN: And why do you make exceptions for rape and incest, I mean if it's murder it's murder...

RANDALL: I don't make exceptions. Those exceptions have been made by politicians out of political expedience but the logic is flawed, it's not consistent with what we believe.

MEGAN: Oh.

RANDALL: Would you like another glass of wine? *(Randall points to the two empty glasses to signal waiter.)*

MEGAN: No, I have to get home.

RANDALL: Why? Do you have a dog waiting for you?

MEGAN: I have a roommate.

RANDALL: And you're worried that your roommate is worried?

MEGAN: I'm worried that my roommate is lonely.

RANDALL: But if you leave, I'll be lonely.

MEGAN: But you must have a wife waiting for you.

RANDALL: I'm afraid not.

MEGAN: But you have children.

RANDALL: I'm divorced.

MEGAN: Doesn't that fly in the face of family values?

RANDALL: It wasn't my decision.

MEGAN: Was there another man?

RANDALL: Another woman.

MEGAN: Oh. Where are the children?

RANDALL: With her. But I hope to get them back.

MEGAN: Why?

RANDALL: Because I miss them.

MEGAN: Because they're with a lesbian couple?

RANDALL: That too.

MEGAN: Are they good parents?

RANDALL: They're not parents They're not married. There's no stability there.

MEGAN: In fact, lesbian couples are more likely to stay together than straight couples.

RANDALL: I'm sorry I'm not able to discuss this abstractly yet. Do you think you'll ever get married?

MEGAN: I don't know. Most of the men I meet are married. Everybody's married. Happily married. I sort of wonder where I was when all that coupling was going on. I mean. I always had a boyfriend, but suddenly it was like musical chairs, all of a sudden the music stopped and there was no chair for me.

RANDALL: Maybe I'm a chair for you.

(Megan laughs.)

RANDALL: You don't think so?

MEGAN: We're very different. We have different beliefs.

RANDALL: Are my beliefs so bad? I believe in getting married and staying married. I believe in raising the children I help to create.

MEGAN: But what if your wife didn't want to have the child?

RANDALL: But you do.

MEGAN: What?

RANDALL: But you'd like to have a child.

MEGAN: But what if I didn't? What if we slept together tonight and I got pregnant and came to you and told you I decided to have an abortion, what would you do?

RANDALL: Are you thinking about sleeping together tonight?

MEGAN: Well it is implicit in the situation, not that we will but that we might. I mean we're in a bar. We're drinking wine.

RANDALL: It's a business meeting.

MEGAN: Is it?

RANDALL: I just want you to be comfortable. I want to frame it in a way that makes you comfortable.

MEGAN: I'm not comfortable. I'm extremely uncomfortable. If my roommate knew where I was and who I was with…

RANDALL: Isn't it funny that we always need to be sneaking around behind someone's back, first our parents, then our spouses, and then our… roommates.

MEGAN: You didn't answer my question.

RANDALL: What question?

MEGAN: What would you do if I were pregnant with your child and decided to have an abortion ?

RANDALL: I would probably cry.

MEGAN: You wouldn't stop me?

RANDALL: How could I stop you?

MEGAN: You wouldn't abduct me…

RANDALL: Abduct you? We're not…criminals. We're not…vigilantes.

MEGAN: Well you are in fact.

RANDALL: I can't be responsible for every faction of the movement. My own organization takes action within the law.

MEGAN: The letter of the law.

RANDALL: Yes.

MEGAN: You stand fifty feet away or whatever but you still harass those poor women who are going in to…

RANDALL: We reach out to them…

MEGAN: Oh come on…

RANDALL: We try to remind them that we're there for them…

MEGAN: You attack them! You throw things at them! You show them bloody pictures!

RANDALL: Did that happen to you?

MEGAN: Yes.

RANDALL: I'm sorry. That must have been horrible. At sixteen.

MEGAN: It wasn't because I was *sixteen*…

RANDALL: No, I know.

MEGAN: I had nightmares. That day was a nightmare. *(Laughs.)* It was Valentine's Day.

(Mom enters living room area wearing a bathrobe.)

MOM: Megan, is that you?

(Megan crosses to her. Randall watches.)

MOM: I need you to run to the market for some mint jelly. What is it? What's wrong?

MEGAN: Nothing. I just…hate mint jelly.

MOM: Since when?

MEGAN: I mean, I like it with lamb.

MOM: That's what we're having. *(Hands her a valentine.)* Happy Valentine's Day. And Daddy got a box of chocolates for you. They're good.

MEGAN: You ate some already?

MOM: Not some of yours. Some of mine.

MEGAN: These stupid hearts. Hearts aren't shaped like that.

MOM: You look tired. Why don't you take a little rest before dinner?

MEGAN: What about the mint jelly?

MOM: Daddy can get it when he comes home.

MEGAN: He'll be tired too. Why can't you go?

MOM: I'm in my bathrobe.

MEGAN: I didn't get him one.

MOM: Daddy doesn't care about that. Would you like some hot tea?

MEGAN: I don't like hot tea! I've never liked hot tea! You're the one who likes hot tea!

MOM: Did Brad give you something for Valentine's Day?

MEGAN: No.

MOM: No roses?

MEGAN: No. *(Megan starts to cry.)*

MOM: Megan, what is it? Did you and Brad have a fight?

MEGAN: I felt sick at school today. I wanted you to come get me.

MOM: Well why didn't you call me at work?

MEGAN: I knew you'd be all mad. I knew you were out of sick leave.

MOM: Well I could have taken some personal time.

MEGAN: That's for the beach this summer.

MOM: Well Brad could have driven you home.

MEGAN: He couldn't. He had a test in Chemistry and I felt sick. And then I have to go to the store for mint jelly!

MOM: You don't have to go. I said you don't have to go. Daddy will go.

MEGAN: Why can't you go?

MOM: Well I will if you're gonna get so upset about it.

MEGAN: You're the one who does the grocery shopping. You're the one who forgot the mint jelly.

MOM: I'll go get some clothes on.

MEGAN: Mom?

MOM: What is it?

MEGAN: I'm sorry Mom.

MOM: Sorry for what?

MEGAN: I'm sorry I didn't get you a Valentine.

MOM: That's all right.

MEGAN: I usually get you a Valentine.

MOM: Daddy got me one.

MEGAN: Did Julie?

MOM: Not this year.

MEGAN: Every year you give us one and we just…expect it and then we forget to get you one.

MOM: We want to, we like to. We've done it ever since you were children.

(Mom exits. Megan and Randall walk through the same park that we saw earlier.)

MEGAN: I wondered if she knew who I really was and what I had just done if she would have loved me anymore…

RANDALL: How could she not love you?

(Their eyes meet. Beat.)

RANDALL: I've wanted to meet you since the first moment I saw your tape.

MEGAN: So this has all been about you getting laid?

RANDALL: No! You were right for the ad. You looked…wholesome.

MEGAN: But I'm not wholesome, am I? By your measure. I'm a sinner.

RANDALL: We're all sinners.

MEGAN: But I'm a baby-killer.

RANDALL: Megan, listen to me. I have total sympathy for who you were and what you went through…

MEGAN: You're a very handsome man.

RANDALL: Thank you.

MEGAN: But there's a part of me that feels that this is just a body you've appropriated for your purposes.

RANDALL: And what are my purposes?

MEGAN: Conversion.

RANDALL: I'm not trying to convert you. I'm trying to woo you.

(*Megan laughs.*)

RANDALL: Why is that funny?

MEGAN: I just...I just had this flash. I imagined you with horns.

RANDALL: A cuckold.

MEGAN: No! A devil. Like you were the devil tempting me.

RANDALL: I'm glad you find me tempting.

(*Megan laughs.*)

RANDALL: I'm sorry I don't know if you're laughing at me or with me.

MEGAN: I'm just. I'm very nervous. I don't really go on dates.

RANDALL: I've never met anyone like you.

MEGAN: Well you wouldn't. In your circle.

RANDALL: That would be the seventh circle, I suppose.

MEGAN: I insult you and you just shrug it off.

RANDALL: I think you're externalizing an inner struggle. I think I represent your issues.

MEGAN: My "issues?"

RANDALL: Right.

MEGAN: What a load of crap.

(*Randall suddenly kisses her. She kisses him back. Chance appears.*)

CHANCE: Boys. Chair-offerers. Trash-emptiers. Jar-openers. Flower-pickers. Housepainters. Grass-cutters. All this can be yours. All this can be yours. Boys. Suit-case carriers. Car-fixers. Fire-starters. Valentine-givers. Honor-defenders. Mother-worshippers. All this can be yours...

(*Lights up on bedroom.*)

RANDALL: Where are you going?

MEGAN: I have to get home.

RANDALL: That is not how we do in my country.

MEGAN: I just sleep better in my own bed.

RANDALL: Would you like the bed? The whole bed? I can sleep on the floor.

MEGAN: I'm not going to kick you out of your own bed.

RANDALL: I'll set you up in another bedroom.

MEGAN: I just...feel weird.

RANDALL: Why?

(*Silence.*)

RANDALL: It's two in the morning. I don't want you out on the streets.

MEGAN: I'll hail a cab.

RANDALL: What if you can't?

MEGAN: The doorman will help me.

RANDALL: What if you get a cab but it's a phony cab driver who murdered the real cab driver?

MEGAN: I'll check his hack's license.

RANDALL: It's too late then. You're already in the vehicle.

MEGAN: Are you sure you're not a native New Yorker?

RANDALL: The stories you read…

MEGAN: You should stop reading The Post.

RANDALL: I don't read the Post.

MEGAN: I saw your recycling bin…

RANDALL: Once in awhile I read the Post. For the comics.

MEGAN: I used to read Newsday.

RANDALL: You did? I've never met anybody who read Newsday.

MEGAN: I read The Times too of course.

RANDALL: Of course.

MEGAN: I just wanted Ann Landers and the horoscope.

(He strokes her stomach.)

MEGAN: Don't.

RANDALL: What? I like it. I like your little belly.

MEGAN: It makes me feel fat.

RANDALL: In medieval times they built armor with space for bellies.

MEGAN: There were no gyms in medieval times.

RANDALL: There were famines.

MEGAN: If this were medieval times, we'd be dead by now. Did you know Lady Capulet was twenty-five years old? At *most*. Juliet was thirteen and her mother says she was younger than she was when she had her.

RANDALL: But they always have like…

MEGAN: I know. When in fact not only am I too old to play Juliet, I'm too old to play Lady Capulet!

RANDALL: There's still the nurse.

MEGAN: Fuck you.

RANDALL: Making love to you was…usually the first time is…

MEGAN: Awful.

RANDALL: Stay.

MEGAN: Oh Randall…

RANDALL: That's the first time you've said my name.

MEGAN: It isn't.

RANDALL: It's so…intimate. When somebody says your name. My four year old has taken to calling me Randall. Rather imperiously I think.

MEGAN: That seems very unconventional. Very 1960s.

RANDALL: Well I was a '60s kind of guy after all. I traveled to D.C. at age ten for my first anti-war demonstration. I told my parents I was going to an auto show which they still considered pansy-ass because it wasn't a truck show.

MEGAN: You were against the war?

RANDALL: Why does that surprise you? I'm against killing, Megan.

(Beat.)

MEGAN: Will you watch me while I fall asleep?

RANDALL: Just watch you?

MEGAN: Watch over me.

RANDALL: Would you like me to sing a lullaby?

MEGAN: Do you know any lullabies?

(Randall begins to sing "All Through The Night." Chance appears in the doorway. Intermission suggested.)

(Megan's apartment. Cat enters. Megan sticks a stick into the jar of urine. Sets a timer. Megan talks to an actress wearing cat ears. Sound of timer ticking.)

MEGAN: Stop staring at me.

CAT: I'm not staring.

MEGAN: You're following me with your eyes. You're like one of those paintings.

CAT: I'm not staring.

MEGAN: I fed you already. I'm sorry I took your kittens to the ASPCA.

CAT: The ASPCA?! You told me you found them a home!

MEGAN: I'm sure they did.

CAT: Are you mad? They got feline leukemia!

MEGAN: They test all the cats. They put down the contagious ones.

CAT: They also put down the ones that don't get adopted!

MEGAN: Kittens stand a better chance. Do you still think of them?

CAT: Do I think of my babies? Do I think of my babies!?

MEGAN: I mean you only knew them for six weeks. I mean you have a fulfilling life without them. The birds out the window. Kibbles. Catnip mouse. Don't you? Don't you?

(Timer goes off. Megan lifts the stick out of the jar.)

CAT: Well?

(Megan nods yes. Cat smiles.)

(Restaurant.)

RANDALL: I've missed you.

MEGAN: How was your trip?

RANDALL: You're supposed to say that you missed me.

MEGAN: I did miss you.

RANDALL: I missed you more.

MEGAN: We talked on the phone.

RANDALL: I would have called every day but I didn't want to look desperate. So I called your answering machine, when I knew you weren't home, just to hear your voice.

MEGAN: You didn't leave a message?

RANDALL: I didn't know if we were going public. Have you told your roommate about me?

MEGAN: No.

RANDALL: Where did you tell her you were going tonight?

MEGAN: To the gym.

RANDALL: Wearing that?

MEGAN: That's what she said.

RANDALL: I think I know how mistresses must feel.

MEGAN: You're not my mistress!

RANDALL: No? What am I?

MEGAN: I don't know.

RANDALL: I want to be your boyfriend.

MEGAN: Boyfriends have acne.

RANDALL: Your lover then.

MEGAN: You are my lover.

RANDALL: I wasn't sure if that was a one-time thing.

MEGAN: I don't have one-time things.

RANDALL: I was afraid that you'd thought better of it. Of me.

MEGAN: Things are happening very fast.

(Dinardi enters.)

DINARDI: Randall. I thought you'd be here. I found the article I was telling you about, about the financial persecution of Catholics at the highest levels of police departments, fire departments...

RANDALL: This is Megan, Tony. Say hello.

DINARDI: Your last name's Tony?

MEGAN: No. Healy.

DINARDI: I was gonna say. That's weird. Her last name is my first name.

RANDALL: I just made an introduction, Tony. Remember we talked about introductions?

DINARDI: You're the one who had the abortion.

RANDALL: That's a commercial, Tony.

DINARDI: Were you just pretending to be sorry? Or were you really sorry?

RANDALL: It's a fiction, Tony. Megan is an actress.

DINARDI: If I ripped a baby from my womb I'd be sorry.

RANDALL: Thank you for bringing this by, Tony.

DINARDI: *(Sitting, to Megan.)* I have guns.

RANDALL: Pleasure guns.

DINARDI: Pleasure guns. But they could kill someone.

RANDALL: Well that's what guns do.

DINARDI: At the range I can hit the head everytime. One two three four five six seven.

RANDALL: You have an automatic?

DINARDI: They're trying to ban them. That's ironic, isn't it? They kill babies and they're acting like we're the killers. Have you seen these pictures?

RANDALL: I don't think this is the time and place.

DINARDI: When is the time and place? Church? This is all church. We should be acting like this is all a big church. Not just, you know, you're good in church, and then you go screwing and drinking and...

MEGAN: Excuse me.

RANDALL: No stay. Megan and I need to talk privately, Tony. About the ad campaign we're shooting.

DINARDI: Shooting! That's ironic, isn't it?

RANDALL: Well commercials are weapons Tony, as we've discussed, probably more effective than violence.

DINARDI: Violence? I'm not violent! I'm trying to stop the violence. But if you had a chance to kill Hitler, would you? I think so.

RANDALL: But you can't shoot every woman in the world who wants an abortion...

DINARDI: No, I can't shoot every woman in the world, but there are targets, Planned Parenthood, the doctors. NOW, that woman who runs NOW, that lesbian...

RANDALL: I urge you to keep these thoughts to yourself, Tony. You will hurt the movement.

DINARDI: I'm hurting the movement?

RANDALL: You frighten people.

DINARDI: Are you going to eat your ice?

RANDALL: Help yourself.

DINARDI: How much do I owe you?

RANDALL: Let me get it.

DINARDI: No way.

RANDALL: Let the organization get it. For all your hard work.

DINARDI: Okay. If you're sure.

RANDALL: Please.

DINARDI: I like your hair color. I like the honey undertones.

MEGAN: (Tersely.) Thank you.

　　　(Dinardi exits.)

MEGAN: I think I'll take a bath now.

RANDALL: He's out of his mind.

MEGAN: I got that.

RANDALL: I am trying to defuse a potentially bad situation.

MEGAN: And you would consider assassinations to be a bad thing?

RANDALL: I recognize the hypocrisy of people murdering to prevent murder.
　　　Megan. This particular foot soldier is spinning out of control and I'm
　　　trying to rein him in.

MEGAN: He works for you. But you know he's out of his mind.

RANDALL: Better to have him under somebody's control than to have him out
　　　there running wild.

MEGAN: Your control.

RANDALL: Yes.

MEGAN: Why don't you have him committed?

RANDALL: I'm not his *father*. I can't have him committed!

MEGAN: Why are you defending him?

RANDALL: I'm not defending him. I'm defending myself. I'm trying to under-
　　　stand why you're sleeping with me when you're ashamed of me!

MEGAN: I'm not ashamed of you. I'm ashamed of myself.

RANDALL: Why?

MEGAN: I thought I had principles, I thought I knew what those principles
　　　were, and yet I'm sleeping with someone who violates those principles.
　　　Because my biological clock is ticking I seem to be walking around in
　　　some kind of hormonally-induced cloud…My need to love and be loved
　　　is taking precedence over everything.

RANDALL: What is wrong with wanting to be loved? I want to meet your
　　　roommate.

MEGAN: No you don't.

RANDALL: I do.

　　　(Megan's apartment. Liz watches television. Randall stands awkwardly in
　　　his coat.)

LIZ: (Yelling.) Megan, your "date's" here.

RANDALL: What are you watching?

LIZ: Television. Are you allowed to watch T.V. in your cult?

RANDALL: Oh yes indeed. It's one of our instruments of power.

LIZ: I forgot.

(Randall points to the wine.)

RANDALL: May I?

LIZ: Whatever.

RANDALL: No plans tonight?

LIZ: I'm planning to watch television.

RANDALL: No date?

LIZ: Does it look like I have a date?

RANDALL: I guess it's hard to meet men in this town.

LIZ: It's not hard to meet assholes.

RANDALL: Tell me how you define asshole. What constitutes an asshole?

LIZ: An asshole is someone who doesn't know he's an asshole.

RANDALL: No seriously, what kind of men do you meet that you wouldn't date?

LIZ: Married men. Divorced men. Substance abusers. Lotharios. Republicans. P.S. I'm a lesbian.

RANDALL: My wife is a lesbian.

LIZ: Very funny. Are you and Megan fucking?

RANDALL: Why don't you ask Megan?

LIZ: She won't tell me.

RANDALL: Maybe she's respecting your feelings.

LIZ: Maybe she's ashamed.

RANDALL: It's a little sophomoric, don't you think, not being able to agree to disagree.

LIZ: If I make that agreement, suddenly you're in charge of my body.

RANDALL: If you became pregnant.

LIZ: Right.

RANDALL: Which is unlikely given your…lifestyle.

LIZ: What are you exactly? I mean what is your profession?

RANDALL: I run an organization.

LIZ: But with what qualifications? Are you a lawyer? An MBA?

RANDALL: Some have greatness thrust upon them.

LIZ: You dress pretty well.

RANDALL: Thank you.

LIZ: I hate to think that some of those hard-earned anti-choice funds are getting siphoned off into your bank account.

RANDALL: I do get a salary. I do buy clothes. Have you seen the commercial yet?

LIZ: I saw it.

RANDALL: What did you think?

LIZ: I thought it was a pile of crap.

RANDALL: But what about Megan's performance?

LIZ: It was the biggest abuse of talent I've ever seen.

RANDALL: Did you ever think that she was tapping into real regrets she had about her own abortion?

LIZ: She doesn't regret her abortion.

RANDALL: Maybe she does. But she wouldn't tell *you* about it.

LIZ: You know, you might think that Megan is desperate. But Megan is not desperate. Megan has always been surrounded by men. And she's talented. In demand. She doesn't need to compromise her beliefs in order to reproduce.

RANDALL: Are *you* going to get her pregnant?

LIZ: Better me than you. Better my DNA than your missing chromosome hillbilly genes.

RANDALL: So this is really a class issue for you? This has nothing to do with your political beliefs. This is really about me being from West Virginia. This is really about you resenting the fact that a little white trash kid could make it.

LIZ: Oh please.

RANDALL: If a black boy from the ghetto becomes a general you buy his book, but if a cracker wears Armani…

LIZ: Why does it not surprise me to discover that you're a racist?

RANDALL: What did I say that was racist?

LIZ: You resent the fact that black people are getting ahead in this world, that they might be infiltrating the…

RANDALL: I most certainly do not! I have more in common with that boy from the ghetto than you do!

LIZ: "Boy!"

RANDALL: Yes boy! We were talking about a child! I grew up in a house where there were only two books—the Bible and the Sears catalogue…

LIZ: And you read both from cover to cover.

RANDALL: Yes I did, indeed I did, I was hungry, I was starved for words. You don't know what that's like, to not only be starving for food, but starving for some kind of…and I can tell you that there is nothing in that Bible that says babies are there to be disposed of, that women are there to be used as sex objects, the Bible talks about a man and a woman going forth and multiplying…

LIZ: A man and a woman, a man and a woman, is there any room in this world for people like me?

RANDALL: Have you ever had an abortion?

LIZ: That is none of your damn business!

RANDALL: If there's nothing wrong with it, then why don't you want to talk about it?

LIZ: I don't want to open the door to some right-wing evangelical…

RANDALL: Women tell me they see the children they lost in dreams. The children come to them. In dreams. Has that ever happened to you?

LIZ: If I eat pepperoni pizza.

MEGAN: *(In the doorway.)* I've had dreams. I dream of a boy running down a dock and I know he's going to fall in the water but I'm powerless to stop him. I open my mouth but no sound comes out. I try to run but my legs don't move. I try to get someone's attention but nobody sees me. I hear him cry out.

(Chance appears.)

CHANCE: Never played hooky. Never played doctor. Never took a teddy bear to bed. Never ate Spaghetti-O's. Never played with GI Joes. Never played baseball. Never made an ashtray. Never felt a girl up. Never had a wet dream. Never had a skinned knee. Never lost a kite to a tree. Was never called a faggot. Never missed my father. Never got a rake thrown at me. Never lost my bathing suit. Never had a dog die. Never went hungry. Never saw Ohio. Never got born. Never got born. So what? Take my soul elsewhere. Circle back. Check it out. Lay low.

(Randall's car, suggested by four chairs. Crystal and Dinardi sit in the back seat. Randall "opens the door" for Megan.)

RANDALL: I'm sorry about this. I've got the company car and they're late for the demonstration. They've got the flyers, the placards, everything.

(Megan and Randall get in the car.)

DINARDI: Hey Randall, how do you spell 'decapitation?'

RANDALL: Say hello to Megan, Tony.

DINARDI: Your last name's Tony?

MEGAN: No. Healy.

DINARDI: I was gonna say. That's weird. Her last name is my first name. If we got married I'd be Tony Tony. No wait.

MEGAN: Hello Tony.

RANDALL: You met Megan at the restaurant.

DINARDI: At the hair salon actually. She had highlights. Hence the honeyed
    undertones.

CRYSTAL: I was thinking about going blonder. Like me in the commercial.

RANDALL: I know you've met Megan, Crystal.

MEGAN: Hi Crystal.

CRYSTAL: I told her my story. *(To Megan.)* Remember? About the pail.

MEGAN: I remember.

CRYSTAL: Where are you two going, Randall?

RANDALL: To dinner.

CRYSTAL: Where?

RANDALL: I don't think you know it.

DINARDI: How do you spell 'suction?'

CRYSTAL: What's it called?

RANDALL: The Zen Palate. S-U-C-T-I-O-N.

CRYSTAL: Is it near Pre-Term?

RANDALL: No. Why?

CRYSTAL: I was wondering if we could have a ride home.

DINARDI: We won't need a ride. I've got my truck there.

RANDALL: Why is your truck there, Tony?

DINARDI: Cause I knew I was going there.

RANDALL: Well if you had parked your truck at the office, I wouldn't have had
    to drive you.

MEGAN: What's that smell?

DINARDI: What's it smell like?

MEGAN: Like vomit.

DINARDI: That's me.

RANDALL: *(Warning.)* Tony.

DINARDI: It's butyric acid. If you toss a pellet into the clinic the whole place
    reeks.

RANDALL: That's not acceptable.

DINARDI: Since when?

RANDALL: Give it to me.

MEGAN: Don't touch it!

RANDALL: Throw it out the window.

DINARDI: *Why?*

CRYSTAL: It's a gross-out, that's why.

DINARDI: You thought it was funny a minute ago.

CRYSTAL: Did not.

DINARDI: Did so.

RANDALL: That's enough! Both of you. Or you're taking the subway.

CRYSTAL: But we're late.

RANDALL: I've apologized for that.

CRYSTAL: You should have dropped us first.

MEGAN: Why are you demonstrating at night?

RANDALL: It's a candlelight vigil.

DINARDI: CNN is coming.

RANDALL: Maybe.

DINARDI: Definitely. They called.

RANDALL: Give the statement to Leon. Is that clear? Under no circumstances are you to read the statement.

DINARDI: I can read, you know.

RANDALL: I know you can read Tony. But Leon has more experience with the press than you do.

CRYSTAL: I smell perfume. *(To Megan.)* Are you wearing perfume?

DINARDI: Yeah, it's called Vomit.

RANDALL: Tony.

CRYSTAL: You're so gross. What kind is it?

MEGAN: I don't remember.

CRYSTAL: You don't remember? You just put it on.

MEGAN: Arpege, I think.

CRYSTAL: What's an arpege?

DINARDI: It's a perfume you dork.

RANDALL: Hop out. Before the light changes.

CRYSTAL: You should take her to the place we went. Remember, Randall? *(Calling after him.)* With the shrimp!

RANDALL: I'm sorry about that.

MEGAN: They're like the Munster children.

RANDALL: They're just teen-agers.

MEGAN: On the dark side of the moon.

RANDALL: Now then, are you hungry?

MEGAN: How can I be hungry? Everything smells like vomit.

RANDALL: Were you hungry before you got into the vehicle?

MEGAN: Yes.

RANDALL: Good.

MEGAN: You can just go and have dinner when there's a demonstration going on?

RANDALL: I'm an administrator. I delegate.

MEGAN: Kind of like God.

RANDALL: Let's leave Him out of it, shall we?

MEGAN: Sorry.

RANDALL: Tonight is important.

MEGAN: Why?

RANDALL: Don't rush me. I have to find a parking space.

MEGAN: Why is tonight important?

RANDALL: Just look for a space.

MEGAN: There's one.

RANDALL: Hydrant.

MEGAN: Are you going to propose to me?

RANDALL: Megan, please. Is that a space?

MEGAN: You need a sticker.

RANDALL: What makes you think I'm going to propose?

MEGAN: I figured those family values would kick in.

RANDALL: You could do worse. I'm a good man.

MEGAN: And a good man is hard to find.

RANDALL: Are you taking me seriously? I don't think you're taking me seriously.

MEGAN: I'm sorry.

RANDALL: I make a good deal of money. You wouldn't have to live with lesbians in railroad flats anymore.

MEGAN: "I Lived with Lesbians," you think I could sell it to The Star?

RANDALL: Oh forget it, we'll talk about it inside...is that a place?

MEGAN: The curb is yellow.

RANDALL: I don't see a sign. I'm parking.

MEGAN: Let's talk about it now.

RANDALL: You're being very flip and honestly Megan it's irritating.

MEGAN: Well you said that stupid thing about lesbians...

RANDALL: It was a joke...I mean you didn't take offense on behalf of the railroad flats, did you?

MEGAN: I don't know when you're joking. I don't even know you. How can I marry you?

RANDALL: Let's eat.

MEGAN: I'm not hungry.

RANDALL: I am. Get out of the car.

MEGAN: You go eat. I'll wait.

RANDALL: Don't be ridiculous. It's not safe.

MEGAN: I'm paying for my meal.

RANDALL: Fine.

MEGAN: I don't like this patriarchal intimation that I need you because of your superior paycheck which is supplied by creepy right-wing organizations.

RANDALL: As opposed to your paycheck?

MEGAN: My paycheck used to come from the NEA but thanks to your pal Jesse Helms...

RANDALL: Yeah, I was thinking he'd be my best man.

MEGAN: I don't want to go to a restaurant. I don't want to fight in public.

RANDALL: I'm trying to make this a memorable night.

MEGAN: I liked the vomit pellet touch.

RANDALL: Come on Megan, please, I'm hungry.

MEGAN: I'm not.

RANDALL: Of course you're hungry.

MEGAN: I feel nauseous.

RANDALL: You're overreacting.

MEGAN: I'm not overreacting! I'm pregnant!

RANDALL: You're pregnant? That's wonderful.

(Megan starts to cry.)

RANDALL: Isn't it?

MEGAN: It all just seems so...random. You. Me. It.

RANDALL: It's not random. God has a plan for us. I know all this God talk must seem slightly blue collar to you, like you've suddenly entered a tent in Mississippi where cripples are walking and women are wearing enormous false eyelashes, but I just know that this has always been here, waiting for us to catch up to it. Megan, marry me.

(Megan's apartment.)

LIZ: Look, I sort of promised Tricia you were coming to the demonstration tonight...

MEGAN: Liz...

LIZ: She's one of the organizers. I met her at Girl Bar.

MEGAN: The one you have a crush on?

LIZ: Well yeah sort of...is it his?

MEGAN: He wants to marry me.

LIZ: Oh I'm sure he does. I'm sure he'd be very happy to have you in some Connecticut suburb picking up his dry cleaning and watching Barney...

MEGAN: I haven't said yes.

LIZ: Look at it this way, CNN is coming tonight, this could be like a chance for you to...atone.

MEGAN: Why the hell should I atone? I was acting! I was playing a role!

LIZ: Without any thought to the consequences?

MEGAN: The consequence is that I can pay the rent, *our* rent, for the next six months!

LIZ: It's a *loan,* I'm gonna pay you back!

MEGAN: Look, when I've got the money you can borrow the money, just don't attack me for how I made the money!

LIZ: I'm not attacking *you...*

MEGAN: I can't demonstrate.

LIZ: You have to! CNN is gonna be there!

MEGAN: No I mean I really can't demonstrate. Legally. I signed a contract.

LIZ: You what?

MEGAN: They could sue me. They could sue my agency.

LIZ: Don't you see that this is just...these people want to control your body in every way?

MEGAN: Of course I see that. But I needed the job.

LIZ: If he finds out you're pregnant he won't permit you to have an abortion, you do know that.

MEGAN: I don't want an abortion...

LIZ: *(Singing Barney song.)* I love you, you love me...

MEGAN: If I married Randall...

LIZ: We're a happy family...

MEGAN: The baby would have a father.

LIZ: And what a father!

MEGAN: I don't know how else I could keep it.

(Beat.)

LIZ: If you say you'll marry him, you'll have to move in with him.

MEGAN: Well of course I will, eventually.

LIZ: No. I mean. You will no longer be welcome in this apartment.

MEGAN: Is this about who I'm marrying or the fact that I'm getting married to a man?

LIZ: Contrary to popular belief, I am not sick with love for you. I mean I was at one time, but when I was convinced of your heterosexuality I moved on. I mean I'm not a *masochist.*

MEGAN: That doesn't mean you're not ambivalent about...

LIZ: I don't give a fuck that you're getting married! Some of my best friends are married! But I do care that you're getting into bed with every right wing interest in this country...

MEGAN: Isn't that a lot of symbolic weight to put on one man?

LIZ: I don't think so. Actions have consequences. You want this baby, okay, have this one baby. You want this man, okay, have this one man. But this man and his minions will see to it that every right wing fuck gets elected into office and before you know it there will be no welfare, no health care, no reproductive rights, no arts funding, which means no theater, no actresses…where are you going?

MEGAN: I don't know.

LIZ: To *him?*

MEGAN: You'll probably see him before I do. He may be at the demonstration.

LIZ: You're not going to tell him?

MEGAN: I already told him.

LIZ: Oh my God.

MEGAN: Stop it! Just stop it! You only march to meet girls, you don't write letters, you don't volunteer, you don't give money, you don't run for office, you just get into lame-brained dinner party arguments. Somebody knocks your little left-wing knee with a hammer and it kicks. At least he's putting his life where his mouth is.

LIZ: And what do you do?

MEGAN: I don't do anything! Because I don't know what I believe! How the hell do I know when life begins?! How the hell do any of us know that! *(Megan puts her coat on and walks out.)*
(Demonstration.)

DINARDI: BABY-KILLER! BABY-KILLER! You want to see what you just did? *(Shoving photographs at the audience.)* That was your baby. That was your baby. Before. After. Before. After. Your baby's body is quivering in some bucket. His blood's splashed on the linoleum floor. Your baby's wondering why you betrayed him, why you let him be twisted, burned, cut…Who are you? Her lover? Some dyke telling her the choice is hers? Who chooses for the baby? He's gasping for breath, but he can't breathe, he's dying in some *pail.* I hate you, the Pope hates you. God himself hates you and he will strike you down. When you want a child, he will take that child, strike him down, polio, leukemia, Down's syndrome… *(Randall's apartment. Voices are arguing offstage.)*

RANDALL: Megan.

MEGAN: May I come in?

RANDALL: What are you doing here? At this hour?

MEGAN: Liz kicked me out.

RANDALL: But it's your apartment.

MEGAN: It's her lease.

RANDALL: Do you want to stay here? Of course you'll stay here.

MEGAN: I've been thinking about your proposal…

(The phone rings. Offstage voice calls "Randall!)

MEGAN: Oh. You have guests.

RANDALL: Colleagues.

VOICE: *(Offstage.)* It's the lawyer!

RANDALL: I have to take this.

MEGAN: A lawyer? In the middle of the night?

RANDALL: There's been an incident.

MEGAN: What kind of incident?

RANDALL: Dinardi had a gun at the demonstration and he opened fire.

MEGAN: He didn't have a gun in the car…

RANDALL: He had a truck parked nearby. He got it out of his truck.

MEGAN: Did he hit anybody?

RANDALL: He killed three people…women who worked there, one of them was seven months pregnant.

MEGAN: Oh my God.

RANDALL: One of the women didn't even have anything to do with PreTerm, she was just the janitor for the building…he threw the butyric acid in and forced them out…

MEGAN: You mean that she was innocent?

RANDALL: The women who work for PreTerm at least know the risks…I'm afraid I have to take this call.

MEGAN: Why are you talking to a lawyer?

RANDALL: We're arranging a lawyer for Tony…

MEGAN: You're defending him?

RANDALL: He is entitled to a lawyer.

MEGAN: You're paying to defend this man?

RANDALL: I'm not paying, the organization is paying. We need to make clear that Tony did what he did on his own, was not representing Life Force in any way.

MEGAN: So the organization is funding his legal defense in order to prove that he is not tied to the organization…

RANDALL: He was our volunteer, on some level we're responsible, but the fact is that Tony did what he did because he's insane…

MEGAN: If you knew he was crazy, then why did you have anything to do with him?

RANDALL: Please Megan, I need you behind me, don't you think I'm agonizing over what I could have done…

MEGAN: You don't seem to be agonized, no, you seem energized.

RANDALL: It's a crisis, it is my job to handle crises...

MEGAN: It's not a crisis, it's a tragedy.

RANDALL: Look Megan, if you think that I am untouched by what happened out there tonight, then why the hell are you thinking about marrying me?

MEGAN: I don't know.

RANDALL: Jesus, Megan, you do too! So I called it a crisis when it's a tragedy, so I was unable to marshal my language skills and choose the precise word. If I could precisely choose the right language, if I could precisely convey my deepest feelings, wouldn't that make it more unlikely that I was actually feeling anything at all?

MEGAN: If one of the women was pregnant, why didn't you say he murdered four people? That's what you believe, isn't it?

RANDALL: It was a body count, it wasn't a metaphysical discussion.

MEGAN: You count the bodies however it serves your needs. When it makes you and your people MORE guilty then that fetus quickly loses its personhood.

RANDALL: It was an oversight, it was a mistake, I'll change the press release.

MEGAN: Press release?

RANDALL: Don't be naive Megan, the whole organization could go down in flames over this, over one sociopathic teen-ager's fuck-up.

MEGAN: Fuck-up? Fuck-up?!

RANDALL: You know what I mean!

MEGAN: A fuck-up is when you oversleep on the morning of your SAT's. Taking four lives is not a fuck-up!

RANDALL: Listen to yourself. You believe four lives were taken. In your heart of hearts, you're pro-life. You and I believe the same things.

MEGAN: If that were true, you'd understand when I tell you I've decided not to marry you after all. You'd understand when I tell you I've decided to have an abortion.

RANDALL: The hell you will! It's my child too!

VOICE: Randall!

MEGAN: Your foot soldiers are calling you.

RANDALL: Do you have any idea what it means to have an abortion?

MEGAN: I think I have a better idea than you do.

RANDALL: Do you have any idea what they do to the child? Do you know what happens when saline solution is injected into the womb? The child suffers the equivalent of third degree burns! Or, if the baby is farther along they reach in to pull out a foot, they pull the child out alive, by its legs, and then when it's in the birth canal, they take a scissors or a scalpel and puncture the child's head, through the fontanel where the tissue is the softest…

MEGAN: I think I've got the picture, Randall…

RANDALL: They say that fetuses feel no pain but that's what they used to say about newborns and animals…

MEGAN: What if my mind is made up? What if I've decided on an abortion?

RANDALL: I'll get an injunction to stop it!

MEGAN: Good-bye Randall.

RANDALL: What was that? Some kind of test?

MEGAN: Yeah. And you fucked up.

RANDALL: Megan wait!

VOICE: Randall, come on! He's about to get on a plane!

(Randall looks after Megan, then goes to answer the phone.)

CHANCE: She got that job in Japan, the soap commercial. And there she heard about the Buddhist shrines for the unborn—the mizuko, the water children. In Japan, abortion is not a bad thing. It's not a good thing, but it's not a bad thing. They acknowledge that every child has a soul or something like a soul, but that doesn't mean you can always welcome the child into the world.

(Scene at shrine in Japan. There are three tiers of child-sized stone statues, some holding pinwheels, toys, some partially clad in kimonos and sweaters. They look like thinner, miniature Buddhas.)

PRIEST: You like buy statue?

MEGAN: I couldn't…I'm flying home.

PRIEST: You leave here. One statue is your child.

MEGAN: I thought I'd just…pray.

PRIEST: You pray to your child. You ask forgiveness. One statue is your child.

MEGAN: Oh.

PRIEST: Any one. You choose.

MEGAN: I like that one. The one with the pinwheel.

PRIEST: That statue taken. The mother bring her that. Choose one without toy.

MEGAN: How about the one in the middle?

PRIEST: That your child. No problem.

MEGAN: I don't exactly know who I'm asking to forgive me. The child? God?

PRIEST: Statue both. The child you return and a bodhisattva.

MEGAN: The child I return?

PRIEST: You sent back. You returned the child to underworld.

MEGAN: The child's soul?

PRIEST: The unborn fetus, even newborn, no soul yet. Soul enters body gradually. We have ceremony at three years old, five years old…

MEGAN: In America we argue about the exact week the soul enters the body

PRIEST: Maybe five years old the soul is filled in.

MEGAN: What is the underworld? Is it hell?

PRIEST: Underworld is lonely. Like rocky cliffs on island in northern Japan. That's why you hear child crying out to you sometime. Has to be lonely. If it's too good they would not come when we called them. That statue your child. No problem.

MEGAN: Thank you. I won't be long.

PRIEST: You bring a toy for your child?

MEGAN: I guess he'd be too old for toys now.

PRIEST: I have E.T. dolls.

MEGAN: No thank you.

PRIEST: You want buy kimono? Silk. Very beautiful. Then they are not cold.

MEGAN: It's a statue.

PRIEST: Cold here in winter.

MEGAN: I think I'll just light a candle.

PRIEST: You want to buy matches?

MEGAN: I have matches. Thank you.

PRIEST: These are better. They are blessed.

MEGAN: I'd like to be alone now.

PRIEST: Forgive me. Please. *(Priest exits.)*

MEGAN: Hello?

(Chance appears.)

MEGAN: I wasn't sure I'd find you here.

CHANCE: Souls are kinda like world travelers.

MEGAN: No, I mean I wasn't sure you'd want to see me. The priest told me to ask your forgiveness but I don't expect you to forgive me after what I did…

CHANCE: Forgive you?

MEGAN: How can you forgive me, when you know and I know, there's always been some secret part of me that felt I…

CHANCE: What?

MEGAN: Killed you. And I don't deserve a second chance.

CHANCE: Everybody deserves a second chance.

MEGAN: But I…

CHANCE: You didn't kill me. Obviously. You returned me. You weren't able to welcome me at that time.

MEGAN: But maybe I could have welcomed you, maybe I should have welcomed you…

CHANCE: No. A good parent invites the child only when it's a propitious time.

MEGAN: But what if it's never a propitious time?

CHANCE: In retrospect Ohio would have been a drag. But New York, that would be awesome.

MEGAN: It's very expensive, very dangerous…

CHANCE: Aw Mom…

MEGAN: You don't know anything about it. You've been living on another plane!

CHANCE: I was hoping this time I could come.

MEGAN: Are you sure you want to? I'm a single mother and I haven't got very much…

CHANCE: YEAH. I mean, whatever. If you want me.

(Megan touches his cheek. Sound of whispering, wind chimes.)

MEGAN: What's that noise?

CHANCE: The water children are talking. Safe journey and such.

(Into sound of jet. Megan's apartment.)

MEGAN: You knew?

MOM: I suspected. I didn't know until I found a card. An appointment card in your Seventeen magazine.

MEGAN: Why didn't you tell me you knew?

MOM: I found it afterwards. It had already happened.

MEGAN: If you had found it beforehand would you have tried to stop me?

MOM: Oh no.

MEGAN: But you're Catholic.

MOM: I wouldn't have wanted you to go through all that.

MEGAN: But you think abortion is wrong…

MOM: I'm glad you had the abortion.

MEGAN: Did Daddy know?

MOM: No.

MEGAN: He would have hated me.

MOM: Oh honey no. Babies should be wanted.

MEGAN: I'm going to have this baby, Mom.

MOM: I know.

MEGAN: I haven't got a husband.

MOM: Just as well. You won't have that extra half a grapefruit.

MEGAN: Mom, do you think you could come back when the baby's born?

MOM: I thought you'd never ask.

MEGAN: I never really thought of you. I mean I knew I could go there but I never thought you could come here. I just assumed you couldn't handle the subways or the locks or the…

MOM: When is it that children start to think of their parents as children? You'll always be my child. Even when you're a mother, you'll still be my child.

MEGAN: I'm so sorry.

MOM: Hush now.

MEGAN: I'm so so sorry…

MOM: For what? You haven't done anything wrong.

(Spot up on Chance.)

CHANCE: Children also choose their parents and I chose her. Other souls made their move, but I got there first, placed my dibs. I like the smell of her neck, the softness of her breasts. She likes a lot of balls for a woman—basketball, football, baseball. She knows how to tell a story, sing a silly song, be a tyrannosaurus rex. She believes in bedtimes but not exactly, she believes in pajamas when convenient, she understands the need for an occasional Happy Meal, and is philosophical about grades. Which is not to say she doesn't insist on mittens, use the television as a babysitter, and snap when she's tired. But other than that she's perfect. *(Blackout.)*

END OF PLAY

TRUE CONFESSIONS OF A GO-GO GIRL

by Jill Morley

To everyone who's been along for the ride…
and you know who you are.

THE AUTHOR

Jill Morley is an actress, writer, filmmaker, and ex-go-go dancer. She wrote and performed the critically acclaimed play, *True Confessions of a Go-Go Girl.* It was produced in Manhattan, San Francisco's "Solo Mio Festival," along with John Waters and Eric Bogosian, The "Texas Fringe Festival," LA's HBO Workspace, and opened Women's History month at NYU.

Besides being published periodically in *The New York Press, Playgirl,* and various newsletters, she is a monthly columnist for *Shout* magazine.

Currently, Morley is directing her non-fiction feature film, *Stripped,* about topless dancers in New York, which is scheduled to be completed in June of 2000. She co-produced two radio documentaries for *The World* and *This American Life,* which aired on NPR. As a theatrical director, Morley has worked on many Off-Broadway productions. Most recently, she directed Maryann Towne's *Springtime in New York* at the Westbeth Theatre. The play was a finalist in the Actors Theatre of Louiseville's 10 Minute Play Contest. Recent highlights in Morley's acting career include a role in Hal Hartley's *Henry Fool,* working as a correspondent in Michael Moore's *The Awful Truth,* and an appearance on the Howard Stern show as an erotic dance coach. Other highlights include being directed by Paul Sills, founder of Chicago's Second City, in an original story theatre production, playing Jackie Kennedy for Japanese television, and Queen of the Goggleheads for the Sci-Fi channel. Current projects include a book of monologues for women, a collaborative work of short stories, and a screenplay she has co-written that has nothing at all to do with strippers or go-go bars.

AUTHOR'S NOTE

True Confessions started out as journal writings when I was a go-go girl, bikini dancing in New Jersey bars. I would bring a composition book to the dressing rooms and write about everything that was going on around me and inside me.

The play began as a way to humanize the women who did this job—the women who commodified their sexuality for money. It ended up humanizing me as well.

I am grateful to be able to bring you inside the walls of these bars and to meet some of the women that I have met. The women who have inspired and touched my life.

ORIGINAL PRODUCTION

Jill Morley
Maria T. Eldridge
Melanie Vesey
Heather Kenneally
Jason Jaworski

Directed by Maryann Towne

Two Go-Go dancers enter. One turns on a light and sits in a window sill. The other takes a seat in a chair. They get ready for work, pulling up stockings, checking make-up, etc. A loud bang and Jill enters. All three women speak and strike poses coincidentally with lights and sound. The girls are to improvise lines in rehearsal, then set them for performance. Should be things they would be saying in a go-go bar to customers, the manager, their driver, or each other. For each line, they strike a pose and freeze. There are four loud bangs before the music starts. House music starts. Dancer's stop speaking and dance sensuously as Jill breaks the tableau, dancing towards the audience. She is wearing a zebra g-string bikini covered by a red vinyl evening gown. She picks a white feather boa off the chair on stage, dances with it, and tosses it aside as she unzips the evening gown. She strips out of that and goes into the audience to take a tip from a man. After getting back to the stage, she stares at the audience. The music fades.

JILL: Do you have the urge to take out a dollar, fold it lengthwise, and tuck it in my g-string right along the sensuous curve of my ass? That's the sort of response this sort of dancing is supposed to evoke. And after two years, I've evoked that response several thousand times. Especially when I do this. *(Bends over with ass facing the audience.)*

This is the classic go-go signal for, "Your time is up, now give me the damn dollar." Sometimes I still don't get it, so I'll try being coy. *(Smiles and waves while bent over.)* As coy as I can be bent over half-naked with my ass in his face. If that doesn't work, I'll be aggressive. *(Smacks ass, turns around and growls.)* If that still doesn't work, I'll do this. *(Turns around seductively.)*

That never fails…to get old George Washington to give me a great big kiss, Abraham Lincoln, Alexander Hamilton, or if I was really getting lucky, my favorite pres, Mr. Andrew Jackson would nestle himself right between my breasts. I love those guys. I dance straight go-go in New Jersey. No topless, no flashing, no "sidework," straight go-go dancing. I dance in Hackensack, Passaic, Carlstadt, Newark, Elizabeth, Hasbrouck Heights, even Lake Hopatcong! You name the club, I'll name the exit. I take the bus from Port Authority to wherever I have to go and my driver takes me home for twenty dollars plus toll. He drives a bunch of the New York girls from Jersey to Manhattan. Most of us are actresses, singers, professional dancers or used to be. We all bond together, fill in shifts for each other and share the same driver, John.
(Slide.)

JILL: He's very dependable, probably because he still lives with his mother.
  (*Slide out.*)

JILL: A lot of us go by other names to fulfill that "other life" fantasy. My real
  name is Jill Morley. My go-go name is…Dylan—after Dylan Thomas,
  that famous alcoholic poet who died face down after twelve shots of
  whiskey. I didn't know the true power of being a woman until I started
  go-go dancing. I grew up in New Jersey in the seventies. It was the
  height of the sexual revolution and I was the most butch girl you'd ever
  want to meet. I had "boyface."
  (*Slide of Jill at age twelve and music—"If you think I'm sexy and you want
  my body," cut.*)

JILL: Come on sugar, let me know. No one thought I was sexy, no one wanted
  my body, no one sugar, no, no, no. But look who I was up against…
  (*Slide and music—Charlie's Angel's Theme.*)

JILL: …Farrah. She had it all. Feathered back blonde hair,
  (*Slide.*)

JILL: Lee Majors,
  (*Slide.*)

JILL: beautiful friends,
  (*Slide.*)

JILL: and a gun.
  (*Slide.*)

JILL: The comparison was not an easy one. Jill,
  (*Slide.*)

JILL: Farrah,
  (*Slide.*)

JILL: Jill,
  (*Slide.*)

JILL: Farrah,
  (*Slide.*)

JILL: Jill.
  (*Slide.*)

JILL: Confused? I was.
  (*Slide out.*)

JILL: Wendy, Virginia, Siobhan and I used to play Charlie's Angels. But since
  there were four of us and Virginia was the only blonde, they used to
  make me play Bosley. I wanted to play Farrah! Her name was Jill in the
  show! I wanted to say things like, "I would've had him Charlie, but my
  hair was in my eyes." But Wendy, Virginia, and Siobhan would go on

the exciting assignments and I was stuck in my bedroom in New Jersey scalding my scalp with a curling iron in the pursuit of wings. I knew I would one day have the poise, style and sensuality of Farrah Fawcett Majors.

(Music—Charlie's Angel's Theme comes up—girls enter as Angels. When Jason is in the show, he rolls in with a blonde wig. Jill sits in chair talking into "intercom" as Bosley. Girls and Jason strike Charlie's Angels Tableau.)

JILL: But I didn't even start getting in touch with my femininity until two years ago.

(Girls look at her and strike a pose upstage.)

JILL: This is the man who finally got me in touch with my feminine side,

(When Jason is in the show, the girls spin him around, Vanna White style and he plays himself, sans slides. Slide.)

JILL: my roommate, Jason.

(Slide.)

JILL: He's not an effeminate guy either.

(Slide.)

JILL: He likes to be known as a "Butch Queen." He's got a great sense of style, and an amazing eye for finding clothing on the street.

(Slide out.)

JILL: His best find was this huge bag of clothes from a woman who was exactly our size. We had a ball trying on these clothes. I mean Paris was burning in our apartment!

("To Be Real" comes up.)

JILL: And safely protected by our four walls, we were workin it! *(As Jason.)* "Work it Kitten! You go girl! Go Kitten! Go Kitten! Go—go—go Kitten! K to the I to the T to the T to the E to the N, Go Kitten!"

Unfortunately, since Jason knew how to accessorize, the dresses looked a lot better on him.

(Slide—Slide out or Jason exits.)

JILL: Through these findings, he got me in touch with my funky, feminine, Farrah, side just in time for go-go dancing. I was sick of catering and asked my friend, Tracy, what she did. She introduced me to the world of straight go-go dancing in New Jersey. The secret other life, conceived in Port Authority, birthed into Jersey, and returned to New York to be reincarnated for the next booking. We took the bus to Stats, The premiere sports go-go bar of Hackensack, where the guys would yell at the girls to get out of their way so they could see their games on TV. It was like this huge existential living room, an incredible metaphor for what you'd think we were trying to escape. I waited four hours in the dressing room with Tracy in between sets and watched these wild and sexy go-go girls put cover up on their zits, shave their butts, and glue their nipples into their costumes, when Nick approached me. "Aw Geez Dylan, what are you waiting for, the second coming of Christ? Where's your courage?" The time had come. A lifetime of Catholic school, four years of college, extensive off-off Broadway credits, and here I was, really off Broadway, New Jersey.

(Slide.)

JILL: I had to imagine Jason voguing in that wedding gown he liked to wear.

(Slide—get laugh, take it out.)

JILL: "Go Kitten! Work it!"

(Music—Barry White's Love Theme.)

JILL: I started dancing. Go-go dancing. I got the job. And so began my career. *(To customer.)* What? You want to see my what?

(Music "What?" Girls react and exit.)

JILL: Flashing. Flashing. Flashing! These girls were flashing their breasts for extra money! It was illegal, but they did it anyway. This one dancer, Edna, had me in tears my second night dancing. She was wild! How could I compete with all her flashing?

(Lights fade—costume change. Music—Eartha Kitt's Cu Cu Cu Tu— dancer's dance in a campy-fun style. They exit on Edna's entrance.)

EDNA

Loud Music—lights up. Edna is dancing wildly-uses her tongue…a lot. She flashes a customer, Bob, and responds to her manager.

EDNA: I'm not flashing. Dino, I'm not flashing!

(Fade music.)

EDNA: You can't fire me for flashing. He's the only customer here, he likes me, now why would I flash? *(To Bob.)* Did you see them? Did you see them? AAAAAAAy Poppy! *(Takes dollar.)* Now what the fuck is his problem? He thinks he can throw me out for flashing? What would this bar be without me and Dylan, eh? I'll tell you what it would be. It would be another stinking neighborhood bar with the same stinking neighborhood losers, but instead of looking at us, those losers would be beating the stinking shit out of each other! No Bob, I'm not calling you a loser. Your name is Bob? Oh, Bob, where is the justice in this world? And don't walk around the bush with me, Bob, I want to hear it. I know I don't have to do this job, but when the place is packed, I make good money. You know, I make more on a good night here than I did in a week in my old job? Mira, I used to be a cashier at Jorge's Liquors, minimum wage. He used to rub his crotch up against me every time he walked behind the counter, and he made me wear a T-shirt that said, "Jorge's Liquors, Liquor in the Front. Poker in the Back." Think about it. All the men in the neighborhood would leer at me. But now the ball is in my basket. Instead of them saying to me, "SSSSSSSST, Mamacita, I got your poker." I get to do it to them. And, I get paid for it. AY, customer. *(To customer.)* Ay, Poppy, I want to take you right now. I want you to give it to me, give it to me, give it to me, AY!! *(Poppy takes tip.)* Some men are so stupid. Oh no Bob, I'm not calling you stupid. Dino, I am leaving right now! If my girlfriend knew how Dino talked to me, she would… yes I have a girlfriend. Well don't look at me like I have three tetas. She is my lover. A blonde. Her name is Christine and she is beautiful. I met her at the lingerie shop where I bought this two years ago, and I knew she liked me. She gave me a discount. I asked her to watch me dance one night and we've been together ever since. She still comes to watch me dance sometimes. You've seen her? Isn't she beautiful?…Yes, we're both so beautiful. We could have any man we want. It's not like we're together by default, sweetheart. Like they say, get used to it. I love her. Dino! Bob, I must take my business elsewhere. But before I go, I just want to say, that you are the sexiest, most caliente, macho macho man here and…What do you mean you're not going to tip me? Because I'm a lesbian? Oh Bob, I might be a lesbian, but I could change for you! I want you to give it to me, give it to me, give it to me AAAAAAAY! *(Poppy takes tip.)* I love my job.

(Blackout—music up—dancers—costume change. Music—Beat fun—One dancer gives the other a table dance, until Jill enters and sees them. They exit.)

JILL: Seeing Edna flashing shook me up. She was shocking. So were her outfits. They were loud and tacky, things I'd never buy for myself. They looked like this. *(Take off robe revealing costume with tacky hearts sewed on.)* Actually, I love this outfit. Because whenever I wear it, there's always some joker in the crowd who'll say, "Hey Dylan, ya got a heart on?" And then I'll say, "No, I'm just happy to see you." Hey, it's good for a quick buck. And I was makin lots of them! In the beginning, I made $150 to $200 in a night. I wanted to work even more! I started going to dinner, movies, the theatre! I even went to the dentist. I started buying sexier costumes. I got more aggressive with the guys and most of them were nice and some of them were cute and this was kind of fun. I used all the moves. But it took me several months. In the beginning, all I could do was vogue! My second time dancing, I was so pathetic, the bouncer got on the stage and taught me how to hump the air. "Yo Dylan, you're not even gettin me horny! Watch the door. You gotta get down on your honches here and make like you're fuckin the air. Yeah, that'll get me horny." I was also getting private coaching from Jason. He would put together outfits for me and we would dance to Madonna in the apartment. Then he would come to the clubs and critique me.

(When Jason is in the show, he enters and Jill runs away, exits.)

JASON: "Kitten, that move is all wrong for that outfit. The fringes are for lateral shaking. 'Toot toot, hey, beep-beep!' Definitely a shimmy piece. But those platforms are hot!"

(One of the dancers comes in dressed like a bar patron, Jill plays Jason or another actor can play Jason.)

PATRON: Hey, what's your name?

JASON: Her name is Dylan.

PATRON: Like Dylan in 90210?

JASON: Like Dylan Thomas, You literary wizard.

PATRON: Hey Dylan, those shoes you're wearin. They're clunky.

JASON: Get over it, heathen! It's called fashion. Kitten's fierce!

PATRON: Okay man, Chill.

JASON: Well, who died and made you Betsy Johnson?

JILL: The first bars I worked at had jukeboxes. Waiting for one song to start after one ends is one of the longest moments in the history of go-go.

(Music— "Last ten seconds of song"—dancers and Jill play with the pause.)

JILL: The guys don't want to see us this way. They get all nervous and eat the bar fruit. Without the music, we're just regular women to them, clunking around the stage in our ragged high heels. But when that next song comes on, it's like the director yells "Action!"

(Music—Sexy Beat music.)

JILL: And we are sex goddesses and the guys love us, and tip us and it's a regular sex party.

(Music—music fades.)

JILL: I like DJ's better. One song flows into the next and we never stop moving, like sharks. The hardest thing to get used to was eye contact. Then, dancing for a guy after talking to him.

(Dance for guy, ask him how he's doing, get an answer.)

JILL: See how that just killed our erotic experience? Dancing for the guy next to him was really uncomfortable because now I feel like a slut! I mean I just danced sexually for him, but it was my job, I got used to it. The other girls were doing it. Ex-secretaries, mothers, students, and I finally realized, the sex industry is the only industry where women get paid more than men and I wanted a piece of it! We weren't even selling sex, we were selling the illusion. *(David Copperfield go-go move.)* I got myself a go-go agent, Dominick.

(Slide.)

JILL: He used to be the driver for the New York girls. He'd drive us around in a hearse.

(Slide.)

JILL: And advertise his agency on the back with a sign that said, "Bachelor parties, and then it's over." Dominick formed the agency with his wife, Natalie,

(Slide.)

JILL: an ex-dancer. Between you and me, his clubs are really sleazy,

(Slide out.)

JILL: but I was fascinated with sleaziness. I saw a whole new world!

(Music—"A Whole New World" comes up.)

JILL: I got to meet dancers like Kitty who has a tattoo of a cat...on her pussy. She shows it to everyone! She even takes tips with it. Definitely not something Farrah would do. A whole other realm of womanhood was opening up to me!

(Music out.)

JILL: My feminist friends hated this whole new world. Said I was propelling the idea of women as sex objects to men, giving men the wrong idea, that by seeing me do this, men won't realize that I am a human being with intelligence, sensitivity and strength...but I dance for women too. I dance at the Warehouse in North Bergen, a club for gay women, gay men, and anyone who wants to go there. One go-go boy, one go-go girl, men around the boy, women around me—Its' like an eighth grade dance but no one is trying to get to the other side. I trust women more when taking tips. I don't feel like they are going to sneak in a quick grab the way the guys do, not big tippers, but the thrill for me is dancing in a bikini and combat boots.

(Music—"I'm Every Woman"—up to everything you want now baby pause.)

JILL: I wouldn't work women for tips anyway! I'd feel like I was trying to trick them, my sisters. They would catch me in the lie, but men, I don't think they'll ever find me out.

(Music—"I'm Every Woman"—slide out.)

JILL: I start to feel like a criminal taking these guys money, these hard working guys money when they're giving me tens and twenties just for listening to their stories. One guy wrote me a check for $400 just because he thought I was nice. It cleared! I take their weekly paychecks, their unemployment, their social security, their last alcoholic dollars, and I could give a shit! I'd do it again like that! It's fun. I should be on Riker's with that kind of attitude. I call it "Go-Go Head," and I'm one of the lenient ones. You should see Hailey.

(Music—costume change. Dancer One pulls a bar stool upstage center and sits on it. She does a stylized repetitive movement that reflects the story she is telling.)

DANCER ONE: I saw a dancer in the dressing room.

DANCER TWO: Not tonight.

DANCER ONE: She was fixing her hair and her lipstick.

DANCER TWO: You're joking right?

DANCER ONE: And it was apparent to me from the way she looked at herself in the mirror.

DANCER TWO: Look, I really need this job.

DANCER ONE: That she was giving head to the owner just to keep her job.

DANCER TWO: All right, but don't tell anyone.

(Dancer One continues the movement.)

DANCER TWO: God, I'm going to hate myself for this.

HAILEY

Hailey enters. She is visibly drunk and drugged out on smack. She slowly makes her way to a pole, smoking a cigarette. When she gets to the pole, Dancer One pushes the stool aside and exits. Speed Metal is blaring. Hailey

sees a customer and smacks her ass. He doesn't respond. She smacks it again.
Still no response. She approaches him. Music comes down a little.

HAILEY: Come on, Buddy, give up the fuckin dollar already. Come on, no cash, no flash. You would prefer to drink your orange juice? "I would prefer to drink my orange juice." You cheap fuck!
(Music all the way out.)

HAILEY: Then what are you doing in a go-go bar, eh? Oh, it isn't just for breakfast anymore? Hey, Dylan, Mr. Wall St. here would prefer to drink his orange juice, did you know that? He's not tippin you neither? What's your deal, Mr. White Collar Prick? You come into a bar where there's talented dancers…you sit there in your white collar shirt with a big pile of cash sittin in front of you, drinkin a non-alcoholic drink, makin like we're not even here, I mean you could be at fuckin Denny's across the street! Don't try to throw me! Cause I know what you're about. I got your number, pal. You're gettin off on not gettin off! Your biggest thrill is actin like your not payin attention to a bunch of girls who would never even look at your slimy ass ugly, face if it didn't have a big pile of cash in front of it, Hah! Nailed him on that one, didn't I, Dylan. Hey Dylan, what's your deal? We gotta stick together here…Hey Mr. Wall St, where you goin all of a sudden, huh? Did you finish your O.J. already, huh? You goin to Denny's now to ignore your waitress, huh? *(Picks up drink and sips.)* Nothin Dino, nothin! Just tryin to make a buck, very professional. Dylan and I are off now. You like my perfume? It's called Reality. *(Sniffs.)* —No, it's Escape. *(Sniffs.)* Hallucination. I don't know. Same company makes em. *(To Dylan.)* You gotta kiss Dino's ass, he likes it. So, Dylan, you workin through Dominick? Yeah, he's my agent too. He's got some good clubs, you just gotta stay on his ass. Cause, you do. I use him for bachelor parties and pudding wrestling. You should try it. It's $30 a match, ya roll around for a little while, split the tips, easy. Jello wrestling is worse cause the red jello stains the skin. And hot oil wrestling sucks, cause you gotta win to keep the tips and last time I was paired with a fuckin American Gladiator. Even that is better than foxy boxing. I find that demeaning. Wrestling is wrestling. I do very well at contact sports. I used to be a tomboy. You too? *(Picks up drink and toasts Dylan.)* Lotta tomboys in this business, Dylan. Probably cause we relate to men so well. *(Drink.)* Ya know, I do better than some of those calendar girls? A calendar girl is like a Playboy bunny the club hires to dance to boost business. They don't do it as much now. It used to be a big deal.

They had their own special light on stage and everything. One time this calendar girl was jealous cause the guys were tippin me more. She was a bitch. So she starts complainin that I'm dancin in her light. Miss Prima Fuckin Donna, dancin in her light! I ignore her, keep gettin more tips, I mean, I'm gettin paper cuts, and she goes and tells the manager, who I know, and he tells me to stop dancin in her light. I got off the stage and quit, cause I knew I'd be fired for what I was about to do. I got changed, got back on the stage, and beat the livin shit out of her…in her light! I grabbed her by her calendar hair and threw her to the ground. The bitch's skin was under my nails. And she, she starts kickin her calendar feet like a real "girl" and we start rollin around the ground goin' at it big time, yeah! Meanwhile, the guys are cheerin me on and the dollars are flyin! Not just ones! Fives! Tens! Twenties. When I was done with her, I collected my money and left. No, I can never go back there again, but isn't that a good story? *(Drinks.)* Man, I'm shit-faced. You gotta drink to do this job. It's easier to let loose. Flash. I flash everything. You don't? You'd be surprised at what you'd do when you have two kids to support. You'd be surprised at what you'd do. Just don't get caught, like Edna. Dino don't care if he don't see it. But they could close his club down. Jersey enforcement's weird that way. The time they spend worryin about us flashin' a nipple, could be spent on how to get rid of that smell on the parkway. Like exposing a nipple is gonna drive these guys into a life of crime. Corrupt their morals. I can't afford to lose another club. Dominick would be pissed if I got caught. Better go check on my Harley. I'm bringin my daughter to my mother's house tonight. It's her birthday tomorrow. She's two. Hey Dylan, don't get in my light.

(Fade—music—"Calendar girl" girls dance—costume change. Jill enters.)

JILL: I have never been sexually harassed in my life. Or I've been sexually harassed so much, I didn't know when it was happening. I didn't know what my boundaries were, until recently. Now, if outside a club, a man tries to grab me, crudely propositions me, or even looks at me the wrong way…I won't stand for that. Because now, I get paid good money for that. When it was slow, and no one was around to sexually harass me, my friend, Tracy, would teach me pencil turns to kill time. When Tracy left dancing to go to school, that's when I started to drink. Usually scotch, usually two. My body would become fluid like the scotch and I'd burn deeper into their ice cube eyes melting them into a dollar. Yeah, I worry about this, but there is something about being in an altered state in New Jersey that makes complete sense. At least I work in a place where I can drink. It's not like I work in an office or a schoolroom or something. "Dewars, rocks, thanks." My civilian drink is wine. Red in the winter, white in the summer. My go-go drink is scotch, but it's been leaking into my civilian world, along with the rest of my go-go world. *(Music—Jill, Dylan, Jill.)*

JILL: The sleazy clubs got to me. I missed the straighter clubs where the older dancers taught me how to bump and grind. Watching Kitty take tips with her pussy and Edna deep throating Bud bottles sort of lost its charm. But, I like to explore the unfamiliar, the dark side. My high school was a melting pot, Red Bank Catholic. It was a Catholic melting pot. I'd hang with my "nice girl" girls from "nice girl" neighborhoods, but I also hung with the Jennette sisters.

(Girls enter in motorcycle jackets, a forty ouncer, and cigarettes. Music— "Runnin Free" by Iron Maiden. One verse and stop.)

JILL: The Jennette's were stocky Italian girls from Freehold. I liked them because they chewed tobacco.

(Music—repeat.)

JILL: We used to drive around in their truck and listen to Iron Maiden. All three of us on air drum.

(Music—repeat.)

JILL: One day they took me to their house and we watched their parent's porno videos with their five-year-old brother. I had never seen a porno before and the Jennettes had it memorized! Every nuance of every sound. These girls had bad reputations and no one understood why I hung out with them.

(Fade out.)

JILL: I didn't understand why they hung out with me! I thought they were cool. I'd act a little tougher just to earn their company. Just to go a little further in that direction, a little further down that road. What's missing that makes me want to go down that road? The further I go, the more I grow apart from regular women, the civilians who go to bridal showers and talk about curtains. The women in the grocery store who pay with food stamps or big bills while I pay with many wrinkled ones. *(Jill looks up as if she is looking at checkout clerk.)* I'm a waitress. I like watching the family across the street through my window when I get home from work. They're just getting up for breakfast. I like watching the mother comb the daughter's hair at the table. I wonder if they can see me counting my money! I make sure to keep it dark so no one can see me straightening out dollars in a sweaty mask of make-up, erasing the creases the guys made to slip them between my breasts. Unfolding dollars that were folded up like footballs or bowties by guys who thought that if they folded a dollar like an engagement ring that I was obligated to sit with them for the rest of the night. The guys who wanted me to sit with them between sets. Tell me things. Like don't think I don't know about every zit on my ass. Heard all about them. "Hey, Dylan, why don't you cover up those zits?" Well, I'll tell you, I won't do it. Because there is some part of me that thinks I am getting back at them by making them look at the zits on my ass. They wanted to know if my breasts were real, what's my nationality? Would I go to dinner with them? Would I go to their car with them? Did I shave my pussy? Would I sit with them, sit with them, sit with them, sit with them! Jesus Christ, don't these guys know I do this for a living and not to meet every single guy at the bar? That every night I dance, five or more guys ask for my number? That I don't give it to any of them? That I don't consider them dating material any more than they consider me more than a good lay? That I know they think I'm a whore and I think they are fucking idiots for giving me their money! I don't think that. I am thankful for the money I make. It's my policy to say thank you for each dollar and mean it. I'm lucky to do this job. Not because of the way I look. Most women could get bookings somewhere if they had the guts. I am lucky to have the guts. I am. The money, the attention, makes me feel attractive, wanted, loved. That can fuck up a relationship. When John drives me home at night, I'm wired. I count all my singles and go to bed expecting my boyfriend to be there for me so I can tell him about the jerk that wouldn't tip me or how sick I am of these guys pawing at me, or if one more guy asks me to go to his car with him like I'm a prostitute…how can they think that I'm a prostitute? Honey? But my boyfriend is always asleep. He has to work in the morning. I did try to spice up our sex life one night. Now that I was finally comfortable in these sexy little outfits, I was going to seduce my boyfriend in one. I put on my black leather bustier, thigh highs and heels, and launched a surprise attack on him in the living room where he was watching television.

(Music—Goldfinger—dance for him, don't get a reaction and see the TV.)

JILL: Honey? *(Strike a pose and react to him.)* He wanted to know if this is what I wore to work. Yeah. This James Bond flick was on the television and several bikini clad women were bathing Bond in some bathhouse. "Do we really have to watch this?" He changed it to the Nature Channel where two grizzly bears were mating furiously. "Honey, are you attracted to me? Oh, nothing, never mind." How can I tell him that whenever I wear this particular, black leather bustier, thigh high heel combination, I have the capacity to turn every man in the place on! I just did it the night before, three different places I auditioned. Each of which booked me and each of which, every man there handed me a dollar with zest! But right there in my living room, I couldn't get the man that I loved, my man, to turn his head. I never told him that. And he never told me how he really felt about my dancing. Always said it was "fine." When I first started, he even wanted to come to the clubs and watch. Once he fell in love with me, he didn't want to anymore. I still don't think it was the dancing that broke us up. When he did want to make love to me, I would sometimes…I couldn't make the distinction of the hands, the touch. What made me different from a prostitute was no longer clear. It didn't matter. I'd even nod to them as I walked up 42nd St. on my way to Port Authority. Sharing their tough knowing looks, their working girl eyes. I loved some of my regulars, like Tex. Tex was a millionaire from Texas, but he got his millions by winning the New Jersey lottery. One day, Tex came in looking really sad. So I danced for him, but when I went to get the dollar, I did a very rare thing. I asked him what was wrong. He said he had just come from a funeral, his father's. I wanted to take his head, put it on my shoulder and let him cry. Instead, I gave him a free dance. He tipped me anyway, but when I went to get the dollar, I grabbed his hand really hard, looked him right into the eyes until he was about to cry and left. I can't to this job a lot, because I see people in the men that I dance for. My therapist doesn't think that's very healthy. He says I should see them as tricks or johns, or get out. I guess I should work on that. I only do it once or twice a week now and each time, I pretend I'm going to the land of make-believe, where there's make believe men, and I put on an attitude.

(Dancer comes out to play toad man. Music—Trance music—fades.)

TOAD MAN: Hey, what's your name?

JILL: Dylan.

TOAD MAN: Like Dylan Thomas? You my friend there with a winning air who smiled brassily at my shyest secret. Enticed with twinkling bits of the eye till the sweet tooth of my love bit dry.

JILL: Like Dylan in 90210.

TOAD MAN: Dylan, ya know ya really shouldn't be doing this. You should be somebody's wife or something.

JILL: I would get that a lot. That I shouldn't be dancing. And that would piss me off more than anything. Now when they say, "You really shouldn't be doing this. What are you doing in a place like this?" I say, "Who are you to judge me? I work here. You...hang out here." I can't imagine doing this job long term, but there are some women who have been doing it for twenty to thirty years. After meeting Donna at the palace, I knew I had to take a break.

(Music— "In the Mood" hip-hop.)

DONNA

DONNA: Hi Ike! Did Brad call? Carl is fine, thanks. Everything's fine yeah. Who's working tonight? Dylan? I don't know her. *(Puts on make-up, pays close attention to under eyes. Puts on powder, sees Dylan.)* You must be Dylan, I'm Donna, nice to meet you. *(Checks out Dylan.)* Dylan, guess how old I am. Guess, go ahead, guess! I am forty-five, really forty-five, I know it's a mindfuck! Forty-five. Twenty-two years of this has kept me young. I used to have to dance. I was putting my husband Carl through podiatry school. When our first, Brad, was born, Carl would drive me to work with Brad on his lap, and I would rush out and breast-feed in between sets! The guys would notice my breasts getting bigger and thought it was some go-go trick! Like I had a saline pump in the parking lot. I made some great tips thanks to Brad. Back then, I had to dance to make ends meet. Now I just do it to get out of the house. Between go-go dancing, the women's league and community theatre, I am very active. I recently played Maria in the Sound of Music. "Captain, whistles are for dogs and cats and other animals, but not for children and definitely not for me." Oh yeah. I rocked 'em. The boys? They were away at school. We had a little incident here about two weeks ago. I had just finished getting ready, got on the stage and saw all these young familiar faces staring at me...boys I babysat, boys I chaperoned on trips, even boys who...Dylan, I was their den mother. Then I see Brad. I turned around, told Ike there were some minors at the bar and one of them was my son and if he could just have them leave quietly and without a fuss, I would greatly appreciate it. And he did just that. I tried to stop dancing once...You know how it made me feel, Dylan? Old. I missed it. I missed the costumes, I missed the exercise, I missed the power. It's not about the money for me, I don't make what these younger gals make, I don't need to. And I know I'm not the picture of beauty to some of these younger guys, the ones who think beauty is a Barbie doll puffed up with silicone, saline, or some other toxic waste. But the older men, they know what it's about—pure sensuality. Something these younger gals don't know anything about. Their tools are their bodies and their flexibility. Mine are my eyes and my soul, and I'll tell you, Dylan, to engage a man, stretch marks wrinkles and all, that is true power. And that kind of power is not easy to give up.

(Dance to Peggy Lee's "Fever" with white boa—look back to audience. Fade both music and lights.)

JILL: I missed dancing on my break. I wanted to be one of the girls again! I kicked off my catering shoes, slipped on my pumps, but this time I hit the bigger clubs. John brought me to Shakers. "We like blondes here and your tits, they're...real." Then he brought me to Satin Dolls where I was able to get some bookings. I've been working there for six months now and I like it. I make a lot more money and it's not sleazy. I am glad to be rid of those sleazy dive bars and to work on being a sophisticated go-go girl, like Nina.

(Music—Nina—Costume change. Dancers come out, dancing almost violently. They attack the audience with the rules of go-go.)

DANCER ONE: No Flashing!

DANCER TWO: No Floorwork!

DANCER ONE: No Boyfriends!

DANCER TWO: No Girlfriends!

DANCER ONE: Don't forget to tip the house!

DANCER TWO: The DJ!

DANCER ONE: Oh, yeah, and lose some weight!

(Dancer Two reacts, they both go offstage and react to Nina. They don't like her.)

NINA

Nina dials her cell phone.

NINA: Billy? Nina. Billy, I want the color to be gold. Like real gold. *(Puts phone down and lisps.)* He is such a sweetheart. He is! He's buying me a car. Well he should, I've been with him for six months, it's the least he can do. Mercedes Benz. So, new girl, do you like my tits? I love them, and you can barely see the scars. Did you see Maria's? Her nipples turned blue. She got in a bad car accident and now her left one is permanently dented. Too bad. I have been making so much money with these and Billy loves them. He's the manager over at Gold Diggers. Gave me his card my first day there, told me how much more money the girls with big boobs make and offered to pay for a boob job. He's so romantic. Last month I took him up on it and here they are, bigger and better than ever! No, I'm not worried about them. I know they're supposed to get hard after a while, they could change shape, discolor, the nipples could turn blue, one could sag more than the other, the saline could leak into my muscle tissue and I might eventually have to get them cut off, but I just know, deep in my heart, I was meant to have big tits.
(Phone rings.)

NINA: It's Billy. Hi Sweetie, No, you're joking…but I don't want silver, I want gold.

JILL: I graduated to the high class babe circuit. I learned how to move, act and look like a beautiful woman and sometimes, just sometimes, I even feel like one. I learned how to look deeper into a man's eyes without looking away. *(Take off high heels and place them on stool.)* I still might have a bad night when I come home crying, unresolved about how right this whole thing is. I'm afraid of getting trapped into this easy money lifestyle and losing my own sense of purpose, but in the same way, I'm afraid of marriage.
(Music—Power Switch.)

JILL: A dancer starts dancing never dreams of flashing, sees the cash the other girls make, has a cocktail, accidentally flashes a nipple, sees some more bills, wants to go for it, really drinks to make that real money. Lets that g-string slide, pulls in the big bucks, drinks every time she dances. She's bored, wants to have fun, raises her expenses, buys a car, buys a condo, gets a tit job. She has to dance five times a week, the only escape, marriage.

Where can she meet the guy? Sweet Cheeks. Marries guy, leaves dancing, has a few kids, bakes some cookies, the marriage skids into the rocks. *(Music—Sound of a car crash.)*

JILL: Gets a divorce, she has to dance, with a vengeance, has kids to support. She is older, she has stretch marks, can't work the good clubs. Goes sleazy, goes further, has kids to support, looks harder for a husband, where can she meet him? The Beaver Bar. Marries guy, still has to dance, supports them all, he doesn't like her dancing, leaves her! She goes deeper into the circuit, topless, nude, a pathetic alcoholic turning tricks…She has come to value her self worth by the men who want to fuck her.

Sometimes, I like to think I am an actress and a writer, dancing for the nobler experience, a sacrifice for my art and to pay some bills. But deep down, I know I am a dancer. And whenever any of us tries to fool ourselves about who we are or why we do this, I think we recognize this common bond we share. The money, the attention, the freedom of sexual expression, and the confidence to know that we can support ourselves by exposing our most vulnerable parts, totally open to the judgment of all and make a living from it. I didn't know the true power of being a woman until I started go-go dancing.

My name is Jill Morley, but sometimes…I'm Dylan.

(Music— "Big Spender" plays. Jill slowly makes her way to under a spotlight, strikes a poster girl pose. Lights fade.)

END OF PLAY

MARGUERITE BONET
by Val Smith

To Michael

It is one thing for the human mind to extract from the phenomena of nature the laws which it has itself put into them; it may be a far harder thing to extract laws over which it has no control. It is even possible that laws which have not their origin in the mind may be irrational, and we can never succeed in formulating them.

Sir Arthur Stanley Eddington,
Space, Time and Gravitation

On behalf of those who are suffering now I make this protest against the deception which is being practised on them; also I believe I may help to destroy the callous complacence with which the majority of those at home regard the continuance of agonies which they do not share, and which they have not sufficient imagination to realize.

S. Sassoon,
Finished With The War: A Soldier's Declaration, 1917

The most beautiful experience we can have is the mysterious. It is the fundamental emotion which stands at the cradle of true art and true science.

A. Einstein

THE AUTHOR

Val Smith is the author of numerous plays which have been published and produced nationally. Her first full-length drama, *The Gamblers,* was a finalist at the Eugene O'Neill National Playwright's Conference, won the Playhouse on the Square's Mid-South Playwright's Competition, and was produced at American Stage Theatre in New Jersey in 1992. Her second full-length, *Ain't We Got Fun,* was commissioned and produced by Actors Theatre of Louisville in the 1993 Classics in Context Festival—The Roaring Twenties. She is the recipient of a Kentucky Women's Foundation grant and the Kentucky Arts Council Al Smith Fellowship. Her most recent full-length, *Marguerite Bonet,* was a finalist for the 1997 Francesca Primus Prize. Her ten-minute play, *Meow,* debuted at ATL's 1997–98 Humana Festival.

AUTHOR'S NOTE

This is a play about how people deal with death. It is also a play about survival—spiritual survival in the face of personal holocaust and group guilt on a national scale. I grew interested in these ideas while researching another project on the First World War. Wandering the aisles of the library, I ran across a book called *Raymond* written by a well-respected physicist of his day, Sir Oliver Lodge. His book is divided into three sections; the first is all of the correspondence Lodge received from his son, Raymond, while an officer in the trenches. Banal stuff as epistological material goes; it was easy to be lulled by Raymond's forced cheerfulness and his descriptions of the day-to-day business of building trenches only to have them blown up. I turned yet another page and there was the shock; the telegram sent to Lodge informing him of his son's death. In the second section of the book, Lodge attempts to prove via anecdote and detailed "scientific" observations of seances, Raymond's survival in the spiritual realm. The final section contains Lodge's argument in which he tries to prove, through theoretical fact and imaginative analogy, how psychic survival might simply be viewed as an alternate sphere of his beloved physics—the unphysical world.

I based Crawford on Lodge. Like Lodge, Crawford did not have a close relationship with his son. And like Lodge, Crawford is confronting momentous changes, private and public. Physics is no longer something he understands and as he faces the new century a whole way of life as well as an entire generation has been wiped out. So, like Lodge, Crawford attempts to build structures of thought and belief which are healing but which also deny any personal culpability. The hard truths embodied in *Marguerite Bonet* allow

Crawford some honest redemption at the end of the play. Lodge, on the other hand, would continue the struggle to make the spirit world "real" for the rest of his life.

ORIGINAL PRODUCTION

Marguerite Bonet received an Equity concert reading at the Florida Stage Company in West Palm Beach, Florida on April 28, 1997 for its New Voices series. It was directed by J. Barry Lewis with the following cast:

Dr. George Crawford . . . . Miller Lide
Marguerite Bonet . . . . Susan Gay
Dr. Franklin Peale . . . . Adam Cohen
Paul . . . . Terrell Hardcastle

The playwright wishes to thank the Kentucky Arts Council and the Kentucky Women's Foundation for their generous support.

CHARACTERS

DR. GEORGE CRAWFORD: Respected physicist. Early fifties.
MARGUERITE BONET: Daughter of a medium. A rebel. Twenties.
DR. FRANKLIN PEALE: Physicist and colleague of Dr. Crawford. Late thirties.
PAUL: Eternally twenty-one. Paul is a creation of Dr. Crawford's memory. He also, on occasion, is a creation of Marguerite Bonet's imagination.

SETTING

The play takes place in England

TIME

Circa 1920

ACT I
SCENE I

Shadows. Music. Outline of Paul, faint through a massive window, and Marguerite, in shadow, turns to face the audience. She speaks to the audience.

MARGUERITE: They scream. Shriek. Hell to pay with the neighbors. Yeh, and it's not just women. We've got *old geezers* flingin' 'emselves about. These are not ignorant people. Knobs, real sniff ya know? Cheek really. Come in our rooms, of a sudden they've got license to carry on. I asked Mum once, I said what is this in aid of? And she says to me, the dark frees 'em up to express themselves, Marguerite. I said, Fine. Why don't they go home, close the drapes, and bloody well express 'emselves there? She said he-ah, Marguerite, he-ah they are free to feel the presence of their loved ones. Among strangers, they may speak to their dead in the safety of the dark. He-ah they may grieve propahly, she says.

So shut it ya little sod. *(Pause.)* Used to sit in the corner with me dolls, have me own seance. Silently or christ help you ya know. Got older I sat table. Feels like I've spent my life in the dark.

But as long as I've been a witness, I've never understood the questions people get up. Always the same. "What is it like there?" "Does my dearest miss me?" "Is my beloved happy?"

Well, there's a real roll off a log. *(Puts on her "seance voice.")* "The place is beautiful beyond words." "She misses you terribly, but she would not have you worry. For there, all is peace, beauty, contentment, tranquility in the bosom of God's love—"

Feck. I mean, if it was me, I'd ask some proper questions. Like "Why the bloody hell didn't you leave a will, you stupid old git?" Or—"Where the bugger did you get to, and did ya ever think about us scraping by in your absence, ya selfish bugger?"

Now those are questions I can respect.

(Lights down on Marguerite and Paul.)

SCENE II

Lights change indicating transition to the parlour of the Bonet home. There is the massive window, hung upstage and a tatty over-sized wingchair, center, with its back toward us. Next to the wing chair, spotlighted, is a bottle of sherry and an empty glass. After a moment, the hand of a woman reaches down and pours wine from the bottle into the glass. The hand disappears with the wine glass into the vastness of the chair. Peale and Crawford enter. Both men have had more than a few drinks.

CRAWFORD: At the risk of being redundant—what am I doing here?

PEALE: Have you heard anything I've been saying?

CRAWFORD: Yes.

PEALE: No you haven't.

CRAWFORD: I have.

PEALE: What was I saying?

CRAWFORD: *(Pause.)* Well. It was so incredible, I quit listening. Alright. It was about the war. I don't want to talk about the war. Nobody wants to talk about it. Let it lie.

PEALE: I was talking about poetic justice.

CRAWFORD: Oh. Really?

PEALE: Because this war, of all wars, epitomized our failure. Oh, I don't mean "us" particularly, but us generally. Diplomatic failure. Failure of imagination. Failure of the old minds who fought it, failure of the social order. The *old* order, the *old* visions of science, of politics and rank. I tell you, I've taken a perverse delight in seeing it all swept away. Annihilated.

CRAWFORD: I wish I had a drink.

PEALE: How many did we lose in the war? Eight to nine million? Add on to that another twenty-odd *million* for the disease and famine that followed and then talk to me about irresponsibility.

CRAWFORD: I don't want to talk about it. I want a drink.

PEALE: These asses running about saying the war broke us; the new science will finish the job. "We will never be the same great people." Do you know what I say to them?

CRAWFORD: No.

PEALE: I say hurrah! If this was the end result how were we ever great? George, listen to me. George, focus. You see, we put our faith in materialism, in the material world. That is what I—all of us—speculated about, measured, what we explored, what we pursued daily. In all ways. That was our life. And that was where we went wrong.

CRAWFORD: This place has a peculiar odour.

PEALE: You're not listening.

CRAWFORD: No. That was very good port.

PEALE: George, the material world, that which we study, that from which we derive our methods, our philosophical approach to science, to life even—George, that's the view that led us down the primrose path. That's the world we ended up killing for.

CRAWFORD: Is it?

PEALE: You know it is. So what does that tell you?

CRAWFORD: That I'm not going to get another drink am I?

PEALE: *(Pause.)* I know you're listening. This is your way of ignoring what you don't want to hear. So what I'm saying, I'm saying that, as scientists, as physicists, we have to be responsible.

(Crawford nods.)

CRAWFORD: Heah, heah.

PEALE: But what does that mean? We tried, and look what happened. No, we have to be more ambitious if we are to lead ourselves away from our current patterns of destruction and death. Even if it looks like what we're pursuing seems—well—a bit preposterous. You see, George, the answer is to go beyond death.

(Long pause.)

CRAWFORD: I like you very much Frank. But sometimes I think you need treatment.

PEALE: Oh forget it!

CRAWFORD: I'm sorry you didn't get the funds. I don't see, though, how you could have expected to get them.

PEALE: It isn't the funds. You haven't heard a word.

CRAWFORD: I was out-voted.

PEALE: *(Pause.)* Wait a minute. You argued on my behalf?

CRAWFORD: I'm not allowed to discuss proceedings.

PEALE: Why George, that's unbelievably wonderful!

CRAWFORD: No, it isn't. I didn't argue on your behalf.

(A pause.)

PEALE: *(Explosive.)* *How* can you not see this research has value?!

CRAWFORD: Frank—

PEALE: —hundreds of reports—you've seen them!

CRAWFORD: Yes. You wouldn't let me avoid them. I tried too.

PEALE: George! You're as bad as the rest of those dinosaurs. Waste of time talking to you.

CRAWFORD: Oh now. Frank. We're friends. We have a philosophical disagreement. That's all.

PEALE: Where does the energy go? Ever asked yourself, ever wondered? Here we are, you and I, each in his separate integrity, and we feel ourselves *within this body.*

CRAWFORD: I feel pretty numb at the moment.

PEALE: So this essence of ourselves that we feel, this life, this *energy* that moves us through space and time, what is it. And more, what is it *for?* How does it work? Does it just dissolve with the death of the body? Suppose it doesn't. Suppose you—found this energy persists after death, that personality in some way survives, even for a little while, in the same way that, that the metamorphosed caterpillar retains the shape of its cocoon when it first emerges. The soul in transition still knows what it was, who it was. Suppose you could communicate with it—

CRAWFORD: Oh, I really need a drink.

PEALE: You could speak to someone you thought you'd never see or hear again. Paul—

CRAWFORD: *(Explosive.)* That's it! Not another word!

PEALE: Alright. Alright.

CRAWFORD: I'm not that bloody drunk. *(Pause.)* Where are we, Frank? Those people out there, who the hell who are they?

PEALE: I thought you'd be interested.

CRAWFORD: This was a bloody stupid thing to do.

PEALE: It was sincere. It was clumsy maybe. But sincere.

CRAWFORD: Right, I'm leaving.

PEALE: Hold on, George. Just a minute. Umm. I know you're upset. But you going off in a fluff—well, it's a bit—

CRAWFORD: Yes?

PEALE: Well, it's a bit awkward.

CRAWFORD: Well, I don't care.

PEALE: You can sit it out in here. No one will bother you. It won't take long, I promise. I know I have no right to ask and I admit I've handled this very badly—

CRAWFORD: You most certainly have.

PEALE: And you have every right to be angry.

CRAWFORD: And I am. Drunk and angry.

PEALE: It's—well—I know a lot of those people.

CRAWFORD: So I gathered.

PEALE: And I sort of gave the impression to Mrs. Bonet that you would be willing to participate.

CRAWFORD: Why the hell should I care whether some bug-eyed spiritualist gets her feelings hurt!

PEALE: You're drunk. And you're angry. But you're still a gentleman. So for me. Please? Settle down. Smoke your cigar. And I'll be back in a jiff. And don't kick a shindy.

CRAWFORD: I don't kick shindys! What the hell is a shindy?

(But Peale is gone.)

CRAWFORD: My regards to the Eternal Stare.

(Crawford does a brief impression of the medium's staring gaze. Before this, a thin trail of smoke has become visible wafting up over the back of the wingchair. Crawford pats his pockets for a light for his cigar. He sees the smoke and pauses.)

CRAWFORD: Hallo?

(No answer.)

CRAWFORD: Hallo?

(The hand reappears, dangling an empty glass.)

MARGUERITE: Hallo. *(Standing.)* I'm Marguerite Bonet.

CRAWFORD: Oh. Ah. George Crawford.

(They shake hands. A beat of silence.)

MARGUERITE: Ada is my mother.

CRAWFORD: Ah.

MARGUERITE: She has a thyroid condition.

CRAWFORD: Oh?

MARGUERITE: *(Pause.)* Makes her eyes buggy—

CRAWFORD: *(Pause.)* Ohhhhh. Oh, I'm dreadfully sorry—

MARGUERITE: Why are you sorry? She's the one with the thyroid condition—

CRAWFORD: No, no, I meant—

MARGUERITE: *(Overlapping.)* I know what you meant.

CRAWFORD: *(Pause.)* I thought I was alone.

MARGUERITE: You weren't. The walls have ears. Ha ha. *(Pause.)* I'd offer you a glass of sherry but— *(She turns the bottle upside down. Empty. She puts her cigarette out in the bottle.)* It was cheap anyway. It's hard to get a proper drink around here. You're right.

CRAWFORD: It was not my intention—

MARGUERITE: Na, na, na. I understand. If it helps any, I'm in complete agreement.

CRAWFORD: Sorry?

MARGUERITE: Nobody should be forced into doing something they don't want to do. The Eternal Stare and I had a hell of a row on that topic just this evening.

CRAWFORD: Oh.

MARGUERITE: She wanted me to sit in. I told her to stuff it. Had enough, playing kneesies with a bunch of old duffs. Gets ya down. *(Pause.)* On the other hand, might have been a giggle for you.

CRAWFORD: *(Looking at his watch.)* How long does one of these sessions last?

MARGUERITE: Oh, they'll be in there for a while. Don't worry about it. Finish your smoke.

(Pause. A reluctant Crawford does.)

CRAWFORD: Mr. Peale has great faith in your mother.

MARGUERITE: Mum's good at what she does. Won't find me saying otherwise. *(Looking out the window.)* Raining again. Someday I'll be off out of here to Italy. They say the sun shines everyday there.

CRAWFORD: You have family in Italy?

MARGUERITE: Not likely!

CRAWFORD: It's a complicated country. One can have serious misunderstandings without a proper command of the language.

MARGUERITE: Oh, Experience speaking?

CRAWFORD: I was there once, yes, many years ago.

MARGUERITE: Holiday?

CRAWFORD: Honeymoon. Years ago as I say.

MARGUERITE: Mrs. didn't care for it?

CRAWFORD: Oh no, she liked it a great deal.

MARGUERITE: Should have another go at it then. Maybe you'd like it better.

CRAWFORD: I think not. *(Pause.)* Mrs. Crawford passed on a few years after our marriage.

MARGUERITE: Oh. I'm sorry. Well, finances is my problem. Have to have money to travel. Have to have money to live period.

CRAWFORD: *(Pause.)* I suppose your mother does well enough. I mean she must—

MARGUERITE: Get paid? No, not officially.

CRAWFORD: Not officially.

MARGUERITE: Ya know. Donations from grateful patrons. That's about it. *(Pause.)* Nosy.

CRAWFORD: Forgive me, I didn't mean—

MARGUERITE: Oh, don't fret. I'm nosy. Everybody is. Go on. Ask me anything. We've withstood rigorous scientific scrutiny. Well, save one item. Dad's not dead like Mum tells everyone. Ran off with a neighbor when I was a tot. She'd like to believe he's dead. Might as well be. Who knows, eh? Bastard.

(Crawford, uncomfortable, checks his pocket watch.)

MARGUERITE: No questions? Most people are fascinated with our "bohemian" way of life. Peale's got somebody new in there tonight again, puttin' Mum through the hoops. French woman. You met her?

CRAWFORD: I think I did.

MARGUERITE: It's his little test, ya see. Somebody Mum couldn't know. Then he writes it all down. What she says. Checks it out with his 'subject' after. Years of it, we've been through. Feckin' awful. Gets so you can't fart twice around here without somebody pointing out you've contradicted yourself.

CRAWFORD: These sessions last a long time, do they?

MARGUERITE: So you're a colleague of his? A scientist?

CRAWFORD: A physicist.

MARGUERITE: What do you get up to then?

CRAWFORD: Oh, that would be a rather complicated subject.

MARGUERITE: Give it a go.

CRAWFORD: Oh. Umm. Well. Ah. For the last several years, my chief area of research has been concentrated in—well— *(Pause.)* —you see, for centuries, physics has been predicated—built—built on the existence of a particular substance. A substance called ether.

MARGUERITE: Ether. Got it.

CRAWFORD: Now, ether is invisible but pervasive—that is, it's everywhere. Luminiferous ether—

MARGUERITE: Luminiferous ether. Got it.

CRAWFORD: Luminiferous ether fills all space. Like water fills the oceans. Only it's not water. The etheric stream moves through everything, through and around all matter, connecting everything by its presence. This explains how objects—matter—can act at a distance on other matter. It explains how magnets attract and repel. How light and electricity travel. It's all connected, you see through the medium of ether. The problem has come in proving ether's existence. It's a most subtle substance. That is what I've been trying to do, find definitive proof. Bit of controversy—argument—on the subject because some people have given up on the concept of ether. That it even exists. But I still believe in it. *(A significant pause.)* That's it.

MARGUERITE: How long you been at this then?

CRAWFORD: Oh, nigh onto—what is it now?—nineteen, almost twenty years.

MARGUERITE: Jayz, that's a long time.

CRAWFORD: It is.

MARGUERITE: So you don't invent things then?

CRAWFORD: You mean—lightbulbs, things of that nature?

MARGUERITE: Yeah, lightbulbs!

CRAWFORD: No.

MARGUERITE: Oh. Twenty years. Long time. Jayz.

CRAWFORD: Yes. *(Crawford checks his watch.)*

MARGUERITE: How much longer do you plan to keep it up then?

CRAWFORD: What? Oh. Well, as I say ether is a subtle substance. Subtler than any substance known.

MARGUERITE: I see. Stuff is invisible you say?

CRAWFORD: Yes.

MARGUERITE: Goes through everything?

CRAWFORD: Yes.

MARGUERITE: Walls, floors—

CRAWFORD: Permeates everything, yes.

MARGUERITE: Causes matter to act on other matter. Even at a distance.

CRAWFORD: Yes.

MARGUERITE: Uh-ha.

CRAWFORD: You have a good memory.

MARGUERITE: Well. Sounds a lot like the spirit world, don't it? Spirits is invisible, float through and 'round anything, act on matter at a distance. Spirits rap on things, move things, put thoughts in your head, put their hands on you, perr—meate everything—

CRAWFORD: No, no! That is a completely spurious comparison. Spirits have nothing whatever to do with ether.

MARGUERITE: Alright. You should know.

(A long pause.)

CRAWFORD: Many years ago, I did make a small but significant—umm—invention that had to do with the wireless. Do you have a wireless?

(Marguerite shakes her head.)

CRAWFORD: Well. No matter. You wouldn't find one with the "Articulator" in it these days. That was the name of the part I invented—the "Articulator." It helped clarify—or "articulate"—the signal. In other words it got rid of static. You are familiar with static?

MARGUERITE: Oh, intimately.

CRAWFORD: It worked very well. And then somebody had a better idea. But it was ever thus.

MARGUERITE: Shame. You must have been disappointed.

CRAWFORD: No. One expects that. Progress. One builds on the work of others. The individual's accomplishments fade away and are forgotten.

MARGUERITE: You have a good attitude. Most people hate change. They fear it. It makes them sad. Then they get angry. Then they go ravin' batty.

CRAWFORD: Hardly useful.

MARGUERITE: Who's talkin' useful?

CRAWFORD: I'm surprised that an attractive young lady such as yourself is not out visiting friends. It's a lovely evening.

MARGUERITE: It was. It's raining.

CRAWFORD: Oh, right.

MARGUERITE: *(Pause.)* I have friends, you know.

CRAWFORD: Yes.

MARGUERITE: I even have a particular friend.

CRAWFORD: Wonderful.

MARGUERITE: At present, he's traveling on the Continent.

CRAWFORD: Italy?

(Pause.)

MARGUERITE: Yeh. In Italy.

CRAWFORD: So that's why you want to go—?

MARGUERITE: His family are stacked. Gads and gads of money. We hope to be married by the end of the year.

CRAWFORD: Well, congratulations. What is your young man's name?

MARGUERITE: *(Pause.)* You wouldn't know him.

CRAWFORD: Oh.

MARGUERITE: It's a surprise, see. I haven't told me Mum.

CRAWFORD: Oh.

(Pause.)

MARGUERITE: I'd show you a photograph. But he hates having them taken. He's a—umm—a little taller than you. Fair with black hair and dark eyes. Has a little dimple right there. I tease him about it.

CRAWFORD: Hmm.

MARGUERITE: He was an officer during the war. A subaltern.

(Lights begin slowly to change in the room, darkening, and focusing on Marguerite and Crawford. The effect should be hallucinatory, distorting the present. A wisp of smoke curls up from behind the wingchair.)

MARGUERITE: I tease him a lot. He's the serious type.

CRAWFORD: Is he?

MARGUERITE: He took shrapnel in his leg, you know. Oh, he went through hell. Well, you know. The war. They saw terrible things.

CRAWFORD: Yes.

MARGUERITE: Anyway, his leg, he's shy about it. Nothing, just a little limp. But he walks with a cane. Now, that's a lovely thing, the cane. A gift from his dad it was. Ebony wood with a top in the shape of a woman's face. Solid silver. Told me his father chose it because it reminded him of his wife. She passed on in ah, well, when my darling was born. Anyway, shame I don't have a picture. Tried to weedle one out of him but he wouldn't give it to me. Was of him and some of the chaps in his company. Oh, he looked so sweet in it. They all did. Them all leaning together. Every time the photographer went to snap it, one of 'em would laugh and fall down and they'd have to start all over again.

(Crawford watches Marguerite intensely.)

CRAWFORD: He was fortunate to have made it through the war. So many didn't.

(Crawford turns to face upstage staring directly at the wingchair. A hand with a cigarette is seen. An arm emerges clothed in the sleeve of the uniform of a WWI British subaltern. The hand holds an ebony cane.)

MARGUERITE: Yeah. He was lucky. We was both lucky.

(Sound and light reach an unbearable pitch. The window opens. The shadow in the chair, Paul, stands, takes his cane and walks through the window. He turns, looks at Crawford, then goes. Sound and light return to what they were.)

MARGUERITE: Did you say something?

CRAWFORD: No. I—

MARGUERITE: Jayz—how did I get on to all that? Well, ya know, they're in your thoughts and you get a chance to natter—are you all right?

CRAWFORD: I have to go. I really must go. I must. It's very late. So, I am going to go. Ah, tell Mr. Peale—well—tell Mr. Peale—I couldn't stay.

(Crawford exits. Marguerite looks after him for a beat. Lights down.)

SCENE III

Lights up on George Crawford on another part of the stage, at a podium. Applause. He addresses an audience of physicists.

CRAWFORD: Before we adjourn, I should like to express some brief thoughts on the momentous developments of the week. I know you will join me in applauding Mr. Eddington's achievement—
(Applause.)

CRAWFORD: Yes, yes. We all appreciate the enormous effort and courage of Mr. Eddington in proving what was previously conjecture. His confirmation of Mr. Einstein's theory and all that Mr. Einstein's theory connotes, his theory that light passing a massive star bends its path. Some of you, well, a few of you *at least,* must be thinking, "Well, there goes Newtonian particle theory all to bits." Hahahaha. Yes. Well. I too shall miss the inspiration of Newtonian dynamics, its simplicity and clarity. At any rate, however much we shall miss particular principles of Mr. Newton, I know I look forward, as I'm certain we all do, to exploring the new frontiers Mr. Einstein has opened before us.
(Finished, he smiles uncertainly. Silence.)

CRAWFORD: *(Pause.)* Oh, ah. *(Pause.)* That is all. Thank you very much.
(A smattering of applause and lights change as Crawford moves into the next scene.)

SCENE IV

As Lights change, Peale, in lab coat, enters Crawford's lab and starts the Ether Machine. Crawford joins him. The Machine consists of two large metallic wheels mounted on a wooden frame. This arrangement resembles a turntable with the metal disks balanced inches apart from one another. Light is shone between them. The effect of the light on the floor and walls should be magical and slightly disorienting. Peale watches them, recording results in a notebook.

PEALE: You're still angry. *(Pause.)* It's been weeks, for Christ sake. *(Pause.)* George? *(Pause.)* George.

CRAWFORD: I don't like surprises.

PEALE: Good. In that case, I'm about to say something that couldn't possibly make you angry. It is absolutely no surprise to anyone.

(No response.)

PEALE: Interested?

(No response.)

PEALE: The results are identical.

CRAWFORD: *(Aggravated.)* Let me see that! *(Takes the notebook from Peale and peruses it.)*

PEALE: Go on. Have a good look. My charge, as I understand it, was to observe whether the motion of the disks replaced a bright band by a dark one. Or the other way 'round. No shift in the bands. Go on, go on, go on. That's it. *(Pause.)* Look all you want to. You and I both know what that means. The motion of the disks should carry the ether stream with them. Some appreciable shift in the light bands should be there. No shift, no ether. No surprise.

CRAWFORD: Something's wrong.

PEALE: Oh, c'mon, George. You can't believe you've overlooked anything. The machine is solid, you've accounted for centrifugal force, air thrown off the disks—

CRAWFORD: Again.

PEALE: George! How long have you been at this?! Since I came in. Three hours ago!

CRAWFORD: Time might be a factor.

PEALE: Oh key-ryst!

CRAWFORD: No one asked you to help.

(Peale sighs, takes the notebook. They begin the disks whirling again.)

PEALE: If I'd known a harmless, well-meaning little visit would upset you this much, I would never have invited you.

CRAWFORD: I wasn't invited. I was trapped. And who knows what you might do to get back at me about the funding.

PEALE: What does that crack signify?

CRAWFORD: Keep your mind on the results.

PEALE: Bugger the results. I've apologized. I apologized that very evening. I begged you to spare me some embarrassment. And what do you do but stomp off into the night.

CRAWFORD: —I didn't "stomp off." *(Pause.)* I felt unwell and I left.

(Pause.)

PEALE: Uh-huh.

CRAWFORD: I'm not handy at entertaining young ladies.

PEALE: *(Pause.)* Oh. So you met Marguerite. What happened?

CRAWFORD: Nothing happened. *(Pause.)* I felt ill. I left.

PEALE: I'm sorry if she caused you any distress. I understand she's a handful. Tortures her mother constantly. Once disappeared for a week. Ada was so upset she had a collapse.

CRAWFORD: Ada is it now?

PEALE: *(Referring to the results.)* Look. No shift. Might we stop? *(Peale goes to the window, pulls back drape. Light pours in.)*

CRAWFORD: You trust these people?

PEALE: One doesn't go on trust alone. That would be foolish.

CRAWFORD: What did you tell them about me?

PEALE: Nothing. I didn't even know I was going to invite you until I thought of it that evening.

CRAWFORD: What about my reputation?

PEALE: Oh for god's sakes, you might have been there for an evening's entertainment.

CRAWFORD: Exactly!

PEALE: What?

CRAWFORD: This is your research? Entertainment?

PEALE: I don't see it that way.

CRAWFORD: You're not a stupid man. You might have had a remarkable career.

PEALE: Thank you.

CRAWFORD: If you must ruin your career, I can do nothing. But don't put me into the same situation.

PEALE: Nobody's doing anything to you. Speaking of ruined careers, if it was apparent *I* was going down the wrong street, *I* hope *I* would know when to give *my* research the shove.

CRAWFORD: I need to come at it from a different angle—

PEALE: You need to go into another area of research entirely.

CRAWFORD: Physicists have believed in ether for four centuries—

PEALE: *(Overlapping.)* Michaelson and Morley! Michaelson and Morley! Michaelson and Morley!

CRAWFORD: —ohhhh! Don't throw them at me! There were discrepancies never properly explained—

PEALE: —michaelsonandmorleymichaelsonandmorely—

CRAWFORD: They're Americans.

PEALE: —michaelsonandmorleymichaelsonandmorely—

CRAWFORD: Oh, shut up!

PEALE: Michaelson and Morley. Decades ago. Proved Ether Does Not Exist. Ether is a dead topic. And you know it. Our eminent colleagues might laugh at me, George. They're in stitches over you. *(A long pause.)* Someone had to tell you.

(A pause.)

CRAWFORD: Who?

PEALE: You don't have to listen to me, George. But you should. While there's still time to do something else—

CRAWFORD: —something else?! Something else?! *What else? (An embarrassed silence.)* This made sense to me is all. I know there's very little support for it.

PEALE: No support. We have that in common.

CRAWFORD: Oh, Frank. It's all changed. I don't know anything anymore, Frank. I came home from the meeting the other day. Went out into my garden. And—nothing. I've always enjoyed my garden. A sense of wonder from knowing that millions and millions of processes were at work under the soil, in every leaf, in every rock and every petal. Every drop of dew. I've always believed that behind the physical world lay an intelligence. I could see it. In my garden. I felt—reassured. And now— Physical phenomena observed. Those are the kinds of problems I'm good at. Those are the problems I understand how to solve.

PEALE: *(Referring to the experiment.)* Or not.

CRAWFORD: Oh! One day, you look around and you're left with, with— bloody Einstein! No unifying element in the world, he says. No agent that connects the most disparate entities to one another. In his world, emptiness is not only possible, Frank, it is the *natural* state of things. It is awful! One believes in and works at something all one's life. How does it suddenly become an illusion?

PEALE: Well, George, something new can be exciting too.

CRAWFORD: I don't want something new! *(Sudden fury.)* Christ, I hate Einstein! I hate, I hate, I hate his genius! I hate his theories, his logic! I hate him! I hate—him! His rotten little German—he is German, isn't he?—

PEALE: *(Quickly.)* —I believe so, yes—

CRAWFORD: —I hate his rotten little German guts!

PEALE: You're furious! See! *That's* exciting!

CRAWFORD: You, with your fairies and your spirits.

PEALE: At least my research tends to support *my* hypotheses.

CRAWFORD: Yes, all those *anecdotes*. Worse possible methods. *(Pause.)* Frank, don't you ever have a doubt?

PEALE: Your results give you the faith you need to go on. Einstein had to have felt the same.

CRAWFORD: As did a number of generals in the last war.

PEALE: I have nothing to say to that.

CRAWFORD: Alright. I'm sorry. It isn't the same.

PEALE: No, it isn't! I am your friend, George! You could be a little more understanding. We don't have anybody else in the professional establishment who gives a fig what we're doing! We are the codgers and the dodgers and the cranks and the rebels who have not and probably never will be anointed by majority opinion. And who cares. You'll be tolerated, but you and I occupy the same fringe now, the same No-Man's Land of science. We are the lepers of our community.

CRAWFORD: Lepers?!

PEALE: Oh, but you are, George! How many of your peers drop by your lab anymore? How many of 'em even bother to inquire what you're doing? I was honest with you, George. Many haven't been and won't be. I'm not asking for you to embrace what I believe.

CRAWFORD: That's just as well.

PEALE: You, you reject things so off-handedly and so absolutely!

CRAWFORD: I do not—!

PEALE: —Oh yes you do!

CRAWFORD: Frank, that's unfair. So many of us lost family in that butchery—you lost a brother—

PEALE: Yes! I know! That's precisely why this work is so important!

CRAWFORD: How can I endorse research that might be nothing more than wishful thinking? I can't do that. I daren't.

PEALE: "I can't" "I dahhhhren't!" Oh come along! Have you ever thought you—and the Society—would be better off being a bit more dahhh-hhring.

CRAWFORD: No. That is not their job.

PEALE: Ten years ago, you thought Einstein's work on inertia and energy was "interesting but without substance." Now you hate his guts because he's *right!*

CRAWFORD: I still don't concede he's right on ether.

PEALE: Oh, gawd! Gawd! GAWD! Give me strength! And he accuses me of wishful thinking! Fine. Think on this then. According to the laws of probability, the sheer volume of *verifiably accurate* "anecdotes" from my mediums *already* proves something. And what does it prove? What you were looking for here? *(Indicates experiment.)* Some, *any* distortion however slight, and ether, George, ether would have *existed.*

CRAWFORD: I'm not getting the connection.

PEALE: What do *my* results prove? One bit of information impossible for the medium to know any other way? One piece of information that could come from one place and one place only? And what have we, George? In that one case? In that one single case, we have proven communication with the other world. All you need is one undoubtable instance. Turn your grizzled visage upon it, and con-sid-ahhhhh!

(Peale retreats as lights grow bright on Crawford, then dim out.)

SCENE V

Lights up on Marguerite sitting in wingchair this time facing upstage in the Bonet parlour. She is reading a book. Peale sneaks silently up behind her.

PEALE: Afternoon, Marguerite.

MARGUERITE: Jesus, Jack and Johnny!

(Marguerite tosses the book in the air. Peale laughs and catches it.)

PEALE: Oh, did I startle you?

MARGUERITE: Sod.

PEALE: *(Looking at the book.)* "Rome, City of Myth, City of Wonder?"

MARGUERITE: Did you need something, Peale?

PEALE: How long have we known each other?

MARGUERITE: An eternity.

PEALE: The point is I think you know me well enough to call me Frank.

MARGUERITE: Did you need something?

PEALE: Do I have to *need* something in order to spend time in your charming company?

MARGUERITE: Oh gah!

PEALE: That's what I like about you. Your unique way of putting things.

MARGUERITE: Pull the other one. It's got bells on it.

PEALE: Mr. Crawford said he had a nice conversation with you. Do you remember Mr. Crawford? Chap came with me a few weeks back, sat out the seance in here? You kept him company.

MARGUERITE: I didn't keep him company. You plonked him in here. What of it?

PEALE: I wondered what happened.

MARGUERITE: Whajamean what happened?

PEALE: He left in a cloud of dust. I thought something happened.

MARGUERITE: I didn't do noffink! All of a sudden, the old duff turned green and powdered off. I didn't do noffink to him.

PEALE: Marguerite.

MARGUERITE: What's he saying?

PEALE: He's not saying anything. He left and I thought it odd. Got my curiosity up.

MARGUERITE: Well, it doesn't take much. You like poking about in other people's business, don't you?

PEALE: What did you two talk about?

MARGUERITE: We talked a little about what he does. Twenty years worth of some bloody silly gas or something. And then he got tired, he went home. *(Indicating book.)* Now, if you please.

(Peale looks at the book.)

PEALE: What's the sudden interest in Italy?

MARGUERITE: Jaysus. *I* don't work for you.

PEALE: You could.

MARGUERITE: Forget that.

PEALE: Planning another getaway?

MARGUERITE: Why would I tell you?

PEALE: I'd be the perfect confidant. Does Ada know?

MARGUERITE: She sees and knows all. With you around, she will.

PEALE: I won't tell.

MARGUERITE: Oh yeh.

PEALE: I will miss you awfully. You're not *really* going to Italy? I don't want you to go.

MARGUERITE: I'm marrying an Italian named Guccioni. Guido Guccioni. Maybe you know him.

PEALE: I hardly think we travel in the same circles with a name like Guccioni.

MARGUERITE: That's what I don't like about you. Snob. We're going to open an ice cream parlour. You're not invited.

PEALE: Oh, and I like ice-cream too.

MARGUERITE: Why shouldn't I go to Italy?

PEALE: Why should you?

MARGUERITE: Plenty of reasons. You're one of them.

PEALE: You're a cruel woman. Well. If ice-cream doesn't work out, you can always go back to telling fortunes.

MARGUERITE: That tears it! *(Starts to exit.)*

PEALE: Marguerite. Marguerite! I was joking!

MARGUERITE: Piss off!

PEALE: Don't go. Please? I didn't mean to upset you. *(Pleading.)* Please? *(She relents.)*

PEALE: I meant what I said about missing you.

MARGUERITE: I'll bet.

PEALE: You know, Marguerite, we have more in common than you think.

MARGUERITE: I wish we did. I'd have more money.

PEALE: You see, you're a person who feels passionately about things. And so do I. And you're someone who appreciates honesty. And so do I.

MARGUERITE: Right!

PEALE: Why is that funny? We aren't afraid to say what we feel. Most people are so hemmed in by the niceties, by appearances, or they're so mired in politics, or are frightened what others think, they forget finally what the truth looks like. But honesty. Well, it's a rare quality. Refreshing. That's what I like about you.

MARGUERITE: You left out place.

PEALE: Place?

MARGUERITE: Hemmed in by "place." As in "know your." Most people don't have the luxury of honesty, Peale. They can't say anything because they have a great deal to lose if they do. You wouldn't bloody know about that.

PEALE: You're wrong. I would know. But you're not afraid to say what you feel. *(Marguerite doesn't answer.)*

PEALE: Are you?

MARGUERITE: I say it's all rubbish.

PEALE: Some people have a kind of talent. Don't you think?

MARGUERITE: I wouldn't know.

PEALE: Your mother has given me some astonishing results.

MARGUERITE: And howdya know your subjects don't go bleating behind your back to her?

PEALE: Do they?

MARGUERITE: *(Pause.)* No. *(Pause.)* You'd have to have a reason to do that. They have no reason. I mean, look where they come from. No, you'd be the one who twigs her. *(Peale laughs but is a bit taken aback.)*

PEALE: What a peculiar idea.

MARGUERITE: People try to get what they want. Even unawares.

PEALE: You're too young to think so little of people.

MARGUERITE: Maybe I've spent too much time in the dark with the bastards. I've seen widows scream, tear their hair, carrying on for husbands they hated. Hated. Husbands sobbing over wives they cheated on for years. And the children. The children they gave not a whit for when alive. Quite a show. But gets a bit old after awhile.

PEALE: And that's why you won't sit in anymore? There are plenty of people who loved, who love. Whose grief is genuine. You don't think they deserve some help?

MARGUERITE: I made things up in there. *That* I know. *That* I'm sure of. More lies to add to the pile of rubbish that gets higher everyday around here! *(A long pause.)*

PEALE: Do you remember Mrs. Creighton-Lee?

MARGUERITE: Who?

PEALE: Mrs. Creighton-Lee.

MARGUERITE: Oh yeah. That bloody great garnet ring of hers cut into me hand.

PEALE: I'm remembering a particular session, last year. You told her to wait for leaves, wait until the leaves turned you said. And there would be a message.

MARGUERITE: What I mean. Crap.

PEALE: I saw her last week. Radiant, a different person from when she was here. You wouldn't recognize her. You see, she thought, as I did, that leaves turning meant the change of season. Fall came. Nothing. So— counted a miss. But then a few months ago, she was clearing out the old nursery. She happened across a favorite storybook of her son's. And there it was. She "turned the leaves" and there it was. A note written his last time home. The message. In it, he poured out to her his deepest feelings, his fear of death, his agony about having to go back, his love for her. At the end he vowed no matter what, he would come back.

MARGUERITE: Well, he got that wrong.

PEALE: Mrs. Creighton-Lee doesn't think so. The woman is transformed. *(Pause.)*

MARGUERITE: If you were a young man going off to war, with a better than good chance you'll never see your mum again, what are you likely to do? And if she'd never found anything, what? She would forget it. Count it a miss. You don't give coincidence enough credit, Peale.

PEALE: Frank. You just don't want to believe the truth.

MARGUERITE: I could say the same for you.

MARGUERITE: What exactly do you get out of all this? What is it with you, really?

PEALE: You mean, why am I interested in being the person who finally and definitively proves what human beings have desired to know for as long as recorded time?

(Long pause.)

MARGUERITE: There's no money?

(Peale laughs.)

MARGUERITE: Oh, I forgot. Money is such a comical topic.

PEALE: If I tried to exploit the situation, I assure you I would lose whatever small amount of credibility I've earned.

MARGUERITE: Lucky you don't need any money then. She's not a well woman. In case you haven't noticed.

PEALE: Mediums tend to be fragile. That's part of their receptiveness. I won't push her too hard, I promise.

MARGUERITE: There's a comfort.

PEALE: See, you are concerned for her. Though you pretend otherwise.

MARGUERITE: She's me mother. And for your information, most of your "subjects" are tight bastards.

PEALE: I wish I could help you. Honestly I do.

MARGUERITE: Then do it.

PEALE: My coming here enhances her reputation. It brings in more people.

MARGUERITE: It makes her life more difficult.

PEALE: You could help her.

MARGUERITE: You don't want me in there. I get the chance, I'll have their wallets off them.

(Peale laughs.)

MARGUERITE: I mean it.

PEALE: I know. That's why I'm laughing.

MARGUERITE: You are a queer duck.

PEALE: I'll take that as a compliment. I think you do like me.

MARGUERITE: You fancy yourself.

PEALE: I think you want to believe me. Your attitude—

MARGUERITE: My attitude. Why I'm so popular.

PEALE: I was going to say your attitude towards your own talent astonishes me—it's just—mind-boggling. Because, Marguerite, compared to what you can know, to what I believe you can know about anyone—Rome, City of Myth, City of Wonder—well, it comes off as boiled pudding.

(Lights begin up on Crawford with Paul in dim light upstage.)

PAUL: Help me.

MARGUERITE: You're entitled to your beliefs.

PEALE: If I could purchase with all my worldly goods—all my money, Marguerite—what you have, the gift you possess, give everything I have, I would do it. I would do it.

MARGUERITE: Pity I can't hand it over then.

PEALE: Marguerite, it's a mystery. It's a miracle. To be able to speak to another world, to know what nobody else can. What I wouldn't give—What I wouldn't do!—I'd—I'd drool down my shirt—

MARGUERITE: Oh, that's attractive.

PEALE: I'd become an aesthete, shave off all my hair. Rub myself all over with ashes. And mud. I'd eat—grubs and raw eggs—and brussels sprouts—I would—

MARGUERITE: *(Giggling.)* You're bats!

PEALE: You see? I would reduce myself to a muddy-ashy-bald brussels-sprouts eater!

MARGUERITE: A muddy-ashy bald brussels-sprouts *and grubs* eater. Get it right, mate.

PEALE: That's how important your talent is!

(Marguerite goes silent. She and Peale look at one another.)

PEALE: It's not the kind of gift you should ignore.

PAUL: Help me.

CRAWFORD: *(Overlapping.)* I need your help.

MARGUERITE: I told ya. I don't want to sit in there. It's depressing.

PEALE: I'm in there. Your mother's in there. We're not depressed!

MARGUERITE: That's only because you're a potty maniac! *(She throws a pillow at him. Peale chases her around the chair.)* Help! I'm being chased by a nutty grub-eater!

(They toss pillows at each other. Finally he stops.)

PEALE: I'm out of breath.

MARGUERITE: Poor old thing. You've got the wrong diet. *(She throws the pillow again.)*

PEALE: Shh. Listen!

(Marguerite ignores him, throws the pillow, hitting Peale.)

PEALE: Enough foolishness for one day.

MARGUERITE: Coming from you, that's good.

PEALE: This is what you do to me. I want you to listen to me, Marguerite.

MARGUERITE: Ahhhhhaaaa!

PEALE: Listen!

PAUL: Help me.

PEALE: Listen! Are you listening?

MARGUERITE: Yeh? Alright. I'm listening.

PEALE: Marguerite. I care about you.

MARGUERITE: Do you?

PEALE: Yes, and what I see is—well, you're not going anywhere quickly. You're not going to Italy. You're not going to open an ice-a-creama parlour. There's no Guido. No one's going to come in and, and sweep you off to some romantic little paradise no matter how much you spend your time dreaming of it.

PAUL: Help me.

PEALE: I'm sorry, Marguerite. I know that was cruel. But I like you because you're like me. You hate hypocrisy. You hate the hypocrisy of people who only pretend to feel something. You hate pretense. But, Marguerite, what are you doing? Dreaming, and if you're not careful you'll end up pretending, just as much as those people you despise, pretending about what should have been. I'm asking you to help your mother. Alright. Alright. I'm asking you to—help me.

PAUL: Help me.

MARGUERITE: I don't want to talk about it.

PEALE: Marguerite. Please.

MARGUERITE: I said no!

PEALE: Alright. Alright.

(Peale defeated, exits. Paul's presence remains a shadow. Transition to Crawford in the Bonet parlour.)

SCENE VI

Marguerite is sitting in the wingchair, listening to Crawford.

CRAWFORD: *(A pause.)* Your friend. Your fiancé? You said he wrote you letters. I was hoping if—I might see his letters. Not the contents. Just the envelope. If I could see the handwriting on the outside. My interest is of a personal nature. It's crucially important. I wouldn't even think to ask otherwise.

(Marguerite rises. A pause.)

MARGUERITE: I burned them.

CRAWFORD: Sorry?

MARGUERITE: I said I burned them.

CRAWFORD: Burned them?

MARGUERITE: Yes.

CRAWFORD: But—?

MARGUERITE: The relationship ended. I can't help you.

CRAWFORD: I'm sorry. But can you at least tell me where the young man lives? How might I contact him?

MARGUERITE: No, I can't. I don't know.

CRAWFORD: But surely—you said he has a home here. His parents—

MARGUERITE: You can't contact him!

CRAWFORD: I hate to insist but it is important. I wouldn't mention your name—

MARGUERITE: You can't contact him. You can't contact him because he doesn't exist.

(A long pause.)

CRAWFORD: I don't—understand.

MARGUERITE: I was a bit pissed—alright—had some sherry, and I just made him up. Made the whole thing up. *(A long silence.)* I'm not having you on. I made him up. He doesn't exist. There never were any letters.

CRAWFORD: But—why? Why would you do such a thing?

MARGUERITE: Oh, I can't explain—

CRAWFORD: But you must. You must explain it.

MARGUERITE: I was pissed. And, stupidly as it seems now, I trotted him out to—I don't know—show off. Something like that.

CRAWFORD: I still don't understand.

MARGUERITE: Look, what does it matter? I've told you the truth—I lied.

CRAWFORD: But that can't be.

MARGUERITE: What's all the panic about anyway?

CRAWFORD: I thought the young man was someone I knew.

MARGUERITE: Oh. Well. I'm sorry for that. I mean I didn't think it would matter. If I'd of known, I would have made him a short blond.

CRAWFORD: You described my son. You described him. His cane. You described my reason for purchasing it.

MARGUERITE: No, no—

CRAWFORD: —and the photograph—

(Crawford takes the photograph out of his pocket and shows it to her. Marguerite looks at the photograph for a good long beat. She recognizes the face.)

MARGUERITE: He's dead.

CRAWFORD: Five years now. This came in his effects. I was stunned when you mentioned it. I've not shown anyone that photograph—ever. Never. (Crawford looks at her, appraising her closely.) How old are you? (Marguerite looks at him.)

CRAWFORD: Very young. How could you have known him? How would that even have been possible? Did you? Did you know him?

MARGUERITE: (Looking at the photograph.) That's daft.

CRAWFORD: Did someone tell you these things?

MARGUERITE: I made them up. I told you.

CRAWFORD: Five years now. Five years is a long time. All these men. All died in the same battle on the same day. I never saw my son's body. No one saw them. Except those who buried them. He's buried in Belgium. I've not shown this to anyone.

MARGUERITE: Mr. Crawford, I don't know how to say—

CRAWFORD: —no, no, no. It's all right. When you told me these things, well, you can imagine—can't you? I thought Frank said something. He's been after me for ages to—but these were things he couldn't have known. He knew my son but I never told Frank these things. And then I thought well it has to be somebody else. But who? All of Paul's friends—they're all dead. All of them. I suppose what I was hoping for was madness. I was hoping that I'd find he was still alive. Somehow he'd escaped and had for some reason forgotten or wanted to be someone else. It's not that mad, is it? Desperate. But strange things happen.

MARGUERITE: Coincidence. Happens all the time.

CRAWFORD: What would your mother say?

MARGUERITE: I don't know. You will have to ask her.

CRAWFORD: I'm asking you.

MARGUERITE: I say it's coincidence.

CRAWFORD: I am ridiculous. Everything about me is ridiculous.

(Pause.)

MARGUERITE: Mr. Crawford. If you love someone, it's natural not to want them gone. Not to believe they're gone.

CRAWFORD: I'd thought the people who went to seances foolish, credulous creatures. And yet here is where I find myself. Here I am, Miss Bonet. And I am willing to believe.

MARGUERITE: I can't help you.

CRAWFORD: But I believe you can!

MARGUERITE: Then you're wrong. You should speak to my mother.

CRAWFORD: But this came from you.

(Pause.)

MARGUERITE: Have you spoken to Peale? About this?

CRAWFORD: I'm sorry?

MARGUERITE: Peale.

CRAWFORD: Mr. Peale knows nothing about this. *(Pause.)* I'm willing to pay.

MARGUERITE: No.

CRAWFORD: You won't even try? *(Crawford has taken out a number of bills.)*

MARGUERITE: Try what?

CRAWFORD: Telling me about my son. Telling me about Paul. You did before.

MARGUERITE: That was a fantasy. You've confused things.

CRAWFORD: One might be the same as the other.

MARGUERITE: They're not. They're very different. They're very different, Mr. Crawford. And Peale doesn't pay for his experiments.

CRAWFORD: How Mr. Peale conducts his business is none of my concern.

(Pause.)

MARGUERITE: I wouldn't feel right about this.

CRAWFORD: How much would you need? I wouldn't be ungenerous.

MARGUERITE: You should go home now.

CRAWFORD: Is there nothing I can say? It would mean so much to me.

(Pause.)

MARGUERITE: Are you sure you've not said anything to Peale?

CRAWFORD: No. He'd be insufferable.

MARGUERITE: That's the word for it. *(Pause.)* It's daft, Mr. Crawford.

CRAWFORD: Yes, it is. Miss Bonet. I've spent twenty years of my life in the pursuit of a what everyone else knew was a fantasy. You can't possibly deceive me any worse than I've deceived myself. So I'd just as soon pay for fantasies, knowing that's what they are. And as long as we're both clear about it, where's the harm?

MARGUERITE: Did you love your son, Mr. Crawford?

CRAWFORD: Naturally, yes.

MARGUERITE: No. I mean, did you?

CRAWFORD: It wasn't for lack of wanting—it just came too late. I don't know how to answer that question exactly.

MARGUERITE: And this stays between us.

CRAWFORD: Yes.

MARGUERITE: This is cracked. Absolutely cracked.

(Crawford gives her his card. After a pause, he places the photograph gently into her hand and quickly exits. Marguerite puts the card in her pocket and goes to do the same with the photograph, but then stops and looks at it as lights change and become more intense and focused on her.)

MARGUERITE: That night, Mum and I had a right knock-down. I called her "old." And it's true. She doesn't keep the lights low just for the spirits. I don't know. I suppose I'd reached a limit. Never having a proper dress. Never having a thing that hadn't belonged to somebody else. I was sick of it. All the posturing, and the marble-mouth, and the fret, and the struggle and her being ill from the strain of it, and going three-sheets into the wind on cheap brandy after they'd gone and taking it all out on me. I said to her (and I was cruel, why wouldn't I be) You think Peale gives a fig about you? When he grows disenchanted with his "line of investigation," you won't see a golden ass-hair of his around here. Wait and see. Wake up, you fusty old cow, I said. Wake up. We have to *do* something. We have to do something! Well. She went into her room, closed the door. And that was that.

SCENE VII

A spot remains on Marguerite in her part of the stage, while lights come up full on Crawford in his lab, pouring himself a drink. He holds in his hand, a formal photograph of his son Paul, as a child, framed. He downs his drink. Crawford puts down the photograph, continues looking at it, as Paul approaches. He is dressed in civilian clothes, young and vital as he exists in Crawford's memory.

CRAWFORD: *(Looking up at him.)* Drink?

PAUL: No thank you, sir.

CRAWFORD: You don't mind if I have one. *(Crawford pours himself one. He drinks. After a long pause.)* Puts me in mind of when I was young.

PAUL: Sir?

CRAWFORD: I wanted to go to Holland. There was a conference of physicists and I wanted to go. And ah, we didn't have the money at the time. So it was arranged that I should ask my Uncle Dink, who was a terrible miser but who loved my mother his sister very much, it was arranged I should ask him for the funds. And I went to his house, and was shown into his great study, lots of portraits and dark wood, and leather, that sort of thing. Very intimidating and there he was, this little crinkled dwarf of a man with white hair. And he said to me, "So. You're Eleanor's boy?" And I assured him that I was. And he said, "Do you drink?" And I was so grateful. There was nothing I needed more in that moment than a drink. And so up I piped, "Oh, yes, sir. Please, sir." And he said, "Never touch the stuff!" A teetotaler. My luck. The interview went downhill from there. I never got a drink. And I never got to Holland. You're sure you don't want one?

PAUL: No thank you.

CRAWFORD: I should be proud of that, I suppose. But I don't know how you get through the day.

PAUL: You wanted to speak with me, sir.

CRAWFORD: Well, yes. *(Pause.)* How are you, my boy?

PAUL: Fine. Thank you, sir.

CRAWFORD: Quite certain about that?

PAUL: Sir?

CRAWFORD: Paul. I am—I am compelled to speak to you about—

PAUL: Oh, yes, this is about school.

    (Pause.)

CRAWFORD: Yes, school.

PAUL: They've told you I'm being sent down.

CRAWFORD: Came as something of a surprise. I thought we were doing better.

PAUL: Obviously, *we* were not.

CRAWFORD: Do you really think this is a good time for impertinent comment—well.

PAUL: Well.

CRAWFORD: You have anything to say?

PAUL: Not really.

CRAWFORD: Nothing.

PAUL: I can't imagine what there could be.

CRAWFORD: I should have thought you would have—some explanation.

PAUL: Oh c'mon. It can't be that great a s-surprise, Father.

CRAWFORD: Oh. Why would we think that?—

PAUL: Because it was crystal clear to everyone, most emphatically myself, and you if you'd wanted to see it, that I have no aptitude for physics.

CRAWFORD: Well. And you've proven yourself correct.

(Pause.)

PAUL: I will have that drink afterall. *(He pours himself one.)*

CRAWFORD: I have to say, I don't think you applied yourself.

(Paul, in pouring himself a drink, spills a little of it.)

PAUL: Damn it! Do you have any idea what's it's like to realize no matter how hard you "apply" yourself, you'll never do b-better than fail.

(Pause.)

CRAWFORD: You could have told me—

PAUL: —I tried, at Christmas—

CRAWFORD: —If you did, I can't recall the effort!—

PAUL: Perhaps because you were too busy—

CRAWFORD: —alright, it was a busy time. It was.

(Paul drinks.)

CRAWFORD: If you could have just straggled through somehow—many brilliant men have not shown their stuff right off the mark—if you could have just—once you graduated, I would have been able to help—

PAUL: Then help now! Allow me to do what I want.

CRAWFORD: *(Disgusted.)* Poetry.

PAUL: Yes. Poetry.

CRAWFORD: That is not a profession. That is a hobby. Even if it were a profession, only the very best are able to sustain themselves by it.

PAUL: Thanks for the vote of confidence.

CRAWFORD: Well. You've got the money. You flunked school. So now you can sit around and write poetry and entertain those friends of yours—pack of layabouts!—and use it all up.

PAUL: I don't care for your friends either. Bunch of withered mummies.

(Pause.)

CRAWFORD: And when you come to the end of your money, what then?

PAUL: I'll think of something.

CRAWFORD: The world is not an easy place, Paul, though it's been made that way for you. That's my fault. Those who take command of their destinies are the ones that it rewards.

PAUL: I'm taking command of my destiny.

CRAWFORD: You need a plan. Some larger vision of your life. Because if you don't, you float through the days, and at the end you can't even remember how you came to be nothing.

PAUL: That's almost poetic, Dad.

CRAWFORD: You always were a little bugger.

PAUL: Thank you.

CRAWFORD: *(Pleading.)* Oh, Paul, it's still salvageable. I have friends. I can write some letters—

PAUL: I don't want you to write any letters!

(Silence. A sullen Crawford pours himself another drink. After a pause, he takes Paul's glass and pours him another.)

PAUL: Always willing to help, eh, Dad. Unless, and until you're really needed. At Christmas, I was this close—this close—to breaking.

CRAWFORD: Oh come along. It wasn't that bad.

PAUL: Well, of course not. You're imminently qualified to judge. Think what it would mean if you were wrong.

CRAWFORD: The rest of the world isn't going to coddle you as I have.

PAUL: When I was little I wanted to be just like you. Now everything about you seems ridiculous to me. Strange how things change.

CRAWFORD: And I think you are a stupid boy. Do as you like with your friends. Don't come back here when the money runs out.

PAUL: Wouldn't think of it

MARGUERITE: No, I mean did you *love* your son?

PAUL: You know, Dad, surprising as it may seem, I do have a plan. I was going to wait but now is as good a time as any. My friends and I enlisted. Orders should be through in a day or so.

(Lights change to a harsh white as Paul rises from his chair. Under the following he will transform from his younger optimistic self to the emotionally drained soldier he will become as he changes from his civilian clothes to the uniform of his rank. This happens as a choreographed visual accompaniment to the following so it should be graceful and the transformation underscoring Crawford's speech.)

CRAWFORD: I thought at the time it was all right. He surprised me. And I thought it was just and honorable he go off and do his bit with the others. I did not know what I felt. We didn't know one another. By this time, I didn't know at all who he was. He felt the same of me it seems. The devastating thing is—I hadn't a notion of how that came about. All I could think of, all I could remember, was the little boy. The one who looked up to me. Who wanted to be like me. We had times then. That's it for all you gave. Of what value was it? That for your care, and your pain. That and he's gone. Day after day. Each one, creeping further and further into some delusion of one's own making. Is that what it is? Nothing I thought I knew matters. I have lived a life and I know nothing.

(Crawford hands Paul his cane. As Crawford watches, Paul walks downstage with the cane, a slight limp evident. Paul stops, realizing he does not know where he is. He takes out a cigarette. He tries to light it but his hand is shaking. Marguerite rises and watches.)

PAUL: Help me.

(Marguerite goes to him, takes the matches and lights his cigarette. He looks at her as if she's a ghost. They stand, a tableau, as the window opens onto darkness. Paul backs away through it into darkness. Marguerite watches him go, then turns. Spot lit, Crawford also looks out into the future.)

CRAWFORD: Perhaps he'll speak to me. If I could have that. Just that one thing. Where is the harm?

(Lights dim out on Crawford. They linger for a moment on Marguerite.)

MARGUERITE: Right then.

(Blackout.)

END OF ACT I

ACT II
SCENE I

Marguerite and Crawford are in his lab. The Ether machine is dismantled, a shambles. The disks lie propped up, pieces of the machine are piled in a heap. A small table has appeared in the middle of this rubble on which sit two teacups and a pot of tea with cream and sugar. An old radio prototype sits to one side. Crawford sips his tea and looks at Marguerite expectantly. Marguerite takes a small notebook out of her coat.

MARGUERITE: I wrote down what I imagined. Help me remember.

CRAWFORD: Very good.

(She clears her throat.)

MARGUERITE: I wrote it in third person because—well—I don' know why—

CRAWFORD: Quite all right.

MARGUERITE: *(Taking the dive.)* Okay. Here goes. *(Reading.)* "There they sit, on a rainy afternoon, she, demure, her skin as white as alabaster, her hair a flowing mass of nutbrown tresses thrust upward and pinned, a becoming flush upon her cheek, her new shoes—a dainty size five and nobody has a foot like hers—and never will, ash, oak or elm—modestly crossed, elegantly though simply attired, pouring tea for the young man, the poor tormented young soldier sitting across from her in her bedsit."

CRAWFORD: Sorry. The young woman you describe is—yourself?

MARGUERITE: Yeh! What I said.

CRAWFORD: Oh.

(Paul appears.)

MARGUERITE: *(To Paul.)* How do you like your tea? *(To Crawford.)* She asks him. But he does not answer her at first and so she prompts him with her lovely smile. *(Smiling.)* One lump? *(To Crawford.)* She asks. He nods but seems hardly to care. What has he seen, she wonders, that he should have that look, so world-weary, so full of sorrow? And what must he think of these dreary surroundings? How could she tell him of her family's misfortunes? That, but for a certain father's love of drink and the fact he'd powdered off, leaving herself and her mother in dire straits, but for fate, she might have ridden in carriages and worn silk? *(To Paul.)* Are you tired? Would you like to lie down? *(To Crawford.)* She asks. But he says nothing. Oh, but that he would take her in his arms, his sheltering arms, strain her to him with all of his passion. She would be his strength, his shield against an uncaring world. She would wipe those lines from his brow. Put hope again into those dark eyes. He has a dimple. Oh! And he is so shy! Love knows no locksmiths.

(Crawford, uncomfortable, clears his throat.)

MARGUERITE: *(To Paul.)* Music? *(To Crawford.)* She asked. *(Marguerite turns on the old radio. It plays an old slow tune.)* But again, he says nothing. Worlds upon worlds unto himself, and she wants nothing more than for him to kiss her, long and passionately, and for them to lose themselves in one another. With all the heart of her, she longs to be his, this delicate yet manly soul, who knows more than his years. She longs to be his bride, his only, for riches and poor, in sickness and in health, 'til death us two part, from this day forward. *(To Paul.)* Is the tea alright? *(To Crawford.)* She asks.

PAUL: Yes. Topping. Thanks.

MARGUERITE: And they would go to the continent for their honeymoon. To—Italy! Rome. City of Myth! City of Wonder! And the hot Italian sun, the warm sands of the Mediterranean would burn all shadows of the past away. They would be free! Free forever! *(To Paul.)* Warm enough? *(To Crawford.)* She asked.

PAUL: Yes, fine. Thanks.

MARGUERITE: Afterwards, they would settle in a cozy, snug little homely home with bright and cheery rooms (that would never smell of dank, and gas and ancient duff) with chintze covers on the armchairs which she has so cleverly fashioned, she bein' such a whiz with a needle, and every morning they have their brekky, and he kisses her good-bye on his way to work. A long, lingering, passionate, hot kiss. And those nasty two-faced moggies down the block can think whatever they like—

PAUL: Perhaps we can have something a bit more— *(He adjusts the tuning on the radio, finding something more lively and dangerous like a tango.)*

MARGUERITE: Oh! Yes! *(To Crawford.)* She exclaimed. Then it came to her. She'd been thinking of this all wrong. Marriage. Ha! That's for bourgies. As it is, men drop at her size fives by the dozens. And she, she kicks them from her path with cool abandon. How could she, given her boundless appetite for excitement, be satisfied by one mere man. No. Why fool one's self? This is but a mere affair! Torrid. Passionate. But, like life itself, transitory! Dance? *(To Crawford.)* She asked.

PAUL: I'm afraid—

MARGUERITE: *(Taking his cane away and pulling him to his feet.)* —you never forget how.

(They dance. He is an excellent dancer with little sign of a limp.)

MARGUERITE: She could be wearing a man's suit, and smoking a cigarette. But—eh. No need to frighten the boy this soon. *(A flourish.)* Yes, she must remember only to live for today, only for now. His eyes burn into hers as though they would read her very thoughts. And she, she would read his before the night was through. She would raise the very devil in him. And not care one whit for the consequences!

(The music crescendos to a finish. Paul vanishes into shadow. We are back in Crawford's lab again. Marguerite sits. Crawford is stunned. He does not know what he expected but it wasn't this. Marguerite is obviously pleased with her creation.)

MARGUERITE: Well.

CRAWFORD: Very nice. Yes.

(A pause.)

MARGUERITE: You asked for a fantasy.

CRAWFORD: And—it certainly is!

(Marguerite taps the table. Crawford twigs to the fact she is expecting her pay. He takes an envelope out of his inner coat pocket and puts it on the table. She takes the envelope, checks the contents.)

CRAWFORD: Well. That's it then?

(She rises and goes to put on her coat and hat. Sees Crawford still sitting.)

MARGUERITE: What? Oh jaysus. You got what you asked for.

CRAWFORD: I didn't say anything.

MARGUERITE: No. You didn't. So what was it you did want? Eh? Let's have a guess, shall we?—our gallant lad on the other side. Tramping lovely cloud trenches, playing football on the fields of heaven, angels on one side, ghostly chums on other—

CRAWFORD: No, that's not what I expected.

MARGUERITE: I put a lot of work into that!

CRAWFORD: I know.

MARGUERITE: I was up half the night writing that bugger down!

(Pause.)

CRAWFORD: My son was not a dancer. He couldn't dance.

MARGUERITE: Well, he bloody well dances in *my* fantasy! *(A mutter.)* And he doesn't stutter neither.

(Crawford looks at her curiously. She continues her move to exit. He takes out a few more bills from his wallet and puts them on the table. He clears his throat so Marguerite will turn. She does and sees the money.)

CRAWFORD: I was sorry to hear about your mother's illness. I hope it isn't serious.

MARGUERITE: Yeh, well, we hope the same.

CRAWFORD: You know, Miss Bonet, perhaps, and I realize this goes against your wonderful sense of style—but I think it might be interesting to simply hear your fantasies as you think of them. As they occur to you.

MARGUERITE: *(Pause.)* Spontaneous-like.

CRAWFORD: Exactly.

(Marguerite looks at the money. Slowly, she moves away to look at the room. She focuses in on the wreckage of the Ether Machine.)

MARGUERITE: *(Re: the Ether Machine.)* What's this?

CRAWFORD: *(Pause.)* It was designed to measure distortion of light as it moved through ether.

MARGUERITE: Luminiferous ether.

CRAWFORD: Very good.

MARGUERITE: Looks a mess.

CRAWFORD: A least it serves a more honest function. Plain old junk.

(Long pause. Marguerite wanders over to the wireless.)

CRAWFORD: That, before you, is the famous prototype wireless.

MARGUERITE: Your invention. The Articulator.

CRAWFORD: Right. Very good.

(She turns it on. Horribly loud static comes out. She quickly switches it off. A pause.)

MARGUERITE: Thank Christ for progress, eh?

(After a beat, Marguerite approaches the money on the table. She sits. She looks at Crawford. Finally, she takes the money.)

MARGUERITE: Peacocks.

CRAWFORD: Peacocks?

(Paul appears in the window.)

MARGUERITE: Peacocks. Like at the zoo. They shriek. At night. An eerie bloody sound. Makes your flesh crawl. When he hears it, he dreams he's back there, in the trenches. The shrieks are the sound of his men.

(Lights begin to change under the following. Music.)

MARGUERITE: He tells me about a house. Out in the country. They roost in the trees. The peacocks. On the lawn, they walk about with those great tails with the eyes in 'em. There's a pool with lion's heads at either end with water comin' out their mouths. You look into the water, down, down, down, and you can see all the fish, orange and gold, some near the surface, some miles down it seems, glimmering there faintly in the darkness. You're lookin' down, there comes a shadow across the water—

(The lights change slowly so that she is spotlit, with Paul emerging from the shadows.)

PAUL: And the voice says Look out there. And you do and it's the little boat. Flying with the wind. Going across the pond like a real boat on real waves. And you are on that little boat. You feel the spray of the water on your face, and the wind, and there the sails bellying out. You are racing. Going so fast no one can catch you. But the shore comes up quickly. And suddenly you're there, at the lion's mouth, the dribbling water. And the voice says—

CRAWFORD: "Well done, young man."

MARGUERITE: "Very well done."

CRAWFORD: Yes. *(Pause.)* Yes.

(Lights fade on Marguerite, Crawford while spot stays on Paul. Then out.)

SCENE II

Lights up on Peale sitting in the wingchair in the Bonet parlour. Marguerite enters. Peale stands.

PEALE: At last!

MARGUERITE: What?

PEALE: Now I don't want you to worry—

MARGUERITE: What?!

PEALE: —I called my own physician—

MARGUERITE: —Oh Jaysus Christ! What the feck is it! What the fecking hell has happened now?!

PEALE: Your mother had a spell. She couldn't get her breath. No, no, no. She's alright now. She's resting.

MARGUERITE: Jaysus!

(Marguerite collapses in the chair. Peale goes to comfort her. He would like to touch her but restrains himself from doing anything other than patting her shoulder.)

PEALE: He says it's her lungs. He's recommended bedrest. Two weeks of solid rest. She should be back in tip-top very shortly.

MARGUERITE: Well, isn't that just glorious. This happened during one of your feckin' sessions, I suppose!

PEALE: Marguerite. Language.

MARGUERITE: Feck my language! Christ! How long was it?

PEALE: What?

MARGUERITE: Before she could get her breath?

PEALE: A few minutes. I don't know. A while.

MARGUERITE: Feck! They're getting worse!

PEALE: *(Pause.)* You know, Marguerite, *you* are her principle source of worry. You don't tell anybody where you're going, she needs you here, you're off to god-knows-where. I've not seen you for a month.

MARGUERITE: Oh, well.

PEALE: Are you avoiding me for some reason?

MARGUERITE: You and your feckin' work! It's you that's put us in this mess, it's you that should make good on getting us out!

PEALE: We can talk about this later, Marguerite—

MARGUERITE: No—Frank—let's bloody well talk about it now. We have not even begun to go through this. Now she'll have your feckin' doctor's bill to worry about. Who's goin' to pay for that?

PEALE: I—If there's the slightest appearance of personal involvement, believe me, Marguerite, there are people who would love to see everything, everything your mother and I have worked for, compromised.

MARGUERITE: Well, I don't give a flat piss about 'people'! Who the feck are they? You're the one I'm talking about! And you're compromised already as far as I'm concerned.

PEALE: I understand you're upset—

MARGUERITE: Don't you give me that "it'll all look brighter in the morning" rant, you smug bastard! We don't have the money for this. This could put us right under. On the street.

PEALE: Tell Ada I'll stop round tomorrow to see how she's getting along.

MARGUERITE: Don't bother. All she needs is you in the room upsettin' her. As for me, the sight of you makes me sick!

(Fuming, Peale takes his coat and hat and prepares to exit. He stops and turns back.)

PEALE: I have always thought we were friends, Marguerite. For my part, I always relished our exchanges—sprightly though vaguely perverse as they might have been. I never could have believed you could be so—

MARGUERITE: Well, believe it and feck off, you knobby bastard.

PEALE: My work is with your mother.

MARGUERITE: And she's in my care. And as long as that is the case, and it'll be a feck sight longer than two weeks you can believe it, you keep your bloody distance.

PEALE: What in god's sake is wrong with you?! This is unbelievable! How dare you speak to me that way?!

MARGUERITE: Oh, there we are. "How dare you—" How could I speak to your lordship like that? *(Pause.)* No personal involvement. C'mon! I have a gift alright. You're spot on about that, Frank. I see things alright. You'd be surprised at what I see.

(She touches his hand. After a moment, he pulls it away, agitated. A long pause. Peale looks at her.)

MARGUERITE: Fine! Tell me again how it's all about the work. And then tell me how you're any different from that pack of old lechers come in here for a touch, and a little thrill? Eh?

(A pause.)

PEALE: Well. Perhaps it's best you tell your mother I will not be around again.

MARGUERITE: That's it then. That's what you want? *(Pause.)* Eh?

(Peale looks at her.)

MARGUERITE: Look—Frank. I've got a mother who's so ill, she bloody turns blue trying to get air—It scares the shit out of me. A lot of things scare the shit out of me. *(Pause.)* Sometimes I get scared and then I'm just— stupid. I say a lot of stupid things. Look. I'm not gonna cock it up for you. You have my promise. Right? *(Pause.)* Alright. I'm sorry for everything I said. We appreciate the help you've given us. I do appreciate it. *(Pause.)*

PEALE: Alright. We'll leave it at that. I'll stop 'round in a day or two.

(Peale exits. Marguerite sits in the chair.)

SCENE III

Lights up on Crawford smiling, surrounded by a chaos of letters and maps, and newspaper. He is reading a letter silently. Paul dimly lit in the background, speaks.

PAUL: Wednesday, 1 September 1915, 4:45 PM
      Dear Father,
      Last time I wrote I was in very much the same spot (which naturally

must remain unspecified). Last night we had a delightful time digging a trench which was to bring us closer to our friend, the enemy.

After that, we slept peacefully for a few hours until stand-to. Those damn larks send up such a racket at dawn you can't sleep anyway. Fine for poetry, the lark, but in real life, a bugger-all nuisance. Middle of a barrage, shells whizzing over, earth shuddering away, and in the short pauses between teeth-rattling blasts, what does one hear? Larks. Warbling away overhead, singing their hearts out, having a jolly celebration. As if it's a normal day and, look, there's a lovely field and there's nothing whatever unnatural going on down there. Oh no. What's a few acres of death and destruction mixed in with the regular landscape. They sing and they sing and they sing. As if, I don't know, as if they just fly high enough and sing sweetly enough—well, perhaps you'll think I'm a terrible killjoy, Dad, but it's all any of us can do to keep from shooting *them*.

Anyway, the cake and the little knife you sent are proving most useful. As are the sniper-scopes. I have given one to Humphries who is terrifically keen on it. I hope to try mine out once we're up front, away from the support trenches.

Respectfully And— *(Pause.)*

CRAWFORD AND PAUL: —Affectionately,

PAUL: Your son.

SCENE IV

Marguerite crosses to Crawford's lab, sits. As she speaks, he takes out a pad, and begins to take notes. She does not notice him do this until the finish of her speech.

MARGUERITE: Alright. My fantasy. Two of us sitting on a park bench over by the quay. *(Pause.)* It's a lovely afternoon, sun sparkling on the water, the lawn that sort of green you get when the air is clear and fair. And we watch the people strolling by, nannies with prams, mums and dads with little ones running ahead, young people on their day off. And we notice someone's dog has left the biggest pile right in the middle of the walk. People are wondering what we're laughing at as they miss the shit by millimeters. Finally. Ahhh. The prize goes to this poor young sod, bank clerk type, afternoon out impressin' his gal. There he is, trying so hard to be smart and gallant. And he slaps his bloody great platform in it. You can tell, she's wants to bust up. But she can't because he already feels like such a twit on the grass trying to wipe it off. And there we two are, convulsing. Oh, if looks could kill. Ohhh. I don't have fantasies where I laugh much. You may have noticed. What are you doing?

CRAWFORD: I was taking some notes.

MARGUERITE: It's not a bloody experiment!

CRAWFORD: I'm sorry. *(Pause.)* Professional habit. Hard to break. Why they're—habits, I suppose.

(Long pause. Crawford offers Marguerite some tea. She declines.)

CRAWFORD: I've been going over Paul's things. His letters. His diary. Never had much of a taste for it before. Anyway I've written to his captain. And he's written back. Charming chap. I've found out so much I didn't know.

MARGUERITE: That's nice.

CRAWFORD: I feel—I can't explain it really—it's like discovering a whole new world. It is, I suppose, Paul's world. There are things you described. Like the dancing, for instance—

MARGUERITE: What dancing?

CRAWFORD: Our first meeting, you remember? You had a fantasy of Paul dancing with you—

MARGUERITE: Who said it was Paul?

CRAWFORD: No, no. That's me. Anyway, I said to you my lad had two left feet, never danced as long as I knew him. But I was wrong. Here's a letter from the captain saying he knew Paul, at least on a few occasions, stepped out very lively with a local gal from the village—

MARGUERITE: I need more money, Mr. Crawford. I can't waste my time with this unless I have more money.

CRAWFORD: Oh. Well. Alright. I don't see that should pose a problem. Your mother, is it?

MARGUERITE: Yes.

CRAWFORD: I'm sorry.

MARGUERITE: Yeh.

(A pause.)

CRAWFORD: She's been ill for some time now.

MARGUERITE: They're telling me she should go into hospital.

CRAWFORD: Oh dear.

MARGUERITE: Yeah. So. I've been trying to find a proper job but you know. Not much going.

CRAWFORD: Mr. Peale? Does he—

MARGUERITE: Come by? Why should he? She's too sick to work.

CRAWFORD: Yes, but—

MARGUERITE: —but what?

CRAWFORD: Not like Frank.

MARGUERITE: Why shouldn't he vapour? He's got no involvement with us outside the work.

CRAWFORD: Oh. He was fond of you and your mother. He spoke of you, both of you, with the greatest affection.

MARGUERITE: Yeah. Well. *(Pause.)* Look, you should know, Mr. Crawford, we did have words. He and I.

CRAWFORD: Oh.

MARGUERITE: —it was bad. I've got a filthy temper these days. I really went for him.

CRAWFORD: If you like, I can speak to him—

MARGUERITE: What for? What's he gonna do? Other than blow a fit. He'll think I'm after him again for help. That's what we argued over.

CRAWFORD: He refused?

MARGUERITE: Well, he's right. It's not as if he owes us anything. I mean it's his work. And it could cork that up is how he sees it.

CRAWFORD: Let me speak to him.

MARGUERITE: He won't like this arrangement either. He'll think I used you. Which I admit I have.

CRAWFORD: Used me?

MARGUERITE: For money, of course.

CRAWFORD: I don't look at it that way.

MARGUERITE: Well, that's sweet, Mr. Crawford. But he won't. Trust me. Anyway, I can't carry on with this much longer. Mum's sick and I—I— can't is all. I don't want to. I think we should finish it.

CRAWFORD: But you told me you needed the money.

MARGUERITE: Yeah, well, on second thought, I think it's better if we finish it.

CRAWFORD: But I'd be happy to help you in any way I can, Marguerite. I don't mind at all.

MARGUERITE: Look, I don't want to be indebted to anyone at this point.

CRAWFORD: Oh. *(Pause.)* Well, I shall miss you coming by to visit. I've enjoyed our talks. Quite aside from the—other. Your mother must be very ill if she's to go into hospital. I'll help you. I'd like to.

MARGUERITE: Oh, everything is such a fecking mess! *(She weeps.)*

CRAWFORD: Oh dear dear dear dear dear.

MARGUERITE: She's coughing all the time. Ya can't sleep.

CRAWFORD: You're exhausted.

MARGUERITE: Mr. Crawford, I know you want to help but I can't keep this up—

CRAWFORD: Naturally not. We'll get you some help.

MARGUERITE: No, I mean this! This! Coming here! This whole fantasy world—I can't go on with this—!

CRAWFORD: There, there. We'll take a rest from it. Whatever you need, my dear. Don't think of it now. Later on, when you're rested. Let's talk of it then.

MARGUERITE: I can't! I can't!

CRAWFORD: There now. There now.

(He comforts her. She composes herself. He pours her a cup of tea. She sips it.)

CRAWFORD: There, that's better. You'll see. It'll be alright. We can talk about this other matter—later. When your mother is better.

MARGUERITE: *(Pause.)* I should go. I've got the neighbor looking after Mum—

CRAWFORD: Yes. Yes, of course. And Marguerite. I'll see to the hospital. Don't you worry. She'll get the best.

(Marguerite looks at Crawford, then exits.)

SCENE V

The scene shifts to a hospital room, starkly furnished. We are in Crawford's memory and light and music should reflect that. Paul, back to the audience, is in bathrobe. He peruses a drawing. His uniform is hung up nearby.

PAUL: *(Looking up and seeing Crawford.)* Oh. Dad. Come look.

(Crawford approaches and looks at the drawing over Paul's shoulder.)

PAUL: Know what it is?

CRAWFORD: No idea.

PAUL: Guess?

CRAWFORD: A room? Like this one.

PAUL: C'mon, Dad. Don't be thick. It's a dug-out.

CRAWFORD: Oh. *(Looking at the uniform.)* We must get your uniform cleaned.

PAUL: Dad!

CRAWFORD: What?

PAUL: If you're in infantry, Dad, you have to look the part. The messier the better, the duller the buttons the better. Green's the best. Means you've seen gas. Don't want to look too Kitchener.

CRAWFORD: Oh. No.

PAUL: Anyway, *(Referring to the drawing.)* it's going to be bloody marvelous this. Put the rooms half underground, seven-foot-high, this for ventilation here, drainage trench here, boarded floor and walls, and a wooden roof with wooden supports.

CRAWFORD: It's very well drawn.

PAUL: I have talents you have no notion of.

CRAWFORD: Yes. Paul?

PAUL: Yes?

CRAWFORD: I want you to know how proud of you—

PAUL: —of course, where we're going to find wood, God knows but Humphries will manage it—old Humphries, that man can manage anything!

CRAWFORD: Humphries?

PAUL: Yeah, he thought we should do built-ins, tables and so on but I felt we should be more flexible, things free to move about, in case you want to be able to, ya know, shift the table near the door so you see to write—

CRAWFORD: Humphries—

PAUL: Dad, you're getting old. You remember. Eddie Humphries. The architect chap. I wrote you about him.

CRAWFORD: Yes, I do remember now.

CRAWFORD: Anyhow, he's the architect. And I—I'm the engineer. We're the seniors, the old men of the company. Imagine that, at twenty-two. My hair should be white. Don't look so glum, Dad. Everybody thinks it's all slaughter and chaos over there. But, you know, it's really more— ummmm—like a long picnic. With the occasional shelling. You were right. As usual. Seize your destiny. You were right about the poetry too.

CRAWFORD: You stopped writing.

PAUL: They haven't invented the language that could describe that lot.

CRAWFORD: Oh. *(Pause.)* Good to have a friend at least.

PAUL: Eddie. Oh yeah. Of all my friends, he's the one you'd like. Of course, all my friends, the ones you did meet, are—gone. So, you don't really have a choice. Eddie or nobody.

CRAWFORD: I'm sure I will like Mr. Humphries very much when I meet him.

PAUL: *(Referring to the drawing.)* You see, what keeps happening is that the Germans advance and we retire. And every single time our architectural wonders wind up behind enemy lines. We end up having to shell our best creations, bugger-all. So, what we decided, Eddie and I, was we'd design an indestructible dug-out. Don't know if we'll get the opportunity to build the damn thing. But it's something to do.

CRAWFORD: The doctor says the leg's healing nicely.

PAUL: *(Nasty.)* "Healing nicely." Is that what that poofy bastard says? *(Calm.)* Well, that's a good thing. It feels better. And I get around nicely with the cane. Can't wait to get out of this shit-hole.

CRAWFORD: You don't have to go back, if you don't want to, you know.

PAUL: Oh, and how is that?

CRAWFORD: Well. I've got some contacts. And arrangements can be made—

PAUL: Oh, good ol' Dad! Still writing letters! Well, not to worry. Your son is doing well. His leg is doing well. Everything is going wonderfully. What's the saying? "If it wasn't for the unpleasant sights one is liable to see, war would be a most interesting and pleasant affair—"

CRAWFORD: —that's just it, Paul. I don't think you are.

PAUL: What's that?

CRAWFORD: I don't think you are doing well. As well as you'd like to think.

PAUL: Oh? *(Angry.)* The bloody *doctor* says I'm fine!

CRAWFORD: He says your leg is doing fine.

PAUL: Something else then is it?

CRAWFORD: That's right.

PAUL: Oh. Oh.

CRAWFORD: You're not well in your mind.

PAUL: My mind. My mind? My mind is perfectly well, thank you.

CRAWFORD: I think you need more of a rest. You've been out there for months. I want you to—come home with me.

PAUL: No, no, I'm not doing that.

CRAWFORD: There's a position in Munitions.

PAUL: A desk job. Oh, won't that be jolly. Leave all my chaps out there. While I'm sitting here. Diddling papers. Little rubber stamp. Chunk-chunk. Chunk-chunk. Sounds like fun. Sounds like it's right up my alley.

CRAWFORD: You have to have some rest, Paul.

PAUL: No! I bloody well said no! There's nothing wrong with my mind other than the fact that you still have your own bloody plans for my future which you are determined to foist on me whether I bloody well agree with them or not! "Arrangements can be made—" Jesus!

CRAWFORD: Eddie Humphries, Paul.

> *(A pause.)*

CRAWFORD: You did write me about him. Many times. In your last letter before your leave, you wrote me he'd been killed. That he was dead. Did you hear what I said, Paul?

> *(Paul is silent. A pause.)*

PAUL: Well. I forgot. Ha ha. Oh, c'm a long, Dad. Where's ya sense of humour? You wouldn't last out there. You don't like to laugh.

CRAWFORD: He died horribly you said. Believe me, son, you're not ready to go back.

PAUL: Stop telling me what I'm bloody well not good for again!

CRAWFORD: Alright, alright. Lower your voice.

PAUL: *(Sotto voce.)* There's nothing wrong with my mind. How could you know? I know more than you ever will. Who are you, anyway? Some stinking little academic scientist toiling away in a lab. Your little bottles and flywheels and mirrors. What a safe little world, you've carved out for yourself! Meanwhile, my lads are being blasted to fragments, sacrificed so that you lot— *(Of the uniform.)* You want to know why I'm not having it cleaned, Dad. The real reason? See this? That was left by Eddie Humphries' brains.

CRAWFORD: *(Sotto voce.)* Stop it! Stop it.

> *(Paul weeps.)*

CRAWFORD: I'll come back tomorrow, lad. We'll sort this out, have another think, shall we? No rush in deciding. *(Crawford embraces Paul.)*

PAUL: *(Pulling away.)* And that's the whole of it is it? Is that all you have to say? Pull yourself together, keep your voice down, don't embarrass us? That's it, is it? Is it? Is that it? Is it? Is that it? Is it? That's all of it, is it? Is it? You were always a stupid bastard! Always! I'd like to bloody well kill you!

> *(Paul wads the dug-out drawing up and throws it at Crawford, hitting him. He turns abruptly and sits on the bed, his back to Crawford and to us. He is bent over, a humped, anguished figure, ranting. Crawford stands to one side.)*

PAUL: Well, what have you to say for yourself? That's a bloody fine thing. A bloody fine thing. A bloody bloody fine thing. You make me sick, you stupid bastards, stupid, stupid, stupid, stupid bastards.

> *(A shocked silence. Crawford is paralyzed. Paul begins to sob quietly, his back still turned to us. A moment or two passes, then, without us seeing his face*

Paul holds out his hand, perhaps it is to steady himself, perhaps it is a plea to Crawford. Crawford backs away out of the room as lights down.)

SCENE VI

The window opens, and a wind scatters the papers in Crawford's lab. The light is intense and the beginning of the scene should have a slightly surreal feeling to it. Peale enters and stands by Crawford with his hand on his shoulder. Marguerite appears, a black armband on her sleeve.

CRAWFORD: You see, my dear, Frank wasn't angry. Were you, Frank? He understood perfectly—

PEALE: —George has been telling me—

CRAWFORD: —I hope you're not angry, Marguerite. I know I promised—

PEALE: —I always knew you had a talent, Marguerite—

CRAWFORD: Is everything alright?

PEALE: —if you'd prefer to work only with George, I'll understand—

CRAWFORD: We're terribly sorry about your mother.

(Lights change abruptly.)

MARGUERITE: She was a cow. *(Pause.)* But I'll miss her. We should have no illusions about those we care for. Or as few as we can manage, anyway.

PEALE: Your mother and I were friends.

MARGUERITE: And she thought highly of you. Right up to the last gasp, she fretted how she looked in case you came by. Mr. Crawford, on the other hand, is not so concerned with appearances. You were very kind, Mr. Crawford. Everyone did their best. She was always weak-chested. It's in the family. Anyway. She had a right knobby send-off. Looked nice, didn't she?

CRAWFORD: Lovely, yes.

MARGUERITE: What money gives you. Much better than the funeral I could have given her.

PEALE: George, you paid for the funeral?

MARGUERITE: And the doctors. And her medicines. And the hospital.

PEALE: George!

MARGUERITE: Mr. Crawford is a kind and generous individual. Like I said, he's not worried about how things look.

CRAWFORD: I—I felt it was right, Frank.

PEALE: Well. You've been working hard, Marguerite. I had no idea.

MARGUERITE: Don't underestimate the skanky depths the lower classes will descend to in order to get some lucre.

PEALE: That's not what I meant!

MARGUERITE: Oh, I'm shattered. Just shattered. You know, I could use a good holiday. Week or two. Somewhere where there's sun. *(Pause.)* Italy would be nice.

CRAWFORD: Very well, my dear. You shall have it.

PEALE: George! Have you gone insane?

MARGUERITE: Thank you, Mr. Crawford. You're a real gentleman, there's no doubt about that. So, Frank. Do you know how we work—have you filled him in, Mr. Crawford? I tell Mr. Crawford my fantasies. None of this hocus-pocus-I'm-gonna-chase-you-around-make-sure-you're-not-cheating-and-write-down-every-word-and-test-ya-and-drive-ya-to-the-poorhouse-if you-get-it-wrong. Our relationship, Frank, is one of trust. I tell him strict honest fantasies. And he—Mr. Crawford—enjoys them, and more than that, he finds meaning in them. And then I get paid.

CRAWFORD: Actually, that is how we work.

PEALE: You have gone insane.

MARGUERITE: He's told you about the photograph? The dancing? All the other "correlations?"

PEALE: Yes.

MARGUERITE: You were suitably impressed when you walked in here.

PEALE: You've been drinking.

MARGUERITE: Two brandies. Me mum is dead. I'm entitled.

CRAWFORD: Don't upset her, Frank.

PEALE: Upset *her?!*

MARGUERITE: That's right. I'm temperamental. Talented people often are.

PEALE: I've seen enough.

MARGUERITE: You've seen nothing! *(Pause.)* C'mon, Frank. You want to see it firsthand. Sure you do.

CRAWFORD: Are you up to it, my dear?

MARGUERITE: Oh, I'm up to it.

(Though angry, Peale is curious. He hesitates, then sits.)

MARGUERITE: There we are. Everybody all cosy?

(Marguerite settles in. Lights change.)

MARGUERITE: What shall it be today? Let's see. My fantasy is—dark corridors. Smelling of damp and mold. Oh, it's a horrible room. Fallen plaster in bits. A room with old wallpaper. Stained. Peeling. Huge white roses. At least, they were white at one time. Squint at 'em long enough, get up close to 'em, they turn into faces.

(A worn, anguished, disoriented Paul in uniform, the Paul seen at the end of Act I, walks with his cane through the open window.)

MARGUERITE: Playin' with me doll in the dark room. The sobbing starts, the shrieking. Don't turn 'round. Don't. So I concentrate on the faces.

PAUL: They talk to me. Brown skulls in a trench wall. Shard of bone in trickling earth. Who was I, they ask? Did I love someone? Did I look forward to a cup of tea, a wash? There's a bugger. Thirty yards away. Boche, Naked, washing himself.

MARGUERITE: The faces speak.

PAUL: He's just having a wash. You can keep walking.

MARGUERITE: Keep walking.

PAUL: Why not try 'em out. Gift from dad, the scopes. Good old dad. There he is.

MARGUERITE: The sun glinting off his blond hair. Sheet of water running off his head, his white skin. Like the belly of a fish. They whisper.

PAUL: The skulls in the trenches.

MARGUERITE: Walk on.

PAUL: Some of them say—

MARGUERITE: For Christ's sake, walk on.

PAUL: A nice wash. Another cup of tea. The sun on our shoulders. We would like to feel those things. I hear them. Shut up, for godsakes, shut up!

MARGUERITE: Look at that. It's as though I'm right up close. Right next to him. I can see his face. How content he looks.

PAUL: Sharp push against my shoulder. What have I—the bucket—

MARGUERITE: —falls. Dot of crimson on the forehead. Blur of white limbs, sliding, sliding, sliding. Out of my sights.

PAUL: Ah gawd!

MARGUERITE: For feck's sake, stop that crying! Don't turn round. They're in the darkness, sharing their sorrow. In the darkness.

(Paul vanishes. Marguerite comes out of the trance.)

CRAWFORD: I gave him those sights.

PEALE: *(Excited.)* And he killed a Boche with 'em. That could be checked. Paul's captain, he might remember.

MARGUERITE: *(To Peale.)* So. What do you think?

PEALE: Good. Very good. What is amazing is the detail. Ada, gifted as she was, had trouble with that.

MARGUERITE: I'm sorry, Mr. Crawford.

(Crawford looks at her. He is upset by what he has heard.)

PEALE: Can we have another go?

MARGUERITE: Mr. Crawford?

CRAWFORD: What? Oh. If you feel up to it?

MARGUERITE: I don't have to.

CRAWFORD: Frank would like you to.

MARGUERITE: *(Pause.)* This is the last.

(Again, the lights change, music up, more ominous now. Marguerite in trance. Paul again, and this time, it's a replay of the action of the end of Act I. He limps forward with the cane, disoriented. Loud city sounds. He tries to light the cigarette but can't. Marguerite rises and lights it for him.)

MARGUERITE: He's come out of hospital. That's obvious.

CRAWFORD: Hospital.

MARGUERITE: He was there. Put on his uniform and walked out. No one tried to stop him. No one even saw him. Already a ghost. Shaking like the palsy.

PAUL: People staring ahead, pushing past.

(Marguerite takes his arm.)

MARGUERITE: God knows, she doesn't need the bother. But he's in the uniform of an officer. A subaltern. And he has a nice face. A kind face. She could leave him here. Somebody would come. Copper maybe. Take him back.

PAUL: The next thing he's aware of—

MARGUERITE: Dank, nasty little room, it was—but what she can afford. She's run away. For the moment anyway. And to what, another nasty little room smelling of sweat and gas. No heat. She sneaks him up the stairs.

PAUL: Cold, so cold.

MARGUERITE: In under the covers, only way to get warm, huddled together like children. Kind of funny. And they lay there. He relaxes. They sleep. Like children. They go in and out of sleep. All afternoon. 'Til the sun goes down through the curtains.

PAUL: She started to talk, I dunno about what—

MARGUERITE: How it is she lives, her dreams. How she's dying for something to happen. It's so feckin' boring where she is.

PAUL: Not really listening, but it's nice—just having a voice, a woman's voice talk to you. Telling you things. She has a nice voice. Soothing. She wanted to know about me. I couldn't answer her.

MARGUERITE: So I told him, I says, you're not daft, you know. You can too remember. Why don't you try. Tell me everything you can remember.

PAUL: Comes very hard. But she made me start when I was little, and things came. Happy times, you know? I thought I'd lost them. But they were there. They were there. The boat, and our house in the country. And how it used to be. Everyday, some new thing. Something wonderful. She kept on. Wouldn't be satisfied, had to have it all. Know everything. So I told her. The worst of it, I told her. About Humphries. I remember being furious, just furious. You know. At her. At everybody. How could you not go back. She didn't understand. There's only one place you can go and that's—to your mates—She didn't like hearing that. None of 'em do. Bastards—I wanted to throttle her, tear at her—scare the hell out of her—But she came at me there, not frightened at all. And she kissed me—

(Light intensifies on Marguerite and Paul. She kisses Paul. He kisses her back.)

MARGUERITE: He told her about the Boche. His friends. The hospital and his dad. A lot about his dad. His dad couldn't wait to get out the room. Don't blame him. Anyone'd have done the same.

PAUL: So he thought he'd leave the hospital and go back. On his own. Nothing left here.

MARGUERITE: But I said, you stupid bugger. *I'm* here. I'm here. We can have a life. Can you see it? Just us two. Great times. A lark. Like now. I was fifteen. And then, I come back one day, he's cleared out. Lasted a week. And he was gone.

(Paul vanishes. Lights change. Marguerite looks at Crawford and Peale.)

PEALE: You were there.

CRAWFORD: These were fantasies.

MARGUERITE: No. No, Mr. Crawford.

CRAWFORD: Oh god.

MARGUERITE: I'm sorry.

PEALE: You should be!

MARGUERITE: Shut up! I'm sorry, Mr. Crawford. I didn't mean to lie to you. You wanted it so badly—

PEALE: And the money.

MARGUERITE: And the money.

CRAWFORD: He showed you the photograph.

MARGUERITE: Yeah. Jaysus! I nearly fell over when you showed it to me. And you, his father. He never gave me his right bloody name. I didn't know. Really.

PEALE: Bloody cruel thing to do!

CRAWFORD: Oh, shut up, Frank! He thought I abandoned him. I did too.

MARGUERITE: He was ashamed of himself, of how he acted in the hospital. Don't you see? He thought the world of you, Mr. Crawford. Why else would he tell me all that? Why would his every happy memory have you in it?
(Silence. Crawford puts his head into his hands. A long pause. Marguerite looks away, Peale shakes his head.)

MARGUERITE: You're a fine one to be judging me.

PEALE: Who said I was?

MARGUERITE: That smug look on your face. You're a fine one. Not one feckin' visit you could manage.

PEALE: I did see her!

MARGUERITE: In her coffin, you liar!

PEALE: I saw her that morning. It was early.

MARGUERITE: And where was I then?

PEALE: I didn't want you to see me.
(Pause.)

MARGUERITE: So. You saw her.

PEALE: I apologized for not seeing her.

MARGUERITE: She forgave you. I'm sure.

PEALE: George?

CRAWFORD: Eh?

PEALE: How are you?

CRAWFORD: I'm fine, thanks, Frank.

PEALE: Well, I'll be going.

MARGUERITE: Yeh. Do that.

PEALE: Will you be alright, George?

CRAWFORD: It's all right, Frank. You go on. *(Looking at him.)* Go on. It's alright.
(Peale with some hesitation, exits.)

MARGUERITE: I could use a drink.
(Crawford is amused. Marguerite understands. This is where they came in.)

MARGUERITE: Typical, eh? Can't find one to save your life.

CRAWFORD: He's not a bad chap, Marguerite. *(Pause.)* And we can all use a little forgiveness. *(Pause.)* Thank you for being kind to my son.
(Marguerite stays silent. She wanders the room. She turns on the prototype radio. Loud static. Crawford does not react. Suddenly, music, sad and beautiful, comes through. Crawford hears it, looks up. It works after all. He and Marguerite share a smile.)

MARGUERITE: You know, I made that bit up about him dancing.
(Lights down.)

SCENE VII

Music. Lights change. Crawford rises, comes downstage, into a spot, taking a letter from his pocket.

CRAWFORD: I gave Marguerite her holiday in Italy. I don't know if she'll see Frank again. I think she will. I hope she does.

The captain wrote me that Paul had been buried on the right of the Ypres-Menin Road, just past where the Zonebecke Rail cuts across. Buried in a garden adjoining a ruined farmhouse. He writes, *(Reading.)* "It is well enclosed by hedges and your son's grave is under some tall trees that stand in the garden. His is the first cross on the far right of the cemetery garden."

He writes "If you can get hold of Sheet 28, Belgium 1/40,000, the reference is I.16. b.2. Any soldier can tell you how to read it." So I did. I got hold of the map and I got hold of a soldier, and armed with directions, I went to Belgium. Hired a driver and a wreck of a touring car. After several days and many automotive adventures, we came at last to the Ypres-Menin Road. The road winds 'round the countryside. It is farm country, beautiful because no one is allowed to farm it. Too many accidents from unexploded shells. Still a No-Man's Land.

And on that final hill before our destination—the bloody car broke down naturally. So I took the packed lunch and left the driver to fiddle with the thing and walked the last leg myself. It was a lovely day, the slight breeze through what is left of one's hair, the hot arm of the sun on your shoulders. And I looked at this—battlefield. You might pick out some craters, a bit of wire. But all has become waving grass, a blaze of wildflowers and scarlet poppies.

I wondered how much of the farmhouse would remain. I reached the top of the hill. There I was, on the right of the Ypres-Menin Road just past where the Zonebecke Rail cuts across. Where my son, Paul, was buried. *(Light has intensified on Crawford. The floor and walls around him, are illuminated with small crosses.)*

CRAWFORD: No sign of a farmhouse anywhere. No trees or hedges. Nothing except rolling hills, wildflowers, red poppies. And in every direction, on every hillside reaching away to the horizon were crosses. Identical. White. Crosses.

A lark sang overhead.

I sat on the edge of the road—ate my lunch in the sun. I had not realized how hungry I was. The lark's song floated above, the breeze sighed in the grass. And for the first time, I knew this is what it came to. This is what it was. All illusion and delusion, all hypothesis and speculation, all of it ended here and no matter what we believe, we should try to know that always.

I ate my lunch. It tasted wonderfully. And everything was alright. Everything was quite all right.

(The lights dim slowly on Crawford, Paul appears for a brief moment. Blackout.)

END OF PLAY

GIVE ME SHELTER

by Wendy Weiner

THE AUTHOR

Wendy Weiner is the author of the plays *Liquid Identity* and *My Gay Neighbor* and the solo pieces *Defying Freud* and *Give Me Shelter*. *Give Me Shelter* premiered at the New York Fringe Festival and subsequent "Best of the Fringe" Festival, and went on to runs at Surf Reality and the San Francisco Fringe Festival, where it was again chosen "Best of the Fringe."

Wendy has performed her own work in New York City at Dixon Place, HERE, NADA, One Dream Theater, Surf Reality, Caroline's Comedy Club, and 46 Walker Street. She has also performed at La Mama Experimental Theater Club and at various venues with Avalon Theatre Company and the Actors Theatre of Manhattan.

An affiliated artist of the Obie Award-winning theater company New Georges, Wendy wrote and performed with their comedy group, Kinda Personal, for four years. She has also written articles published in *American Theatre* magazine, *Mademoiselle,* and *FYI,* the journal of the New York Foundation for the Arts.

AUTHOR'S NOTE

I've never really liked the term "one-woman show." It implies a solitary state that is anathema to what I love about theater. Theater involves a group of people (and in our hyper cyber hooked-up world, it seems to me anything that gathers live people in a room is somewhat revolutionary). It involves collaboration—between performer and audience, performer and technical people, and in my case, though not the case of all solo performers, performer and director.

My director, Julie Kramer, guided both the writing and performing of *Give Me Shelter* from its inception. It was magical to me that, during rehearsals, she often explained things to me about my own text that I didn't understand. It was as if she was the bridge between the part of me that wrote the piece and the part that came to it simply as an actor approaching a piece of new text.

But maybe Julie summed it up best when, during the tech of my solo show *Defying Freud,* she looked around the theater—at the stage manager setting lights, the assistant stage manager cueing up sound tapes, the director of the video insert working with the visual artist who designed the video projector—laughed, and said "One-woman show, my ass."

I would also like to thank Aaron Beall, Artistic Director of the fertile and vibrant Lower East Side theater Todo con Nada, who presented the first play I ever wrote—and the second, and the third.

ORIGINAL PRODUCTION

Give Me Shelter, developed with and directed by Julie Kramer, was first presented at New York's Surf Reality by New Georges and The New York International Fringe Festival, a production of The Present Company, Inc. Wendy Weiner played all the roles; the lights were designed by Kristina Kloss; the stage manager was Kimmarie Bowens; the assistant stage manager was Valda Lake.

WELCOME TO NEW YORK!

A map and biased glossary to New York City neighborhoods

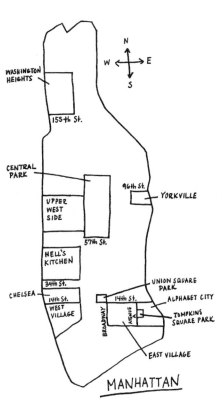

MANHATTAN

ALPHABET CITY: Encompasses Avenues A, B, C and D. Until the last few years, it was known as a place of drug deals and homeless people's bonfires—and a place that young people and artists could afford to live. Now quickly being gentrified, rents have risen sky-high.

CHELSEA: The West 20s and early 30s. Pretty, with historical district and tree-lined streets.

EAST VILLAGE: East of Broadway, south of 14th St. Ethnically diverse area with a lot of young people. Very trendy and still cool, but gentrified; where the Anarchy Cafe used to be, there's now a McDonald's.

HELL'S KITCHEN: Area west of Ninth Avenue, between 34th and 59th Streets. The name tells you that, like Alphabet City, this area used to be considered rough, but due to many factors—including Disney taking over 42nd Street—its reputation is quickly changing.

TOMPKINS SQUARE PARK: Park in Alphabet City. Always thriving with every imaginable form of human life: t'ai ch'i students, chess players, witches, sunbathers, drummers, punks, the elderly. Site of 1991 riots when police ousted the homeless people living there.

UNION SQUARE AREA: Safe, centrally located area a little north of the Village.

UPPER WEST SIDE: Area west of Central Park, home to the characters on *Seinfeld* and *Mad About You*. Very yuppy, very expensive, very Starbuck's.

WASHINGTON HEIGHTS: West area north of 155th Street. A place where you can still get affordable apartments, in part because it's far from Central Manhattan.

WEST VILLAGE: Pretty, European-looking, one of the only areas of New York where the streets aren't in a grid. Very expensive.

YORKVILLE: Still-affordable area very far east on the Upper East Side, not near much public transportation.

Note: Whenever a * appears in the script, that is an acting note indicating that that the unseen character has spoken.

This voiceover plays in darkness. Phone rings.

MALE VOICE: Hi, you've reached the home of Jim,

FEMALE VOICE: Karen, and *(Other female voice.)* Julie. *(All together.)* Please leave us a message.

MALE VOICE: If you're calling about the apartment share that was advertised in the *Village Voice,* the room has been taken. Thanks. Bye.
(Phone rings.)

FEMALE VOICE: *(Friendly.)* Hello! *(Cautious.)* Who is this? *(Abrupt, rude.)* Yeah, it's taken.
(In building pace: ring.)

VOICE: It's taken.
(Ring.)

VOICE: Taken.
(Ring.)

VOICE: Taken!
(Ring.)

FEMALE VOICE: *(Annoyed.)* Hello, where have you been? *(Laughs.)* Oh, sorry, I thought you were someone else. * Yeah, we're still lookin' for a roommate. You wanna come by tomorrow, like noon? * Cool. Catch you later.
(Dial tone segues into very loud rock music which plays into next scene.)

JEWEL, ALPHABET CITY

Lights come up on Jewel, a funky, downtown, woman in her twenties. She is rolling a joint, then looks up and goes over to an imaginary door facing the audience. She opens the door.

JEWEL: Hey, man, come on in. *(Goes to her boombox, turns the music off.)* Sorry. Hey, are you here to check out the squat? * Cool, cool. Sorry, man, don't mean to be paranoid, but this Jehovah's Witness chick came here about half an hour ago and I let her in 'cause I thought she was you. Those people bug me out, man. I thought I would never get her to leave.

But, anyway, hi. Sorry, my mind's... *(She sits in a chair.)* Sit down. * On the floor, wherever. I'm Jewel. You're... * Diana, right. Cool. Where you from? * *(Shudders.)* What a fucking nightmare. Ron, the guy who's leaving here, is from California. * No way, man. No way. I mean, it's like my boyfriend always says to me—want some? *(Pot.)* * No? That's cool. He says, Jewel, there's like only one thing you can be sure of, right, and that's that the ground's underneath your feet...But in California, fuck, you wake up, pots are flyin', your legs are over your head, the ground buckles up, your linoleum's staring you in the face. I'd rather risk it here, you know?...You ever been mugged? * Me neither. *(Holds pot out again.)* * No? That's cool.

Me? I'm from New York. * Naw, not Manhattan. Outside Manhattan. * No, not the boroughs...New Jersey. OK, let me show you the squat, that's why you're here, right, not to stare at my big tits.

Oh, hey, hey hey hey, how did you hear about us? * The guy at Limbo, which guy? * Oh oh yeah yeah yeah, Romé, the guy with the nose ring, yeah he's a friend of my boyfriend's. I met my boyfriend at Limbo. Yeah, it's like everything begins and ends there, right?

* No. A guidebook? No way. You found out about Limbo in a fucking tour book? SHIT! That *kills* me man because I saw these fucking tourists with those, what do you call them, yeah! fanny packs right?, walking up and down Avenue A the other day! It's like why bother, man? Why fucking bother? Avenue A. It's like where do we move now? Amsterdam?

Sorry. OK, so, this is where Tap and I sleep. Tapio, that's my boyfriend. Did I tell you about him? * Oh, right, right. You want to see a picture? *(Picks up picture, hands it to Diana.)* Isn't that cool? This is, it's from *Details* when they did the profile on squats. * Yeah, that's him. Isn't he hot? He's gotten fan mail from this. It's so fucking weird to have a boyfriend that's prettier than you, especially in this neighborhood. 'Cause we'll be like walking down the street and the guys are looking at him and the girls are looking at him and I'm like hello? It's like I'm not even there. But yeah, he's really hot. *(Places picture back carefully.)*

Over there, that's where Cam and Rikki crash. They're weird, man. * I don't know, they're lovers, but...they don't fuck. Whatever, that's cool.

And Tap's mom crashes— * yeah! She lives here, isn't that a trip? She is so cool, though. She was a hooker when the East Village was like Alphabet City and Alphabet City was like…whoa. And I don't know 'cause I never had—well no I was gonna say I never had a mom but that's not true, but it's just that my mom, she's not she's not like a person. But Tap's mom, you can talk to her about anything.

And this whole place is like that. It's a total community, us against them, right? Fuck the pigs. Fuck *Rent*. Fuck TV, the pig's way of getting into us everyday, right? This is the real thing, life, everyday shit.

Sorry. So this is the shower and the kitchen. Yeah, it's OK. Oh, and you know what's cool? Cam *(Laughs.)* Cam, you got to check him out when he's taking a shower. This guy has got the fucking biggest dick I've ever seen in my life. * No, it's a scarf—he could throw it over his shoulder. And he's not even using it, if you know what I mean. It's like this expanse of natural resources just going to waste. Not that I could accommodate him. Fuck, this inn is closed. No vacancies available, ya know? I got limits.

Oh, but don't let Rikki catch you checking Cam out. He'll fucking pull a knife on you. * Oh, it's a chemical thing, flares up, then dies down.

(Sound of ice cream truck.) Man, do you hear that? Wherever that sound is, Tap is. *(Goes to window, looks at street, sees him.)* Yep. *(Opens up window, yells out.)* Tap! TAAAPPPPP! What are you doing, man? *(Laughs.)* This is the chick who's looking at the place. * I don't know! *(Turns to Diana.)* Do you like it? *(Turns back to Tap.)* Hey! Hey! Catch you later. *(Closes window.)* That guy…he's, like, all id, you know?

…So, that's the place…So, what do you do? * Bike messenger? No, man, what do you *want* to do? * I hear where you're coming from. * Me, I'm, I don't know, I hate labels, but I guess I do performance art. * Yeah. Tap's my director. We're working on this piece, "Kentucky Fucking Chicken." It's like all about how fucked up our world is; there's like deforestation and dehumanization and de-everything, you know, and, no!—it's like what I said about TV before, how, how this poison seeps in and then it, just…comes out. Yeah.

Well listen, I go off vibes from people and you've got a good vibe. * No, you really do. So, if you want to crash here, that's cool. *** *(Laughs.)* Oh man, I didn't expect this kind of reaction. It's like you're Miss America or something. * No, it's cool, it's cool!

OK. Uh, OK. So, I don't know, we can do this now or later, I really don't care, but I'll need a check for six hundred. That's a month's rent. I don't need a security deposit or— * what? Free? No man, it's not free.

Free?! Look at this place, we got the whole floor. * Nonono, six hundred each. Each.

    * It is a squat. I don't get where you're coming from honestly. * Well yeah, technically technically you don't pay for a squat but there aren't any squats like *that* left. That's more like being homeless. * *(Disappointed.)* No, no it's cool. You're from out of town.

    Listen, you should come to my show anyway. Wait wait wait I have a flyer. "Kentucky Fucking Chicken," Tuesday, Limbo, eight o'clock. * Yeah? Cool. Oh, and wait, take this *(Picks up newspaper from the floor.) The Village Voice.* It's got like the Koran of classified ads. * No problem. Catch you later.

KATIE, UNION SQUARE

Slide appears of ad from Village Voice:
      Women's residency. Union Square Area.
      $150 a week for single room. Meals provided.
      No visitors, no phone, no smoking, no men.

(Lights come up on Katie, a woman in her late twenties. She is checking items off a list.)

KATIE: Bags packed, key returned, post office notified. *(She looks up.)* Aaaagh! Hello. I didn't hear you knock. * Oh, oh, oh, you're the girl who's moving in here. No, no, they did tell me, I just completely forgot. I have so much on my mind.

    I'm getting married today. * City Hall. I am so happy, so thrilled, so ecstatic, to be leaving this place. * Why? Why? Shared showers, shared kitchen, no visitors, no phone, meals that are—indescribable. To sum, the entire experience has made me want to die.

    What's your name? * Diana! Oh, how exquisite. I've always wanted a name like that. * Katie. Not even Katherine, which has some dignity. Katie. It signifies nothing. It refers to nothing. But Diana! Mmmm. * No, really? You don't know where the name Diana comes from? You really should.

    In Roman mythology, Diana was the virgin goddess of the hunt. She was a very solitary goddess, except for the animals which always surrounded her. Perhaps the most seminal story about Diana recounts an incident where she was bathing naked in a mountain stream, as she was wont to do. A young hunter, Acteaon, came upon her and she was just so extraordinary that he stood there watching. Diana looks up, sees him, and grows instantly enraged. She dips her hands into the water, showers him with a few drops, and he is instantly transformed into a deer. Ultimately, he is hunted down and killed by his own pack of hounds.

* Sad? Hmm. I've always rather liked that ending. I mean, ontologically speaking, if I may, this story is merely an ancient example of the oppression of the male gaze. Actaeon is no different than the men on our city streets who feel entitled to yell out such epithets as "Hey, sugar mama," "Nice butt," "I'm just a baby, I want to suck your tittie." *(Pause.)* But, I digress. It's a lovely name.

* Oh, so you're new to the city? Mm-hmm. Yes, you look it. Sort of that deer caught in the headlights look. Or that Actaeon-caught-at-the-pool look. *(Laughs at her own joke.)* Well, welcome! You're going to adore the city. Well, most of it. There are places you shouldn't go. Hell's Kitchen, Alphabet City, Washington Heights. You never want to go too far east or too far west—or to any of the boroughs. Otherwise, you'll be fine.

Where are you from? * You. Are. Joking. Really. God, I thought that was just a setting for Jim Jarmusch films. So, what's brought you here? Are you on some sort of budget vacation?

* Oh, you're staying here while you look for an apartment? * Hmm. * No, no, no, I just hope you find a place soon. You know they don't let you stay for more than a month. * Mmm-hmmm. It's a new rule. *(Laughs.)* But then, that's not my problem!

* Oh, no, no ring. No, it's not quite like that. See, god, it's all happened so fast; this was just last week. Ron and I were sitting in Loeb— * Hmm? Oh, Loeb Student Center. I'm matriculating at NYU. PhD, Mythopoetic Comparative Anthropology. * *(Smugly.)* Thanks.

Anyway, we're sort of moaning about our lives. He's living in this nightmare dungeon over on Avenue B with god knows how many other people, and I'm—well, look around you, when we overhear this woman saying how she just got married and moved in with her husband to Married Student Housing. Well, here comes the bride!

* Oh, no. I don't even know that he likes women, honestly. Who cares? I'm getting a room, a kitchen, a bathtub!

Well, I'd best be going. *(Looks around room.)* What can I say? Good luck.

BULL, 14TH STREET

Slide of newspaper ad: it's a crow with an open beak. Inside the beak is writ-ten the words "Crowman Realty." Lights come up on Bull, a man in his early thirties. He talks very quickly and with a Brooklyn accent.

BULL: Hello, Diana, and welcome to Crowman Realty where we've got some-thing to crow about. Badabing, badabang. I'm Bull *(Vigorous hand-shake.)* and yes, Bull is my Christian name, not a nickname, nothing to do with my impeccable reputation as the only honest realtor in our fine jewel of a city.

Now, what has brought you to our office today? * Mm-hmm. Mm-hmm. The ad for the $600 studio in the West Village. Beautiful apart-ment, all right? Sun-drenched, eat-in kitchen, working fireplace, not available. * It means, it's taken. Apartments like that—they're gone yes-terday. It's like puttin' a steak down in front of a group of hungry orphans. Before I can even put it on the barbecue, it's gone. Now, what I *do* have is a gorgeous studio a bit further west, only $1200. *

Mm-hmm. All right, all right, you need a lower price range. Have you thought about Brooklyn? * No, no, you want to keep your search to Manhattan, let's see what we got. Ah! Here. If you like the West Village, you might be interested in Yorkville. * Hmm? Well, no, the neighbor-hoods are quite different, but they *are* both in Manhattan and that's what you're looking for, right? Now, in Yorkville, I got what we call a "half-studio" for only $1150. *

Look, I am sensing some attitude here. Did you read the *New York Times* magazine last May? I said—did you read the *New York Times* mag-azine last May? *(Holds up a magazine with the words "Why It's So Hard to Rent an Apartment" on the cover.)* Read it! Then maybe you'll have some idea what we're up against.

(Suddenly beats his chest and gives out a long Tarzan yell.) I'm a war-rior, OK? That's how I see myself. An urban warrior in the most fero-cious jungle of a market that exists, has existed, and God willing, ever *will* exist. And I need to know that you're a warrior too. I can not have a client who's gonna drop dead halfway through—ooh, it's hot! ooh, the mosquitos! ooh, I'm getting blisters—is that an anaconda? Aaahhh! And then, I have to haul your dead-weight carcass out of the jungle. Dead

weight is heavy, my friend…Are you a warrior? * Louder! Are you a warrior? *(Beats chest and yells again.)*

(Instantly business-like.) All right, how much is your annual salary? * You are joking with me, right? My nephew, who is seven years old, earns more than that in allowance. That, I can tell you right now, is gonna be a problem. See, you should be making ten times the amount of your yearly rent. That's the kind of figures I'm looking for.

All right, no salary to speak of. How about your credit? * Your *credit?* Do you have outstanding bills that you haven't gotten around to paying? Are there people looking for you who might want to outfit you with some concrete boots government-style? * All right. And who will be serving as your guarantor in the tri-state area? * No one? No one at all? A cousin, an aunt, an ex-boyfriend, someone your grandma knew from her heyday in the forties? *

You, my friend, are out of luck. Badabing, badabang. I'll be straight with you. I'm the best there is. Studios, one bedrooms, two bedrooms, I got everything from the charming artist's garret on the Bowery to the Central Park penthouse with wraparound views. But with these stats, there's not a damn thing I can do for you. Not one damn thing.

(Pause. He looks at Diana uncomfortably, then takes some Kleenex from a pocket and holds it out to her.) Tissue? *(Slaps hands together, checks watch. Standing up.)* OK, kid. I got a 3:30.

LOUISE, UPPER WEST SIDE

Slide of Village Voice ad:
> Upper West Side. F to share w/F.
> Private room w/closet space.
> $600/month + utilities.

(Lights up on Louise, a nineteen-year-old with a northern British accent and a very sunny personality. She is peering down a staircase.)

LOUISE: *(Yelling down the stairs.)* Hello, are you Diana? * Yeah, it's up here. Number fourteen. *(Waits for quite a while as Diana climbs the stairs.)* Quite a hike, right? I'm Louise. * Yeah, you talked to Karen on the phone, but she had to go out for a bit so I'll show you around the place.

Come on in. *(Walks in, then turns around quickly.)* Ooh, yeah, just watch for the crucifix above the door. * I know, that thing's a bit of a health hazard.

* Yeah, Karen owns the place, right. I've just been staying in the room that's coming vacant. Oh, don't lean. Right, it's just that that scroll was hand-given to her by some pope or priest or whatever and, trust me, you don't want to touch it. She goes a bit ballistic. Well, here we are, this is the living room/common space area, what you will.

And this is the bedroom. It's a bit small, but it's doable. And— * yeah, go ahead—you get a bit of light through that window. Though it's mostly in the morning when you don't want it, right? And there's a closet, which is pretty fantastic. For only six hundred a month, it's hard to beat. *

(She spaces out for a minute.) Oh! Do you want to hear a song? *(She goes to boombox, turns on British pop song and dances, happily lost in her own world. Then, responding to Diana.)* What? * I can't hear you. Oh, wait! *(Turns off music.)*

The neighborhood? Oh, it's right good fun. Are you new to the city? * Oh you're going to love it, you're going to love it! It's brilliant. Everything's here. Right around the corner, there's an Indian restaurant, Tibetan, Chinese, Italian, a fish place. I mean, you could spend your whole life here and never eat all there is to eat. And the clubs, the pubs, just on the street, there's an energy, it's like there's speed in the air and it's just constantly sifting through your skin. * Oh, I like that. Without it, life gets so sleepy. Where I come from is just one big yawn.

* Yeah, I'm going back next week. My visa's run out. Ran out a couple of weeks ago to be honest. Oooh, yeah, just watch out for the crèche. If you move even one figurine, you're bleeding dead.

* Yeah, she *is* a bit of a religious person. Which is all right with me. I mean, whatever someone's into I try to respect. Although sometimes it'll be the morning and I'm making eggs, hungover, and all of a sudden there she is, talking about Jesus. I don't know, I don't really like hearing about the crucifixion when I'm making me eggs. I mean, I think Jesus was a fine person. Did you see *The Last Temptation of Christ?* * Oh it's brilliant! Willem Dafoe plays Christ and he's bloody gorgeous. But really, Karen's all right. The only time she bothers me is in those situation when I'm eating.

Oh, and there are some rules you have to stick to with her. Nothing serious. Just things like the phone is also for her church group so when you answer the phone you have to say "Jesus loves you." And around the big holidays, she leaves leaflets for you and then sort of quizzes you on them later. Oh, it's not like a test you have to pass, it's just that things go better for you if you do. And you have to share Sunday dinner with her, ham and all the fixings.

* Yeah, it did bother me a bit in the beginning. I don't like ham. And I'd find myself chewing and I'd start thinking about my mates out at the pub, and I'd look at Karen and I'd think "I hate you, you crazy old bat." But then I started thinking about my mate Amber, who I met at the pub. She's a hooker, part-time, to pay her rent, you see, and really, acting like a good Christian isn't half as bad as that, is it?

* You're not Christian? What *are* you? * Jewish?! Really? You don't look it at all. Oh. That might be a problem. I do think that would be a problem. * Oh God, I'm making it sound like she's anti-Semitic, aren't I? She's really not. She's more anti-everyone equally. Everyone else.

You know, you could probably hide it from her. I mean, I didn't know, so— * Yeah, that would be a drag, right? Well, all right then. Honestly, I mean, it's not that great a room. I'm sure you'll find something. *(Watching Diana exit.)* Oooh, watch your head.

SAM, SIXTH AVENUE

Slide of Village Voice ad:
    $575/month, Chelsea area.
    Own large room, lots of light.
    F or M to share w/M.
    Must be in good shape.

(Lights up on Sam, a good-looking man in his late twenties.)
SAM: Hey, Diana! Come on in! Come on in! Did you have trouble finding it? * Yeah, when I tell people it's above Billy's Topless, it's usually not a problem. * That place is a classic, but now all these porn stores are moving into the neighborhood, it's really getting sleazy. It's a shame. I even heard there's an S&M palace, or dungeon, whatever you call it, right on 17th Street. Can you believe people pay for that? I mean, maybe in Iowa, but this *city* kicks my ass every day.

(Flops down into a chair.) Ugh, I'm exhausted, been showing this place all day, phone ringing off the hook. *(Reaches out hand.)* I'm Sam. Look, I know the ad in the *Voice* must have seemed weird—it's just that I'm a personal trainer, yeah, I work out of my home, so it kinda looks bad for me if my roommate's flabby, out of shape. For myself, I don't care what you look like. Not that you don't look good—you do. *(Laughs at himself.)* I'm gonna stop talking now. *(Pause.)*

OK. *(Stands up.)* This is the living room. * Yeah, thanks. Of course, you would have total access to this. Kitchen—eat-in. * Oh, yeah, that's real nice in the morning, with the sun comin' in and the view of the Empire State Building. * Yeah, take a look. *(He checks her out while she looks out the window.)* And the bedroom, two closets. And bathroom, which we share. Oh, speaking of bathrooms, do you like golden showers? * I said—do you—

(Blackout.)

JEWEL, LIMBO CAFE ON AVENUE A

Slide of hand-scrawled sign:
> Limbo Cafe
> Today's coffees: Hazelnut Amaretto, Dutch Chocolate,
> Good Ol' American Joe
> Tonight's performance: Kentucky Fucking Chicken

(Spotlight up on Jewel sitting with an open Kentucky Fried Chicken box on her lap. She messily devours a chicken leg. Then, she puts the leg back in the box, stands up, and reaches out to shake imaginary hand, or, as it were, wing.)

JEWEL: Hello, free-range chicken. Now, as you know, we have a position open. What it entails is sitting in a box this big with about eight other chickens. You'll sit there all day, every day, eating. Yeah, that's a real fringe benefit. You'll grow so fat you can't move, then we'll chop your head off, rip you into pieces and serve you to already overfed Americans. How does that sound to you? *(She stands up, overturns her chair, yells.)*

Yeah, thanks for your KENTUCKY FUCKIN' CHICKEN!
(Quick change of pose. She looks at the audience.)

Everybody needs a little KFC.

(End of piece. Faint applause.)

Thanks, thanks. *(Grins at friend in audience.)* Shut up Romé! Anyone stupid enough to get his dick pierced shouldn't be hurlin' criticisms.

(Sees Diana.) Shit! Diana! You came! That is so cool. *(Looking around room, anxious.)* You seen Tapio? * Shit. He's not here. Fuck. Whatever. It doesn't matter. Oh hey, maybe he's in the bathroom. I'm gonna go check. You want something? You want a beer? * Naw, man, it's on me. It's so cool that you came. *(Goes offstage, we hear her pounding on a door.)* Hello? Hello? * Oh, sorry, man, I'm just looking for someone. Give me a fuckin' break!

(Comes back onstage.) People. What's their fuckin' problem? *(Sits down.)* * Oh, thanks, man, thanks. * Yeah, I thought it went OK. I can't really tell without Tap here. But can I tell you something, just between you and me?... *(Confidentially.)* I love that chicken. It's so damn good. * Naw, I feel really guilty about it, the way they oppress those chickens and then kill them for my consumption, but—come on, it is *good.*

...So, how's the apartment thing going? * Mmm-hmm. *(Laughs.)* No way! Golden shower! He *said* that? No fuckin' way! People are crazy man. Shit!

(Looks at Diana.) You OK, man? * I don't know, to be honest you look a little, what's the word? peaked. * Yeah, I know it's hard. I was thinking about you the other day, man, 'cause you got guts. * Naw, you really do. You've traveled like two thousand miles, totally on your own, to this mythically cold-hearted city where you don't know anyone, and now you're going into strange people's homes looking for a place to live. I don't think I could do it. For so long now, Tap has been where I lived. I mean—he's found where we lived. What did I just say? * Whatever.

Did I just depress you more? Shit, I have a way of doing that. Listen, what can I do to, like, cheer you up? *(Sound of ice cream truck.)* * Naw, man, you don't want what they got in there. *(Motions like shooting up.)* Yep. 24-7-365. And not an ice cream sandwich in sight...

Oh, shit! I know what'll make you feel better. I can't believe I didn't think of—OK, listen, there's this guy, Ned, he was the drummer in Tap's band. He's from California and he's like totally over New York. He just snapped, you know? He has got a studio—650. * I don't know, I've never been there, but Tap tells me it's got a fucking *terrace.* * Yeah, yeah, I wanna give you his number. Shit, what is it? * Naw, I know it, it's got like a seven in it…

(Sees Tap through the window, runs over and opens door.) Tap! Tap! * Yeah. Where the fuck were you? *(Reacts to something he does, smiles.)* Hey! What's Ned's number? * Ned's number? *(To Diana.)* Hey, get this. 757-1027. *(To Tap.)* Yeah, I'm coming! *(To Diana.)* Good luck, man. Call me at work after you see the place. *(As she exits.)* TAAAAPPPP!

NED, HELL'S KITCHEN

Lights up on Ned, a sweet and slow slacker dude in his twenties. He's sitting, air-drumming to The Eagles. He hears knocking on the door.

NED: Hey…come on in. I'm Ned…So, you're a "friend" of Tapio's? * Oh, Jewel. Yeah. She's a great lady. Well, let me give you the grand tour. *(Points to right near the bed.)* This is the bedroom. This hot pot is the kitchen. And this *(Pointing again to right near the bed.)* is the living room.

* Yeah, I measured it when I first moved in. It's roughly 6' by 9' by 7'. And, if you put a loft bed in, that would like double the space. * Oh, the bathroom is in the hallway, right down there. You share it with the family on the other side of the hall. They are very nice people. Every one of 'em. * Um, I don't know, there's…six of them, no, seven with the new baby. She was born right here in the building. *(Smiles thinking of her.)* Baby Sally. Oh, and the terrace— *(Lifts up window bars with difficulty, leans out window.)*

I covered this strip of tar with Astroturf and it's really killer. I hung out here all last summer and, as you can see, you have an excellent view of the alley. The rats are awesome. They're more like people than people think—there's families and gangs and sex stuff. If you don't have a TV, you can definitely kill hours that way.

* Oh no, I'm not leaving 'cause of the apartment. It's been real great. Having your own casa in Manhattan is practically unheard of. No, I'm leaving for *(With mystery.)* "personal reasons." *(Long pause.)* Well, since you ask, last Thursday, I had a moment of clarity. NoZone, our band, was playing at Mercury Lounge, and we always end our sets with

this song Tap wrote called "Age of Rage." So I'm playin' the rhythm. *(Starts beating out the rhythm with his foot.)* It's a real constant, driving beat, you know. Like when you're angry. And your heart's slamming against your chest. There's all this blood flowin' through you. You're starting to shake. You can't see. *(Stops beat.)* I don't know why, it was really gettin' to me. So after the set, I took off and walked out onto Houston Street, but the beat was still there. *(Starts beating out rhythm again.)* People pushin'. Horns honkin'. Subway rushing under-ground…all to that same beat. *(Stops beat.)* It's not a wonder people kill each other here, it's a wonder most of us are still alive.

    * Oh, the place? It's yours, if you want it.

JEWEL, KIM'S VIDEO ON AVENUE A

Slide of a tacky movie display for Donnie Brasco. *Lights up on Jewel slump-ing over a counter. A customer comes up.*

JEWEL: Hey. Can I have your card. *(She takes card and video from him.)* Spinal Tap. Excellent. This is my boyfriend's favorite movie. * No, I'm not paid to make film commentary. *(Mutters.)* Fuckin' bastard. * Give me your other film, please, so I can complete your transaction. *(Takes film, looks at it and smiles.)* Naughty Nunnery. Naughty Nunnery. Although I, as you know, am not paid to make film commentary, I must say that *(Yelling out the title.)* Naughty Nunnery is an excellent choice. Now, you have a good evening.

    (Phone rings. She picks it up immediately.) Tap? * Oh, Diana. Hey, what's up? No, I'm cool, I'm cool. I'm just PMSing, you know. Hey, did you know that the hormones women have when they're PMSing are the hormones men have all the time? * Yeah, that's a well-kept secret, right?

    So, what's up? Did you see Ned's place? Oh, hold on. *(Takes video from customer. Looks at it.)* Pretty Woman? I don't rent that. * I said, I don't rent that. * 'Cause if you want a bullshit fantasy about hookers, there's a whole room of perfectly straightforward porn, but this Disneyfied good-for-the-whole-family prostitute-into-princess, I-fuck-but-I-don't-kiss-so-it's-OK-now-will-you-take-me-shopping bullshit doesn't fly with me and I'm not gonna be part of disseminating it!

(Phone rings. She picks up immediately.) Tap? *(Hugely disappointed.)* Oh…Yeah, this is Kim's Video. * No, we don't have *Donnie Brasco*.

(Switches lines back to Diana.) Sorry. So you saw Ned's place? * Yeah, yeah. * You're taking it? That is so cool. I hooked you up. I'm like a real estate guy. * What? Hello, what? How big? *(She measures it out with her body as she talks.)* Six by nine by seven? That's not a studio, man, that's a prison cell. * You are wigging out, man. * Yes, you are. You're like in that desperate place where anything looks good to you, but I'm tellin' you man, you're gonna regret it.

* Naw, I know, I know it's hard. And everyone's telling you: you can't get an apartment in New York, there's nothing for under a thousand, blah blah blah. But you know what? It's all a fucking lie. It's all part of the bigger picture, you know what I mean?

* I mean, from the time you're born, it's like the whole world is saying to you—like here, here's four feet of space. No, we're white, right, so our world is like here's six feet, well no, we're women, so OK maybe five. Here's five square feet—this is what's allotted you. And then everything—school, magazines, fucking TV—is there to train you to keep your eye on what you own, to not ever look up. 'Cause if you do, you're gonna see there's more than five feet—there's a whole fucking world out there that you've never seen or smelled or touched. All I'm saying is, look up. This apartment search is like everything else, you're gonna get exactly what you think you deserve.

* Me? We're not talking about me. * I, I don't know, man, I don't think of the squat that way. It's a political thing.

(Looks at customer, then to Diana.) I gotta go. * Yeah, cool. * Well, think about what I said, man. Catch you later.

CAROLYN, WASHINGTON HEIGHTS

Slide of Village Voice ad:
> F to share w/F. Private room, $600.
> Washington Heights Area.
> Near subways and bus. No smokers.

(Lights up on Carolyn, a woman in her thirties. She's sitting at her computer, typing.)

CAROLYN: Come in!…The door's open. * Hi. I'll just be a minute. Feel free to look around. * Yeah, go wherever you want. The empty bedroom is on the left. *(She goes back to typing, then finishes.)* OK. Sorry. If I'm writing, I have to finish what I'm thinking or it just disappears.

Nice to meet you, Diana. I'm Carolyn. * Did you see the room? * Yeah, it's fine. I mean, I guess for the world at large this is a pretty mediocre apartment, but for New York it's damn good. I feel lucky.

* Oh, I'm sorry, have a seat. *(Carolyn sits too.)* Are you from around here? * Iowa! Where? * You're kidding! I'm from Cow Creek. * I know. Wow. How funny. How long have you been here? * Three weeks? Oh, that's nothing. Oh, when I first came here I had no idea what I was doing.

* No, no, I had no place to stay. Actually what happened was, oh god, I arrived around 3:30 in the morning and I had so little money, I think 500 dollars total, that I started walking from Port Authority over to the YMCA on 23rd Street.

So, of course, this guy comes up to me. Doesn't even hesitate, just comes right up in my face and says—"Give me all the money you have right now. I'm serious." * There's no one around, absolutely no one.

And I just thought "I can't give him my 500 dollars" so I looked at him and said "I don't have any money. I don't have anything." He went to pull something, I thought it might be a gun or a knife, and then, I don't know why I said this, I said "I don't have any money! I don't even have an apartment or a place to stay."

Suddenly, all the aggression just disappeared from his face and he said—really? I said—yes. And he said "Do you want to stay with me? I've got an apartment." I stayed with him for three weeks.

* Oh God, I know, it seems crazy now, but at the time I just felt so lucky. He didn't want anything from me. He just let me stay with him until I found this place…I don't know, sometimes you find comfort in the most unexpected places.

* Now? I'm a freelance writer. * Yeah, and actually I go places on assignment a lot, which is why I decided to rent out the room. It just seems like a waste to spend so much money on an apartment I'm barely ever in.

And…I hope this doesn't sound bad, but I'm not looking for a friend, you know? Or someone to hang out with. I've just found, in my own experience, that when you're living with someone, it's best to keep that relationship really clear, you know? And clean.

So…that's my story. * Um, no, you answered most of my questions on the phone. And you seem very…dare I say it?…normal. And you are from Iowa. So…if you'd like to move in…that would be fine with me.

JEWEL, TOMPKINS SQUARE PARK

Lights up on Jewel, standing, waiting for Diana. She's visibly upset but trying to hold it together. A slide behind her reads "Don't sit on the grass."

JEWEL: Hey! Diana! Thanks for comin'. I hope my note wasn't too weird. * Yeah? Cool. Come on, let's go sit on the grass. * *(She turns to look at slide.)* Fuck that. If there's one thing Tap's taught me it's that if someone tells you you can't do something, you must be able to do it. You'll never see a sign that says "Don't fly over the grass" 'cause you can't fly. It says "Don't sit on the grass" 'cause you *can* sit.

(Sits down.) * Really, man? You found a place? What's it like? * Mediocre? All right!…You got a roommate? * That's great, man, I'm really happy for you. Havin' a home, it's gonna make all the difference.

D, I…I kicked Tap out. * I know. I can't believe it either. *(Dead, not as she said it before.)* He's so hot. But…last week he disappeared for three days. And then, one night, that night I talked to you at work, I go home and he's back, and he's just like prowling around the house. And then he starts getting all sexual with me which is even weirder 'cause we haven't been like that in a long time. * No. And I'm pushing him away like "Tap, get OFF me!" and he—I don't want to use the word rape 'cause I let him—but he just starts having this sex with me that's so violent…I kicked him out the next morning.

Oh, shit. That abyss I saw in his eyes is yawning deep and wide inside me today. I feel this panicky energy vibrating off me like a poisonous gas…It's days like this I know why I came to the East Village. Everyone wears their differences on the outside here—artists, orphans, addicts.

But you know what the test is? It's in the permanence of the difference. Revocable or irrevocable? *(Points to someone in the park.)* Tattoo?

Irrevocable. My fake Doc Martens? Revocable. *(Points out.)* Tongue piercing? Irrevocable. My Fab 208 striped pants? Revocable.

See, I retain my visa to the Upper West Side or this New Jersey wedding I went to last weekend. No lie. I wish it was. My appearance says— I'm here today but one day, maybe, I'm movin' on. The punks, the derelicts, the truly grunge, they say—man, I am here to stay. It's the end of the line and Tompkins Square Park is the center of the universe.

I envy them, man. At least they know where they belong.

* I don't know. I don't know what I'm gonna do. The squat, it is Tap to me. *(With surprise.)* I don't wanna live there anymore. Plus, I've been thinking and it's not a squat. It's just…a lot of people living together.

* Yeah, you did say that.

(Long pause as Jewel listens to Diana talk.) * Really, man? *Really?* You wanna live with me? But what about the mediocre apartment? * I— whoa. I don't know what to say, man, I—yeah. That's what I want to say—yeah. I would.

* Yeah. I guess the search begins again. *(Stands up.)* Come on. Let's go get ourselves a *Voice.*

END OF PLAY

HURRICANE

by Erin Cressida Wilson

This play is for Sean San Jose.

THE AUTHOR

Erin Cressida Wilson is an internationally produced and award-winning playwright and Professor of Playwriting at Duke University. Among the theatres where she has been produced are Joe's Pub at The New York Shakespeare Festival, The Mark Taper Forum, The Brooklyn Academy of Music, Naked Angels, The Magic Theatre, The Manhattan Class Co., Yale Cabaret, The Traverse Theatre in Edinburgh, New York Stage & Film, The Sundance Institute (four seasons) and the New Grove in London.

Among Ms. Wilson's plays is *Cross-Dressing in The Depression,* which opened at Soho Rep in NYC, directed by Marcus Stern. It is published in the Smith & Kraus anthology *Women Playwrights: The Best Plays of 1993.* Ms. Wilson is currently adapting *Cross-Dressing in the Depression* into a musical with composer Jack Herrick of The Red Clay Ramblers at the McCarter Theatre. Lisa Portes directs. Other plays include *The Trail of Her Inner Thigh,* commissioned by Steppenwolf, developed at The Mark Taper Forum's New Works Festival, and produced at Campo Santo; *The Secret Ink War,* commissioned by Playwrights Horizons; and *Dakota's Belly, Wyoming,* currently being adapted into a film. Ms. Wilson is in pre-production with her feature-length film adaptation of Mary Gaitskill's short story *Secretary*—Steven Shainberg director and producer.

Honors include the National Endowment for the Arts Fellowship, The Rockefeller Award, and the California and North Carolina Arts Council Grants. Ms. Wilson co-wrote—with playwright Lillian Ann Slugocki—*The Erotica Project,* which opened for a three week run at Joe's Pub at The New York Shakespeare Festival in January of 1999—John Gould Rubin directed. Ms. Wilson also wrote for *Pieces of the Quilt,* an AIDS benefit produced by Sean San Jose and The Alma Delfina Group; it opened at the Magic Theatre in 1996 and has since opened in over 100 venues—from AIDS clinics to regional theatres.

AUTHOR'S NOTE

This play took a long time to write and many were involved and instrumental along the way. I am grateful to work with and be encouraged and supported by the following…

Thank you to Doug Aibel, The Bay Area Playwrights Festival, Paul Bernstein, Jordan Beswick, Natasha Boas, Allison Boyer, Mary Coleman, Jim Carmody, Patricia Dunnock, Barry Edelstein, Beth Emelson, Florence Falk, Maria Irene Fornes, Lee Hall, Margo Hall, Wendy Vander Heuvel, Israel Horovitz, George Lane, Mark Linn-Baker, Delia MacDougall, John C. Mackenzie, Max Mayer, Tom McCracken, New Dramatists, The New York Playwrights Lab, Jerry Patch, Jeff Perry, Johanna Pfaelzer, Lisa Portes, John Gould Rubin, Natania Rosenfeld, Luis Saguar, Sean San Jose, Steven Shainberg, Ted and Adele Shank, Anna Shapiro, Michael Torres, Leslie Urdang, Michele Valkensky, Paul Willis, Graham & Lois Wilson, Robert Woodruff, and the various casts who realized this play. Also, I was inspired, fueled and am thankful to the memories of Ray Grosvenor, Delfina San Jose, and Barbie Stein.

I would like to acknowledge Catherine Porter's translation of Luce Irigaray's book *The Sex Which is Not One* as helping to hone and focus the Linda/Larry scene.

My suggestion for the "playing" of *Hurricane* is to allow its heart, soul and poetry to be earned through a balance of its satire, cruelty, playfulness, optimism, irony, and the fearless embracing of its stereotypes.

ORIGINAL PRODUCTION

Hurricane was commissioned by South Coast Repertory and was developed at Naked Angels—Catherine Patterson directing, New Dramatists—Robert Woodruff directing, Soho Rep—Lisa Portes directing, and New York Stage and Film—Barry Edelstein directing. Its New York Premiere was in December of 1999 at Classic Stage Company, with Naked Angels co-producing, Barry Edelstein directed. It was also produced at Printer's Devil in Seattle—directed by Paul Willis and at The Famous Door in Chicago—directed by Anna Shapiro.

Hurricane's world premiere was at Campo Santo in San Francisco. The director was Delia MacDougall; the producers were Sean San Jose, Luis Saguar, Michael Torres, Margo Hall, and James Carpenter; the dramaturg was Sean San Jose; the lighting designer was Jim Cave; the composer and sound designer was Beth Custer; the projections and slides were by Matt Beiderman and Arianna Vasquez; the set concept was by Delia MacDougall and Luis Saguar; the costume concept was by Dena Martinez; the stage manager was Lucy Owen; and the poster and lobby art was by Victor Cartagena. The cast was as follows...

Katy . . . . Margo Hall
Esther . . . . Lynne Soffer
Judy . . . . Jamie Comer
Ray . . . . Colman Domingo
Maria . . . . Monica Sanchez
Molly . . . . Cristina Frias
Larry . . . . John Flanagan
Linda . . . . Blancett Reynolds
Lucy . . . . Stephanie Hunt

The play was then published in "Theatre Forum Magazine," and "The American Poetry Review," and was subsequently extensively rewritten at New York Stage and Film. The following script is the result of that work. The director and set designer was Barry Edelstein, the dramaturg was Zak Berkman, the lighting designer was Russell Champa, and the stage manager was Spencer Anderson.

Katy . . . . Adina Porter
Esther . . . . Phyllis Somerville
Young Woman . . . . Jessica Caterina
Judy . . . . Marissa Copeland
Ray . . . . John Ortiz
Maria . . . . Socorro Santiago
Molly . . . . Clea Rivera
Larry . . . . Ralph Buckley
Linda . . . . Jenna Stern
Lucy . . . . Vivienne Benesch

SETTING

The stage is a prison cell. And a "poetic space." Spare. All the action takes place at a very long banquet or conference table.

CHARACTERS

AFRICA:

KATY LONGSTRETH: A woman. A poet. She is in a prison in Africa. She is restrained with an underlying passion. She is African American.

SOUTHERN UTAH:

ESTHER CARDINAL: A woman. A stoner. A hippie. A feminist. Wears long flowing flowering dresses from the Sixties and Seventies, San Francisco. Looks like Janis Joplin if she were still alive.

YOUNG WOMAN: A young and sexy woman. A quote unquote post-feminist. Possibly Esther's hallucination.

NEW YORK CITY:

JUDY: A woman. Thin as a rail. A model. She's not in her twenties anymore.

RAY: A man. A clothing designer. Funny, clueless, flirtatious, unconscious.

Note: The waitress in the Larry/Linda scene is Judy. And the photographer in the Katy/Lucy scene is Ray.

SAN FRANCISCO:

MARIA GARCIA RIVERA VALENZUELA DE LA RIVA: A woman. A mother. Works at Safeway Supermarket. Indomitable spirit.

MOLLY O'CONNOR: Maria's daughter. Seventeen years old. Typical adolescent.

NEW YORK CITY.

LARRY ROBBINS: A man.

LINDA GOTTLIEB: A woman. Runs a children's theatre.

NEW YORK CITY:

KATY LONGSTRETH: A woman. A poet.

LUCY STONE: Another woman. An aggressive magazine journalist. A feminist.

PROLOGUE

A prison cell in Africa. A naked woman tries to wash herself clean from a single drop of water. Her name is Katy Longstreth. Behind her, a conference table full of the women of the play. In silhouette. Katy lights a match and writes on the floors and ceilings of the prison.

KATY: My mother was a hippie. My father was a Panther. I was born in San Francisco. In 1962. And I am writing to you with mascara, with a matchstick, with my blood, with what I have left. From inside a prison, across the ocean. In Africa. This is how I became, not a person, not a woman. This is how I became, finally, a poem. A poem sent home from the war. This is my hurricane. This is my scream. And this is for you. In the next cell. If you can hear me, scratch your name, sing a song, tell me a story, tell me, tell me, you hear me.

ESTHER: My name is Esther Cardinal. Southern Utah.

YOUNG WOMAN: My name is Claire Cardinal. Hurricane, Utah.

JUDY: My name is Judy Finelli. New York City.

RAY: My name is Ray Grosvenor. New York City.

MARIA: My name is Maria Garcia Rivera Valenzuela De La Riva. San Francisco.

MOLLY: My name is Molly O'Connor. San Francisco.

LARRY: My name is Larry Robbins. New York City.

LINDA: My name is Linda Gottlieb. New York City.

LUCY: My name is Lucy Stone. New York City.

KATY: My name is Katy Longstreth. Africa.

(Katy's presence stays on stage for the rest of the play as the ensemble exits and the duets begin.)

SCENE I

Hurricane, Utah. On the top of a mesa above Hurricane, Utah. A young woman sits serenely writing on her laptop computer. Next to her sits Esther. Esther holds a wrinkled and old paper bag close to her heart. She lights a joint. She offers a hit to the young woman.

YOUNG WOMAN: No thank-you.

ESTHER: "No thank you." *(Esther points to the landscape.)* Those are gorgeous aren't they? Those two sticking up like that together? Perfect harmony. Like two female bodies.

YOUNG WOMAN: Uh-huh.

ESTHER: Back in 1973, I cut off all my hair, I boarded a bus to Frisco, and became a lesbian. I had a poster in my kitchen there of a witch with her breasts pushing out of her rags and her eyebrows raised, kind of feisty and naughty, and she's snapping her broom in half. The poster said "Fuck Housework." I'm sure it's a relic now. And next to it, The Grateful Dead, Sister Sledge, Santana and the Airplane.

YOUNG WOMAN: I'm not interested.

ESTHER: Yeah, I went to the Freedom Trash Can and deposited my false eye lashes and my wire cup bras. I chose to live without men. The amazon utopia. Not that I never did. Love men. But that's another story. So, this is the first time I been back to Utah since the day I left so long ago. Sitting on top of my favorite mesa in the middle of the fucking desert.

YOUNG WOMAN: I'm trying to work?

ESTHER: Ah. Oh. So. Then no talking. OK...I never was much of a talker anyway. Never had the *vocabulary.* I was a good seamstress though. And when I felt like I *had* to say something, I just made this vision—it was like my own form of prayer—that I'd sew up my lips, real tight, and then everything I had to say would stay inside of me and bloom into little violet flowers that would appear on yellow wallpaper. In my sweet smelling bathroom in my dream house. That's no shit. What a bunch of crap that was...so...work? Work. Work. Work. Gotcha. So, let me guess. You're a college girl.

YOUNG WOMAN: I graduated.

ESTHER: Oh, that's nice. Ever seen a girdle?

YOUNG WOMAN: No.

ESTHER: Want to see one?

YOUNG WOMAN: That's OK.

ESTHER: Don't really got one.

YOUNG WOMAN: OK.

ESTHER: So that's nice, you go to college.

YOUNG WOMAN: No, I just said...

ESTHER: It sounds like Marilyn, right? My voice. High pitched and breathy.

YOUNG WOMAN: What happened?

ESTHER: They cut my voice box right out of my throat. Special kind of cancer.

YOUNG WOMAN: If you didn't have a voice box you wouldn't be able to speak?

ESTHER: So they say.

YOUNG WOMAN: Listen, whatever, I'm sorry for you, but I got to get this resume done. *(The young woman sprays perfume on her neck and wrists.)*

ESTHER: Oooooh. I wanted to be with men too. Touch what they could do. Be near a man who was doing something important. Yeah, back in the Fifties, you and I would have been in competition. Is that the internet you're on?

YOUNG WOMAN: They don't have phone jacks in the desert?

ESTHER: Right. I suppose you young ones do what you call "Communicate" over the internet. I'd like to see a god damn sexual revolution happen over cyberspace...you want to know what my first sexual experience was?

YOUNG WOMAN: No.

ESTHER: OK...It was seeing the atom bomb. That's right. I was only in third grade, and right across the border there in Nevada they used to test those nuclear bombs. At recess a bunch of us would run up to the top of this mesa here and throw ourselves onto the earth just as the explosion went off, and feel the shiver run through the soil and up into our bodies. It was as if the earth was reaching up and holding us, embracing us like they say, "He's got the whole world in his hand!" It was thrilling. And I knew, right then and there, that I was alive. Then we'd peak our heads up a bit—sort of an erotic version of duck and cover—and we'd *see* that god-like mushroom fill the sky. I'd be down on my belly with my cheek to the soil, and I thought I'm gonna marry a man who works on those clouds, and there was a boy. And his name was Jerry, and he was lying right next to me, and just at that moment he said "I'm gonna work on those sky mushrooms someday." And there you are. He wasn't a scientist or anything. He was what you might call a "nuclear janitor." Cleaned out the area after the "events." So that's not hooked up to a phone in any way?

YOUNG WOMAN: I'm not on the internet.

ESTHER: No online chat groups rallying up women to unite?

YOUNG WOMAN: I'm rewriting my resume.

ESTHER: Does Germain Greer, Angela Davis, Gloria Steinem ring a bell?
(The young woman puts on lipstick.)

ESTHER: Oh no, certainly not, don't look at me, honey. Don't look at me, because I am your god damn history. I am the real deal, Sister. That's the first lesson we women learned in the Fifties, that the best ways to *win* the female competition is to not look. Don't let her catch your eye. Then she'll know you're just like her.

YOUNG WOMAN: I'm *not* just like you. (*She closes her laptop. And begins to squirm into black stockings and high heels.*)

ESTHER: You know what baby?! You have no idea what I went through to get you on this mesa, all by yourself, putting on that lipstick, taking a solo trip, you have no idea. How we fought the establishment, made it safe for women. So you could rewrite your resume on a magical screen. What I did to give you the freedom to be what you are. Let me ask you, would a woman create the atomic bomb? I say no. No. No. Sister, I married this country, this land, and look what it got me. A fucking trash heap. A place you might throw out your used razor blades. Disposable. This country, these people. One hundred twenty-five Atomic blasts detonated in Nevada between 1951 and 1962, and each one about the same size of that Chernobyl. And my voice box cut right out of me. But I stayed in it like a fucked up marriage. The day they started to bomb our own country. Oh, it's not my husband I mourn so much, but don't get me wrong, cause I do, it's my daughter. Born with her heart outside her body. She'd be about your age now. She would be. He'd be sixty. Ha! "Claire." So sweet, like naming your daughter something that will be safe and pure. You know what's inside this bag. My baby girl. Her ashes. I'm *still* holding onto her. Holding onto her like I hold onto those days when we believed.

(*The young woman starts filing her nails.*)

ESTHER: You know the thing about you, is that maybe it's not that you treat me like I'm invisible, but maybe you're not here either. You know I'm proud to say I can have an acid flashback at the drop of a hat at this point. So maybe that's just all you are, an hallucination.

(*The young woman starts tweezing her eyebrows and then waxing her upper lip.*)

ESTHER: OK. Well, I can talk to an hallucination as good as the next gal. So, I moved to Frisco years after my loved ones died, I woke up, embraced the lavender coalition, and now I'm back for two reasons. To bury my daughter. And to die. And when I die, I'm going to leave behind a party. I'm going to buy a trailer down in Hurricane, and I'm going to give away all my dresses, my long flowing dresses from the Height Ashbury, San Francisco, and my trailer, it's going to rock and roll for the girls of the Nineties, and a dress for each one. Cause my hope is in those little girls. Not in you anymore. I'll put a little Post-It on each dress with each of their names. I'll send out invitations for a party the day of my death, and they'll creep into this mysterious trailer that they were invited to, peak in, and see their past. A gift from the lost mother of the Sixties to the daughters of the Nineties. And these will be their dresses.

(The young woman pulls a girdle out of her bag and flaps it out.)

YOUNG WOMAN: By the way, girdles are back in.

(The young woman disappears. Esther holds her brown paper bag closer to her heart. She looks at the spot where the young woman was, as if invoking her dead child.)

ESTHER: Your heart I touched in my hand when you were born, outside your body, and how you did not live to see twenty-four hours—your face, a hole—your heart, in the stones, your touch, in the stream, your torso in the stars, your hair in the wind on my lips, your face... *(Esther pulls out—from a knapsack—all her long flowing Sixties dresses and skirts, she puts them in different piles. Putting Post-Its on each one.)* To Emily, Laramie, Leslie, Johanna, Beth, Dixie, Jessica, Marissa, Jenna, Clea, Socorro, Vivienne, Adina, Phyllis, and the girl with her same name...Claire.

SCENE II

New York City. A photo shoot in Judy's apartment. Ray photographs Judy. Judy is wearing rubber stockings, garter belt, coned breasts. A black dildo is strapped around her waist and her arms are tied back so severely that she appears armless.

JUDY: I gotta get out of New York.

RAY: I picked up a pizza delivery boy.

JUDY: Was Julian in town?

RAY: Julian was gone.

JUDY: Where?

RAY: London. Business. Writing. Did he call you back?

JUDY: Julian? Hasn't called me back since he was heterosexual.

RAY: Well, you aren't exactly Mike Nichols now are you?

JUDY: And the pizza delivery boy?

RAY: I slept with a woman.

JUDY: Stop it!

RAY: In her parents' home. She was eighteen.

JUDY: You're evil. Did you fuck her?

RAY: Yes. It was frightening. I felt lost. *She* liked it.

JUDY: Last night I tried to give Damian a blow job out on one of the piers. I said, "Oh, come on, out here, past the homo's, oh don't mind them." And then I was like to myself "Judy, what *are* you doing?" I mean, I'd like to be a gay man, but let's face it, I'm not.

RAY: Did Damian have a big one?

JUDY: No.

RAY: You can tell.

JUDY: How?

RAY: You can see it in the eyes.

JUDY: You can tell the size of someone's penis from their eyes?

RAY: Yyyyyyup.

JUDY: But you've never met him.

RAY: *Your* eyes, I can see it in *your* eyes.

JUDY: Really?

RAY: You're a size queen honey. The disappointment is evident in your very pupils.

JUDY: Even twelve hours later?

RAY: Uh-huh.

RAY: He was Puerto Rican.

JUDY: Uncircumcised?

RAY: Uh-huh.

JUDY: Ouch.

RAY: Yyyyyup.

RAY: I think he was seventeen. He was walking down 73rd. And then I saw that he walked into the pizza joint on my corner and I guessed that he was a pizza delivery boy.

JUDY: So you ordered?

RAY: Pepperoni. But I wouldn't pay him.

JUDY: You're evil.

RAY: I wouldn't pay him but I answered the door with my shirt off and, well, basically, I gave him a blow job.

JUDY: Then what?

RAY: He ran out.

JUDY: He was terrified.

RAY: He was gay.

JUDY: Are you sure?

RAY: He was gay. Of course he was gay. He was a complete and total Mo.

JUDY: After the fiasco with Damian I went home and watched, that "Scout" movie, what's it called?

RAY: *To Kill A Mockingbird.*

JUDY: Do you relate to anybody in that movie?

RAY: What do you mean?

JUDY: Do you relate to what it's about?

RAY: What do you mean?

JUDY: And also *It's A Wonderful Life.* They are good people in that movie. I just don't get what they are all about. Anyway, are you done with me?

RAY: Do you have any condoms?

JUDY: You know I don't have penetrative sex.

RAY: Paranoid!

JUDY: Yeah, well. Gotta be safe.

RAY: It's OK, I've got one somewhere.

JUDY: Can you undo me?

(Ray undoes her arms and she shakes them out.)

RAY: I was horny the other day and kind of like couldn't be bothered to ride my bike to the Rambles cause I was hung over, so I was fiddling around and I filled a condom with water and it looked just like your breast.

JUDY: Huh. Really.

RAY: Put on that bustle!

(She starts to redress in a chiffon red lace-up bustier and bustle. Ray goes into the bathroom.)

JUDY: The blue make up?!

RAY: That's right!

(Judy starts applying blue make up to her face making her look pale and dead.)

JUDY: I'm not going to do this anymore.

RAY: What?!

JUDY: The first time I ever saw you, you were doing that "Women Who Want to Dress Up Like Little Girls" shoot in Sheridan Square. You looked like David Cassidy, the Fonz, and Vinnie Barbarino all smushed together.

RAY: David Cassidy? You know that turns me on in a kind of ickky way.

JUDY: The second time I saw you, you ignored me and I thought it was because you were so into me and by the end of the night you stared at me. Hungry. Like a fish hook catching my tongue, you reeled me in and made me feel beautiful for the first time in my life. We stared at each other. You took my skin between your lips, and inflated me. We picked lipsticks and we giggled.

RAY: Your bathroom is filthy! Get a fucking housekeeper.

JUDY: And then you started saying "I'm going to marry you." I was yours, you were mine, we were underground, and I was gonna have your turkey baster baby.

(Ray walks out of the bathroom with the water filled condom.)

JUDY: That *does* look like my breast.

RAY: I told you.

JUDY: I'm too old for this.

RAY: You're thin as a rail.

JUDY: You told me to be thin as a rail.

RAY: I told you to appear *dead,* to appear *starving.*

JUDY: On the ground?

RAY: I'll tell you one thing though, you've got a butt on you and that is *in.*

JUDY: Is it?!

RAY: Baby, those are child rearing hips and men are *loving that!* Put more blue on.

(Judy puts on more blue make up to look dead. She is now on the floor, in a dead position.)

JUDY: Would you kiss me.

RAY: OK! That's dead enough looking. And pull up your dress like you might have just been violated or something. Good.

JUDY: Would you lean down and kiss me.

RAY: Oooyyyyyy. *(Ray leans down and kisses Judy on the cheek.)*

JUDY: On my mouth.

(He takes her hand and kisses her hand.)

RAY: OK?

JUDY: I want you to really kiss me.

RAY: I saw Carl, he wanted to "make up." I'm like I don't need Carl's energy on me.

JUDY: Carl was your best friend.

RAY: He does the same work he did when he was nineteen. He's confined to a way small number of people. He hasn't reached out.

JUDY: You mean sold out?

RAY: Oh please. Don't give me that bullshit that anything that is commercial or makes money, or should I say just simply *works* and people *enjoy* is selling out or is somehow sub or beneath the real shit that is going on out there. Besides, Carl's stuff only gets shown in Sweden.

JUDY: Denmark.

RAY: Whatever.

JUDY: I mean Amsterdam.

RAY: Is that part of the Netherlands?

JUDY: I think so.

RAY: Are they Dutch? Or…what country is Dutch?

JUDY: Deutschland.

RAY: Well, one of those Scandinavian countries up there. I mean Jesus Christ, that's where Abba came from, take it from there.

JUDY: Done.

RAY: Sit down with this tit in your hand. Like it was just lopped off, look sad, like you miss it.

JUDY: Like this?

RAY: Where the fuck would you live if you moved out of New York, you'd fall off the face of the earth.

JUDY: San Francisco.

RAY: San Francisco! You're going to San Francisco to get *away?* From the homo's? Christ, you're thin as a rail.

JUDY: Why do you keep saying that?

RAY: Oh, I want a little piece of boy candy right now. I'm hungry. Now lick your lips. Lick them. Lick them. Lick then. Like you're ready for love.

JUDY: I don't exist.

RAY: What?

JUDY: You're a fucking sexist.

RAY: How am I a sexist?!

JUDY: You know what: Ray? You know what the big secret about you is? You're not gay.

RAY: Roger.

JUDY: You're not gay, you're just so scared of me, that this is the easier solution.

RAY: OK, so now my choice of sexuality has nothing to do with me, or my entire history, but now it is *unbelievably!?…about you!*

JUDY: The very fact of your being gay is a violence towards me and all women.

RAY: You know you go out and say that in a public forum and see if you don't get mowed down for homophobia.

JUDY: And the pictures you're taking of me? What will *you* get mowed down for?

RAY: This is art. Fashion. And besides I am affirming your body. Your female body.

JUDY: Did I decide to look like a demented sex starved dead tart? I can't remember the moment of decision.

RAY: They have design and photography classes you can take at the New School anytime Judy. It's a free world.

JUDY: It's dangerous for me to spend any more time with someone who does not desire me.

RAY: Oh I see, is that how you define yourself, as to whether you are sexually desired or not. Maybe that's your problem.

JUDY: And I shouldn't be sexually desired? Is that it?

RAY: Well, you *could* read a book sometime.

JUDY: The reason I fuck so many young men is not because I desire them, but I desire to be them. Why did it frighten you to sleep with that girl?

RAY: Well, it's true Judy, you'll never have a penis, I'm sorry.

JUDY: Because you went inside of her. She held you, you touched and sucked her breasts. And when you were done, she hadn't come, and if she had come, she could have come a million more times, there was no end to her.

RAY: I didn't even sleep with a woman anyway, I just said it to get you going.

JUDY: You know it's one thing to be a beard, even a fag hag, but I do this and stay at home. Now I see your picture at your new Fall Lineup with your arm around fucking Christy Turlington and some other razor sharp six foot tall woman who in most circles would be thought of as a geek, and at first I hate her, I'm jealous of her, she's ugly, I accuse her of having anorexia, and then I realize I'm not jealous of her, I'm jealous of you. I was tricked into thinking it was safe because you didn't want me, but that's precisely what wasn't safe.

RAY: I'm going to Squeezebox.

JUDY: All men are fags!

RAY: OK, so now I'm not gay, all men are fags, which is it? And by the way I am offended by that term. I let you use it, but essentially it strips me of my self esteem.

JUDY: Oh, yeah, you are so right on with the gay language of empowerment.

RAY: Listen!! I marched on Washington. Julian donates half his Gap ad money to charities.

JUDY: That's a publicity stunt *and* a tax write off!

RAY: I attended the Gay Olympics.

JUDY: Who won?

RAY: They're non-competitive.

JUDY: Christ!

RAY: As you know. I have found a community that has repaired a fucking childhood of confusion. I have a *family* now. You remember we laughed at that story I told you, but seriously, when I was about sixteen, I asked that thirteen-year-old boy that I had a crush on but I didn't understand I had a crush on, I asked him to move that lawn mower into my parents' shed, just so I could be in the shed with him alone and say "put that lawn mower over there in the corner." And then he just walked out of the door and left me in the shed in the middle of the afternoon, with me having no idea why I was doing things like that. You can say *nothing*. About my life you have no right. Anyway, you are who I love.

JUDY: Then why don't you love me.

RAY: Listen, you've been uppity since the second I walked in today. If you want to be alone, fine. Whatever. There's nothing I can do about that.

JUDY: Screw you! *(In an act of anger, Judy pulls all her clothes off. She is completely naked.)*

RAY: I think estrogen and argument just don't mix.

JUDY: Do you think I'm pretty?

RAY: Well, that was enough test shots anyway. Until we get the *real* models. Sesh over!

JUDY: You see, my bag is packed.

RAY: Ok, you're right, you do scare me.

JUDY: How do I scare you?!

RAY: Come out with me, we'll have fun. I need you with me.

JUDY: No!

RAY: Settle down.

JUDY: You know I'm going out on the piers, I'm dancing at Squeezebox, I'm trying to exist in one way or another. Even when I successfully imitate you and catch these guys and go to bed with them there is no evidence of me, there is no real proof that I have even come for Christ's sakes. I mean I've heard there are those women who ejaculate, but for me I could fake it until the end of time and nobody would know. There is no proof of where I start, where I end. Even to myself. I want to know where is the evidence? Where is the evidence that I exist?

RAY: Your children.

JUDY: Thank-you.

RAY: Do I look butch?

JUDY: Yes.

RAY: I don't look like a homo do I?

JUDY: No.

RAY: But the second I step foot into Squeezebox I'll look gay right?

JUDY: I'm leaving you.

RAY: Do you like this shirt?

JUDY: Uh-huh.

RAY: OK, touch my cock. Does it feel good.

(She does.)

RAY: I love you.

JUDY: You don't love me you hate yourself.

RAY: If I catch any boymeat, can I bring him here for a quickie? You can go across the street for about a half an hour and have a drink, right?

(She takes his hand and puts it on her breast. He pulls his hand away and giggles. Ray runs out of her apartment. Judy slowly turns around to look into the mirror. She wants to, but cannot see, her own beauty. She grabs a dress, throws it on, puts on lipstick, and runs out the door, following Ray. The lights fade on the scene as Bill Wither's "Ain't No Sunshine" faintly plays.)

SCENE III

San Francisco. Molly and Maria in the kitchen. Molly sits there mad and sixteen, with newly short and dyed hair. She looks like a little boy. A college application sits on the kitchen table. "Ain't No Sunshine" plays lightly in the next room. The slash marks indicate where the lines overlap one another.

MOLLY: He gave me a piece of shit / haircut!

MARIA: / What?!

MOLLY: You heard me.

MARIA: Obviously / I heard you.

MOLLY: / What's that music?

MARIA: What music? Don't say "Shit." I don't hear no music.

MOLLY: He's playing Seventies music.

MARIA: Don't say that / word.

MOLLY: / Shit?!

MARIA: Don't say it!

MOLLY: Shit!

MARIA: Ay! Dios / mio.

MOLLY: / Don't talk Mexican.

MARIA: / Spanish!

MOLLY: / Who does that asshole think he is!

MARIA: He's your father for Christ's sakes!

MOLLY: My *step*father!

MARIA: Your father!

MOLLY: My father had red hair!

MARIA: Watch it!

MOLLY: Not black hair! Why do I have to have black hair Mom! Why did you dye it black!?

MARIA: That's enough!

MOLLY: He's an asshole!

MARIA: Get out!

MOLLY: Don't!

MARIA: Come here!

MOLLY: Don't talk like that.

MARIA: Come here.

MOLLY: Don't tell me get out then come here.

MARIA: Come here.

MOLLY: Don't tell me that!

MARIA: Stop it. I hear you. /

MOLLY: / Shut-up!

MARIA: Shutup!

(Molly turns back to her college application.)

MARIA: Check the box.

MOLLY: Which box?

MARIA: "Other." And use my maiden name.

MOLLY: Where?

MARIA: You got "black," you got "white," and you got "other." And use my maiden name.

MOLLY: Garcia Rivera Valenzuela de la Riva?

MARIA: You'll get into school.

MOLLY: They ask for a picture.

MARIA: You look Mexican enough.

MOLLY: Mom! I used to look so fine before.

MARIA: That's stupid, you know it.

MOLLY: I know it's stupid. But I look like somebody else now. I look like a fucking Cholo Mission Street geek. Who am I? I hate it. Fuck. Mom!

MARIA: It's beautiful hair.

MOLLY: What did you marry a fucking hairdresser for?

MARIA: Here, you keep the hair, you keep the hair, remember the hair. *(Maria starts picking up the hair and putting it into Molly's arms.)*

MOLLY: I look like fucking Frida Kahlo.

MARIA: I'll cut my hair like you.

MOLLY: He took my power, he took my edge. He said it would be OK. It's not OK.

MARIA: Give me the scissors.

(Molly turns back to the application. Maria starts to cut a bit of her own hair.)

MOLLY: Mom, what's my hobbies?

MARIA: Say Amnesty International. You're a volunteer for Amnesty International.

MOLLY: What? /

MARIA: / Say it!

MOLLY: No! /

MARIA: / Write it!

MOLLY: I won't! /

MARIA: / Now!

(She writes it.)

MOLLY: How about clubs?

MARIA: What?

MOLLY: Sports.

MARIA: Put tennis too.

MOLLY: Jesus Christ.

MARIA: A Mexican tennis player, you volunteer for Amnesty, you'll get in.

MOLLY: You always said I was Irish.

MARIA: So what, that's what I said.

MOLLY: You named me O'Connor, dad's name.

MARIA: Your dad left us.

MOLLY: Then why didn't you give me *your* last name? Why did you give me *his* name and why did you *then* name me Molly? You gave me an Irish name, Mom. Obviously.

MARIA: I thought it would help you. But now it won't help you.

MOLLY: Why?

MARIA: Molly Garcia Rivera Valenzuela de la Riva, and we're making it legal! Here, take this lock. Keep it. *(Maria hands Molly a lock of her hair.)*

MOLLY: What do you want me to do with it?

MARIA: Put it in a locket, how the fuck do I know. Keep it somewhere special.

MOLLY: OK.

MARIA: That's good. That's good.

MOLLY: But I hate the name Garcia Rivera Valenzuela de la Riva! And besides you've always told me your were from Spain. Your family was from Spain? What did you think that was gonna help?

MARIA: What?

MOLLY: Madrid!

MARIA: Get on with the application!

MOLLY: What? Now you're from Mexico? Or should I just write down Nicaragua, they might like that, or better yet, Sarajevo!

MARIA: Change it! I got the white out!

MOLLY: No!

(Maria comes up and tears up the application.)

MOLLY: Mom!

MARIA: Don't go to school then!

MOLLY: You can't lie on these things!

MARIA: It's not a lie, you're a Mexican God damn it. That's no lie and that's gonna get you somewhere. *With* a scholarship!

MOLLY: Why?

MARIA: Because the cycle's done.

MOLLY: What cycle?

MARIA: The cycle is that you were born here so you don't know what you have, you are not grateful for the perfumed Charmen toilet paper, the dollars and pennies in your pocket, you're no longer thankful for the smell of American soaps and Dove and Arm & Hammer and Lysol and a clean toilet for Christ's sakes. For books with fine print in a language that you now think is yours, English. Oh, no this is just what your life naturally is, nobody broke themselves to birth you here, you are now one of the privileged because you're a real American, from this soil...here... wait...check...there...American Indian, write Native American. *(Maria hands Molly another application.)*

MOLLY: What?

MARIA: That's what we are, Native American, before the Spanish got in our blood, we were Indians, so put down Native American.

MOLLY: Which one is this?

MARIA: The Stanford one, fuck Berkeley.

(Molly starts writing in her notebook. She speaks what she is writing to the audience.)

MOLLY: My Mom was so beautiful, even when she was sick, she never even got skinny like everyone says you're supposed to. She always was in some way dignified and lovely, especially at Christmas, under the lights of the tree she wrapped my presents in gold and told me be quiet for the Easter

Bunny would come down the chimney. This was Portrero Hill, San Francisco. Why she said Easter Bunny I'll never know, but we left out *carrots* and milk instead of *cookies* and milk, and always in the morning there was a line of orange M&Ms going to the fireplace, and I'd say "Mommy! Mommy! The bunny ate the carrots and pooped it out in a straight line of orange M&Ms…" Then we'd eat them and they'd be chocolate in our mouths and we would feel like we were doing something naughty. We were living the high life, and even though my skin was olive, I was Irish American and I was going somewhere.

MARIA: What did he do, bite you? Did that boy you're seeing bite you? There's teeth marks across your cheek, did he bite you?

MOLLY: It's my scar from when I was two, when the dog bit me.

MARIA: You're becoming passionate then.

MOLLY: Mom, chill, what do you think, no.

MARIA: He bites you like a dog, you become passionate, does he bark, does he purr?

MOLLY: Shut up!

MARIA: Stop!

MOLLY: I won't!

MARIA: What?

MOLLY: I have never even ever French kissed OK?!

MARIA: That's not true.

MOLLY: I haven't.

MARIA: Then start!

MOLLY: What, you want me to end up with AIDS like you? What a turn on. No, I can't make out, have sex, get drunk, get stoned. You did all of that already Mom!

MARIA: I want you to also say that you worked for a phone sex line to work your way through high school, to support yourself and your dying mother. This is good. This is a wonderful, very in, sort of opposite thing you can do that works these days. You show you're smart, underprivileged, and have led a noble and sturdy but safe life on the phone sex lines and then, say that one day you said "Enough, I've done this long enough," and you were hired to write these phone sex things, and that is how you became a writer, the writer that you are today.

MOLLY: It's a lie!

MARIA: They call it "female erotica," and you're the youngest one of our time to write it, and you're hip and sexy and Latina and smart and liberated.

MOLLY: It's a cliché!

MARIA: And for that reason, my dear, it will work.

MOLLY: It's stupid! It's unimaginative!

MARIA: Exactly, you hit it there, that's what goes. Anyway, I'll do the phone sex for you. I'll quit Safeway. That way you don't have to worry, I won't be getting blood in the pastries, croissants, and goo-filled donuts if I cut my finger. I won't be infecting the customers.

MOLLY: Sometimes it gives me the creeps to talk to you. Anyway, you can't do phone sex because of your cough.

MARIA: I have a mute!

MOLLY: What?

MARIA: On the phone! I'll press mute if I cough. I piss while I'm talking on the phone all the time.

MOLLY: What?

MARIA: Now write the essay. You're going to Stanford!

(Molly writes in her notebook again.)

MOLLY: My mother died in the Fall. I was there at her last breath. From the moment she got sick I stopped getting into trouble, I stopped getting arrested. I watched her last breath, and when she died there was a wetness on the sheets where she had been alive. They threw her body in the back of the car like it was lead. I touched her blood and put it to my tongue. Because she was my Mom. I never wore rubber gloves. Because she was my Mom. This is Portrero Hill, 1998. Now I nurse my stepdad. I don't hate him no more. I don't think I hate anything no more. She taught me about anger, she taught me about rage, she taught me how to speak and how to yell, and because of it I don't hate no more. Weird, huh? I wave to her slowly, slowly, I wave to her slowly in my dreams.

MARIA: Help me with the needles.

MOLLY: Why doesn't he do it?

MARIA: They make him faint.

MOLLY: He was a junky!

MARIA: Well, he had a hard time being a junky.

MOLLY: He gave it to you!

MARIA: Yes he did.

MOLLY: You knew!

MARIA: Well…

MOLLY: You killed yourself!

MARIA: No.

MOLLY: You did it on purpose. So did he! To kill me!

MARIA: Come here.

MOLLY: Hold still.

> *(She takes the iv tree and flushes a tube with a shot of saline. She hooks her mother up to the iv.)*

MARIA: I never was a fem libber, you know that. I think they all end up just castrating themselves. But I was wrong. I want you to feel proud of what you do. Ok? That's all. I don't feel well. I can't see too good. I feel swollen.

MOLLY: Tell me about something.

MARIA: I saw a movie.

MOLLY: Oh?

MARIA: With that guy.

MOLLY: What guy?

MARIA: From Cuba.

MOLLY: You mean, what's his name?

MARIA: Uhm, yes...it's...

MOLLY: What is it...

MARIA: He was in that movie with that woman who did that movie with the actor.

MOLLY: You mean the one with the black hair?

MARIA: Yes, it was a vampire movie by that...

MOLLY: What was her name?

MARIA: The one whose kid died?

MOLLY: Yes.

MARIA: What did she die of?

MOLLY: Cancer.

MARIA: What kind?

MOLLY: Uhm, leukemia.

MARIA: What was her name? /

MOLLY: / What was her name?

MOLLY: Who cares!

MARIA: Johnny did.

MOLLY: Who?

MARIA: Johnny, your godfather. He loved to hold you on his knee when you were a baby.

MOLLY: Was he gay? Did *he* die of AIDS too Mom?

MARIA: Leukemia! It was leukemia! Stan Rice, Anne Rice, *Interview With The Vampire,* Tom Cruise, Glenn Close!

MOLLY: Don't you mean Andy Garcia?

MARIA: I don't know what I meant.

MOLLY: If I had a bag to punch I'd punch it, if I had a face to break I'd break it, and then I'd go over and write a novel.

MARIA: Molly.

MOLLY: What did my real Dad look like? What kind of shirts did he wear? What glass did he drink his beer out of? Was his skin like ruddy and white? Did he have freckles?

MARIA: Get back to the application and check the box.

MOLLY: Which box?

MARIA: "Other." And use my maiden name.

(Molly slowly walks up and punches the wall. Then she takes her mother's face in her hands and kisses her forehead. As the scene ends the faint sound of gentrified Muzak can be heard coming from the next scene.)

SCENE IV

New York City. Linda interviews Larry for a job. They are in a midtown restaurant.

LINDA: I see you're married.

LARRY: Yes. She doesn't live here though. She lives in L.A. I tell you, sometimes it feels like I'm married to a phone. And when we fight long distance my voice echoes back at me when the connection's bad. It mocks me.

LINDA: That's awful.

LARRY: You're not married.

LINDA: No, no, no.

LARRY: No.

LINDA: You don't drink?

LARRY: No.

LINDA: When did you stop?

LARRY: I had to stop.

LINDA: I know.

LARRY: I had a problem.

LINDA: When did you stop?

LARRY: So I had to stop.

LINDA: When?

LARRY: I had to stop.

LINDA: Oh.

LARRY: It's been eleven months now. I'm almost one year old. That's what we say.

LINDA: Good. So. Shall we begin?

LARRY: Yes. OK.

(A waitress approaches.)

WAITRESS: Drinks?!

LARRY: Three diet Cokes.

LINDA: Wine. One.

(Larry thanks the waitress.)

LARRY: Thanks Man.

(The waitress leaves.)

LARRY: Did you know I'm also a singer?

LINDA: No!

LARRY: I compose songs.

LINDA: Oh? Piano?

LARRY: Guitar.

LINDA: So, what was your first experience in the theatre?

LARRY: I write my songs from a woman's perspective. I try to express the anger of women also their frailty and their desire to save the world.

LINDA: Really?

LARRY: I dedicate my songs to women. In a way I am a woman when I sing these songs. And being a man, sometimes I can be a woman better than a woman because of the perspective I have.

LINDA: That's cool. Are you a feminist?

LARRY: I'm a lesbian.

LINDA: Oh?

LARRY: I prefer to think of myself that way.

LINDA: I thought I was a lesbian once.

LARRY: Did you?

LINDA: Uh-huh.

LARRY: Really?

LINDA: Uh-huh.

LARRY: Really...?

LINDA: You know I'm always sleeping with married men and my shrink says for me to look at the problem, or the thing I'm doing that's bothering me as the obstacle to my real desire. So I realized that married men were the obstacle to the wife that I really desired. But then I always got stuck with cunnilingus. It stops at the pussy for me. I just can't get into it, you know.

LARRY: Uh-huh.

LINDA: But anyway.

LARRY: Right?!

LINDA: Ok, I note you've played a lot of multiple roles in plays.

LARRY: Yes. I'm not doing that anymore. I'm playing only leading roles now. That's my policy. I'm putting my foot down, I'm taking my power back now. One day at a time.

LINDA: What does it feel like to have founded and basically run? Am I right? You *ran* the biggest theatre in the South for how long? Ten years?

LARRY: Yes.

LINDA: Does it feel strange to return to acting after being this big director?

LARRY: Well…

LINDA: Does it?

LARRY: I been around the world and I been around the block Linda. I lived in Thailand, I traveled through India, got dysentery, screwed the traveling Free Spirits from Ontario to Australia. Lived outside the law, liberated my consciousness through psilocybin, wore the poncho, studied the shadow puppets, meditated and was right on with the Asian gals, lived the hippie dream and read Beckett on the Eurail. Did the contact improv. in Amsterdam, fucked a few Dutch, put a pound of heroin up my ass to support my art, that sort of thing.

LINDA: You're a Renaissance type of guy.

LARRY: I'm a real guy Linda. I'm not on a pedestal. I'm just your average nut.

LINDA: Uh-huh. So what you're saying is that the transition from running a theatre to walking the pavement with your headshot is just part of your journey. You've been there and back and everywhere.

LARRY: I've grassrooted plenty is what I'm trying to say, yes.

LINDA: Grassrooted?

LARRY: I used to be the guy with the dope, Oh man, I was the guy who you called when you needed a little smuggling done. I was the guy whose backpack stank and whose soul was clean.

LINDA: Uh-huh. Where's your wife?

LARRY: My wife?

LINDA: What?

LARRY: She's in L.A.. She lives in L.A.

LINDA: When did she leave?

LARRY: Eleven months ago.

LINDA: Oh. Has she been back?

LARRY: Oh yeah!

LINDA: So she splits her time.

LARRY: She came back for five days at Christmas. She's working on her career and so am I. One day at a time.

LINDA: How long has it been since you've made love?

(Larry spits his gum across the table. The waitress arrives with the drinks.)

WAITRESS: Uhm, excuse me, were you in that play a few months ago directed by that guy, uhm, that guy from Chicago?

LARRY: Yes!

WAITRESS: You were so good! I thought you were so great. Really great.

LARRY: Thank-you. Thank-you. Thank-you.

(The waitress gives them the drinks and leaves.)

LARRY: I was nude in that play.

LINDA: I heard.

LARRY: You heard.

LINDA: Uh-huh.

LARRY: Oh, I've been nude in lots of plays.

LINDA: I've heard.

LARRY: So what, I mean I don't know what that means. Do you?

LINDA: I don't.

LARRY: What does it mean. Who cares, right? Right.

LINDA: Can I see your ring.

LARRY: Yes. *(Larry wets his finger by running it into his mouth. Then he slips the ring off and hands it to Linda.)* Oh! It's been since Christmas! No, actually truthfully, it's been one year and a half. To answer your question earlier. That is. The one about making love.

LINDA: I'm sorry.

LARRY: It's OK. I'm in it for the long run. Even though it's a little dry right now. This run.

LINDA: Do you have photos? From your plays?

LARRY: Yes. *(Larry takes out an envelope of pictures of himself in plays.)*

LINDA: Oh, you're clothed!

LARRY: Yes. I have played clothed characters, but I was wondering—

LINDA: Yes…

LARRY: I would like to sing you a song that I wrote.

LINDA: Did you look into teaching? After you were fired?

LARRY: You know I love the Blacks. I love the Jews. I love the Micks. I love

the fucking Spics. I love the Wops. I love the fucking *Native Americans.*
I love them.

LINDA: Uh-huh?

LARRY: Yes I looked into teaching.

LINDA: Do you think the sexual harassment problem was a factor in your being locked out of institutions.

LARRY: You know, I got groovy with those foreign gals when I was traveling, years ago. I did it in the Louvre, the National, the Sistine Chapel, under all the art, and all the tits, in the London Library, and I got to say, I realized, if I were a woman, I'd be confused. If I were a woman, I wouldn't know what was up. If I had a womb in my belly, I'd wonder, what were those bitches doing back then in those olden days. Were they all weaving baskets, were they all frying the fish, because none of them were picking up a paint brush or a chisel, I'll tell you that much. Making something that lasts through history. It was at that moment that I became a feminist.

LINDA: Bitches?

LARRY: I wanted to see the world, pass the joint and march for Martin Luther. You know? I wanted that.

LINDA: So, you couldn't get a teaching job?

LARRY: The man leans over to me, this is a very reputable, secondary, insignificant, overrated, and underpaying institution in Manhattan, the man leans over to me, he's a New York Eyetie, mind you, and he whispers under his voice, sotto voce, "You'd be great for the job but we need a little color." "Color? What's color? What exactly do you mean?" I said. "Well, for the kids, the kids need to see their own kind," he says.

LINDA: Do you think that's why you didn't get the job, because of your color?

LARRY: So I apply for another job, it says…"Staff diversity grant. Focus is to provide occasions that sensitize *non-underrepresented employees.*" Well, that's me I guess. White and *non-underrepresented.* That's no bullshit.

LINDA: Can you tell me exactly what happened with the sex suit?

LARRY: Hey, I revived Zora Neal, Lorraine Hansberry. I was producing plays about AIDS before Tony Kushner was even born, I was conducting symposiums on nuclear disasters, I was hiring people with black wives, female literary managers. Listen, I loved the blacks, I loved the fucking liberated women and the Jews. I set up a Latino Theatre Lab for Christ's sake, what do you want? I was the first to hire a Mexican to play more than a maid. Where's the balance here, what do they want me to do? One pinch of the old ass, I mean. You want a sob story? Ok, my father was a trash collector. My grandparents were Appalachian…now said to be the "Poorest population in America." My mom was a drunk! Which one of us is the most oppressed around here! No? Ok!

LINDA: You pinched someone's ass? That's incredible. No, that couldn't be it, that couldn't end a career.

LARRY: I'm a fag!

LINDA: What?

LARRY: I'm an African American with an AZT habit, that gonna get me a job?

LINDA: Uhm.

LARRY: I'm gonna move back to Ireland where it's OK to be white. Where the war's on the streets. You know I was as fucking right on as the next guy. I'm perfectly capable of exploiting my own people for a dime like the next guy who makes a nickel off an ad, who makes a nickel off their disease, their *orientation,* their specialness. Hey, I grabbed an ass or two, asked for a date or ten thousand, but I hired them, I hired them. I've done the black thing.

LINDA: Huh.

LARRY: Get me a drink!

LINDA: You want a drink?

LARRY: No man. No. I tell you, I stay away from those meetings too long, my disease is doing push-ups outside the door, just waiting for me. Ok, I'm powerless. I gotta work my Fourth Step.

LINDA: What?

LARRY: Has flirting gone out of style or what?

LINDA: No.

LARRY: I like you.

LINDA: I like you. I always thought these rings were like bulls wearing rings in their noses or brands on animals. *(She refers to his wedding band that she still holds.)*

LARRY: Oh, I believe in them.

LINDA: Do you? *(Linda puts the ring inside her skirt and inside of herself.)*

LARRY: What have you? Uhm. Where? What? Oh?

LINDA: Why are you so quiet.

LARRY: I can't stand up.

LINDA: I hear you have a large dick.

LARRY: I do.

LINDA: I hear you can see it running down your leg.

LARRY: You can.

LINDA: I hear you wear pants tight enough that you can see the veins coursing with blood.

LARRY: So I've heard.

LINDA: Mmmmm.

LARRY: I like strong women.

LINDA: Do you?

LARRY: Yes, I can give myself a blow job! That's how big my cock is.

LINDA: You don't say.

LARRY: I don't like to boast.

LINDA: Boast.

LARRY: I've got my guitar! I brought it with me!

LINDA: Get your ring.

LARRY: Here?

LINDA: Yes.

> (Larry puts his hand under the table and his fingers inside of Linda. He touches her as they continue to talk.)

LINDA: What did you do?

LARRY: A headshot crosses my desk, my secretary asks me "Do I want to audition this girl?"…"No, I don't want to audition this girl," I say. "She's got to learn what's between her legs first before I'll look at her." That was it. She tape recorded it. The board of directors fired me.

LINDA: Maybe she didn't know what was between her legs.

LARRY: Do you think?

LINDA: Maybe she didn't know that her whole body is covered in sexual organs.

LARRY: Maybe.

LINDA: Maybe she didn't know that her genitalia are two lips constantly in contact. That she is constantly caressing herself. That the layers and the contractions and the space between the moment, all of this is kept a secret, even from herself.

LARRY: Maybe you're right.

LINDA: Is it the clitoris or the vagina that is the point of her pleasure, or is it neither, or is it both. Touching the uterus, touching the breast, the vulva, the lips. She has sex organs everywhere. In fact, whenever she speaks, she is involved in the act of touching herself.

LARRY: Ah-hah!

LINDA: She folds in and out, and when she is asked if she wants more or less, she says nothing and everything. She walks into museums, just like you said, and though she sees her naked image everywhere, nothing is signed by a woman. So she must put herself together with scraps and debris, into mosaics and cubism in an expanding and confusing universe that says she does not exist.

LARRY: I should have said that.

LINDA: Maybe she needed to find all that out.

LARRY: What about the interview?

LINDA: Got it.

LARRY: So, my career, my wife?

LINDA: Why don't you write it?

LARRY: Write it?

LINDA: Across my breasts.

LARRY: Breasts!?

LINDA: Waitress.

(Larry orgasms.)

LINDA: What happened?

WAITRESS: Anything else?

LARRY: I came.

LINDA: Could we have the check?

(The waitress writes the check.)

WAITRESS: Sure.

LARRY: I came.

WAITRESS: *and one glass of wine.*

LARRY: I came.

WAITRESS: *and plus tax that comes to…*

LINDA: I want you to write your story across my breasts. I want you to write your life across my body, and down my inner thighs.

WAITRESS: Thank-you.

LARRY: Did *you* come?

LINDA: What do you think?

LARRY: Should I take my hand back?

LINDA: No, I'm just about to release my teeth.

LARRY: Oh! *(Larry quickly pulls his fingers out of her.)*

LINDA: Did you get the ring?

(Larry pulls his hand up. Indeed, the ring is back on his finger.)

LARRY: Oh! Ho ho ho! I like you Linda.

LINDA: I like you Larry.

LARRY: Did I get the job?

LINDA: Was it the role of the Tree or the Chipmunk we were talking about, I can't remember.

LARRY: I would prefer to play the Tree. I have a great idea for the costume.

LINDA: That's fine with me. The Tree it is. *(To the waitress.)* Keep the change.

SCENE V

New York City. An interview. The meat packing district. Lucy Stone and Katy Longstreth eat oysters and drink wine.

KATY: I don't usually do interviews.

LUCY: Who was your mother?

KATY: A hippie.

LUCY: Who was your father?

KATY: A Panther.

LUCY: Where were you born?

KATY: San Francisco. 1962.

LUCY: It's raining in the meat market, it smells like fish and piss. It's the summer heat and I'm here with Katy, Katy Longstreth, with the deep dark eyes, Katy Longstreth back from Africa.

KATY: It does smell like fish and blood.

LUCY: I love this district.

KATY: Ok. You're recording?

LUCY: Yes. OK?

KATY: Uhm.

LUCY: You have come back to Americas with the most extraordinary set of poems. Nonchalant.

KATY: What?

LUCY: Nonchalant!

(Lucy's photographer shoots flash pictures of Katy and Lucy. Lucy tries to act nonchalant for the photo, as if she is being caught off guard mid-interview.)

KATY: What *kind* of journalism is this?

LUCY: Come again?

KATY: What *is* this magazine?

LUCY: It's, Oh! You *have* been gone a long time. I integrate myself into the interview.

KATY: So, you don't just take a picture of me, you take a picture of me *with* you.

LUCY: Yes. It's called "A Conversation With"...you and me.

KATY: And who are you?

(Lucy laughs.)

LUCY: Exactly. Yes. I often ask myself the same question.

KATY: Ok. So, I should ask you questions too?

LUCY: Yes.

KATY: Like what?

LUCY: Like you might ask me, for example, let's see, maybe it may come up about, I don't know, how *I* started writing, and I might harken back to what Auden once penned that—quote—Writers enjoy the sight of their own handwriting much as most people enjoy the smell of their own farts. End quote.

KATY: Huh.

LUCY: Or then Patty Hearst, what she asserted, that she and her fellow prisoners were not allowed to keep typewriters and she assumed because the prison officials thought they might kill themselves with the typewriters which I thought was funny…you know like the way they confiscate belts.

KATY: Right.

LUCY: Yes! I want to peel away the foreskin of this conversation.

KATY: What?

LUCY: And who says rape isn't sexy.

KATY: What are you talking about?

LUCY: I'll tell you, part of the problem is that my editors see this as a "post shame women's story." You know, "boring!" We got to jazz it up a bit, get it into the "style" section, talk a little bit about the new African clothing, puca shells and the like. Katy, now help me out here, do you wear *any* designer clothing?

KATY: Designer…?

LUCY: Rape victims have a recurring dream of melting away like wax.

KATY: I was not raped. I was a prisoner of war.

LUCY: Would you like Blue Point or Fin de Claire?

KATY: I've never eaten oysters.

LUCY: Good, so shall we begin?

KATY: Yes.

LUCY: So, I think this is very interesting. You are an international poe*tess* making history, or shall I say "Herstory," in Africa, living on the Rockefeller, Yale grad, political poe*tess* tasting the war.

KATY: Yes.

LUCY: Now let me get this straight. You were to observe and write about this African Rebel Leader, and in the process you were imprisoned. Yes?

KATY: That's right.

(Lucy refers to the oysters.)

LUCY: Put a little *tabasco,* and a little lemon, that's right, now, just in your mouth.

KATY: Oh, oh, oh my goodness, oh.

LUCY: Does the trick huh?

KATY: Uhm?

LUCY: What did you smell in prison?

KATY: The odor of death, decaying clothing, something sweet.

LUCY: What did you hear?

KATY: I listened for the unspoken, I kept listening for the silence, for the lack of language, for the end of the voice.

LUCY: Katy, you've gone into the Heart of Darkness, and all you've come back with is banality.

KATY: Why?

LUCY: You slept with him.

KATY: Why shouldn't I have slept with him?

LUCY: What did you eat in prison?

KATY: We had a can of mackerel and I smoked cigarettes. We had one bowl of water.

LUCY: Who is "we?"

KATY: Me and the woman that may not have been there through the wall. Of stone.

LUCY: How long were you in prison.

KATY: Six months. My whole life. I still am.

LUCY: Clever. Was there any light?

KATY: The best thing human beings can do in the dark is make up stories. And that's what I did.

LUCY: Why were you in prison?

KATY: There was no reason.

LUCY: What did you do in prison?

KATY: Repeated the words "Snow snow snow."

LUCY: That's beautiful.

KATY: I didn't shower for six months. I was dirty for six months.

LUCY: What did you do in prison?

KATY: Some rooms were the size of coffins.

LUCY: What did you do in prison?

KATY: Remembered the fingers. The women's fingers. They held all ten fingers in my face and then closed their fists and opened them again to show ten more. To tell me how many of their men had disappeared. The women tore through freshly dug graves—identifying their loved ones sometimes only by a scrap of fabric that they themselves had sewn. They pieced together the bones, dovetailing and fitting them together until they reconstructed their husbands and carefully lay on top of them to make love to their shadows as they disintegrated to dust beneath them. As if they had never been there in the first place.

LUCY: What did you do in prison?

KATY: Wrote on the roof of my mouth, spoke to my mother, on the roof of my mouth with my tongue.

LUCY: What did you do in prison?

KATY: Felt with my hand the screaming along the wall, pieced together the invisible, the disappeared, the invisible woman.

LUCY: What did you do in prison?

KATY: I tried not to scream, and to not scream you do this, you put together the woman in the next cell, it was the puzzle and each of her body parts scattered throughout the cell at different points, I kissed her, and I put her back together.

LUCY: What did the Rebel Leader say to you?

KATY: That there is great serenity in horror.

LUCY: Katy, you were violated without consent. You may have acted like you were consenting, you may have seduced him, but only in order to stop him from raping you.

KATY: You know this knee jerk feminism gives me a real pain in the ass.

LUCY: You strike me as someone who must have been incested repeatedly as a child.

KATY: Can you really use incest as a verb?

LUCY: Are you attracted to men that act like international terrorists?

KATY: He came to my cell, he put his breath to my tongue, and he asked me if I wanted to taste murder, if I wanted to touch the ocean, if I wanted to wrench the teeth from the mouths. I could say nothing in response. Because I was struck dumb. He would stand in front of me and I was petrified. His military ribbons brushed against my face. When he chased me, I ran, he made me shake, he made me tremble. It was exhilarating. And it felt better than suffering inside my own skin. What could be wrong with that.

LUCY: That is called rape.

KATY: To you.

LUCY: I've noticed that almost every article about you they've mentioned your beauty first, your artistry second.

KATY: There was blood being hosed from the sidewalks.

LUCY: But no marks on your face.

KATY: No.

LUCY: It is estimated that a woman is raped every one point three minutes in America.

KATY: Give it a rest.

LUCY: Might I just add that one out of eight American movies portrays a woman being raped? What did you do in prison?

KATY: Repeated the words "Snow snow snow."

LUCY: Who was your mother?

KATY: A hippie.

LUCY: Who was your father?

KATY: A Panther.

LUCY: Where were you born?

KATY: San Francisco. 1962.

LUCY: What happened. In San Francisco?

KATY: Fog kissed my face. There were demonstrations and equal rights being shouted. My mother lost me in a crowd.

LUCY: Your mother?

KATY: Yes.

LUCY: What are you thinking?

KATY: That I hate you.

LUCY: Why?

KATY: Because you are another woman.

LUCY: What are you thinking?

KATY: That I hate you.

LUCY: I see. What happened? In San Francisco? At the demonstrations?

KATY: Fog kissed my face. My mother lost me in a crowd. They were yelling equal rights. Sisterhood.

LUCY: When?

KATY: During a riot.

LUCY: What kind?

KATY: There was purple paint in the shape of Angela Davis sprayed across a wall. Rocks were being thrown and we were running, but I stopped to touch the wet paint and put a dot of the purple on my nose. When I turned around my mother had disappeared. I held my fingers up in the peace sign and ran, tears streaming out of my eyes, signs and politics shoved in my face, but I could not find her. She was somewhere else screaming equal rights.

LUCY: What do you hate?

KATY: I hate you because you are another woman.

LUCY: Why did you leave the United States?

KATY: I came to Africa because I wanted to see the violence on the surface. In America I was being raped everyday, quietly, but it was a little louder in Africa. The volume was up and therefore more honest. In North Africa the women are caged. Even their dress covers their eyes, their mouths, their entries, their screams, their bodies.

LUCY: Why did you go to Africa?

KATY: I thought if I go to Africa, people might listen because it is not in their backyards, it's not in their bloods, in their sheets. As a girl I watched my mother march for the rights of women and drop my hand. Wander off. I watched peace signs and gay rights and nuclear awareness and race riots, and where are we now. Where is the fucking promise of the Sixties. Where's the fucking free love and the free world. Where is the promise that I can feel the skin of a man touching my skin and coming inside of me?

LUCY: What is your question?

KATY: Why is it considered disgusting, ridiculous, and hysterical to talk about being a woman. Because there really is no problem at all, right? We've come so far, we're over that. Right? And anyway, if I'm going to talk about being a woman, shouldn't I talk about my weight, or shouldn't I not really be a woman, a sexual woman? So I walk around acting as if there is no problem, because there is no problem at all. I swallow the men over and over and over again, I make a hurricane inside my groin, and I spit it out. The words, the fire, the wind, the brokenness, into your face, into the face of the woman.

LUCY: Why did you go to Africa?

KATY: I went to Africa to turn these violences into poems, and even myself, I would become a poem. But all I thought of was you.

LUCY: Who am I?

KATY: You are the butterfly on the edge of my finger. You are the scream inside my throat that says "Love me, love me, love me." You are the woman I made up to keep me alive. You are my mother, me, the wife, the model, the daughter, the actress, the feminist. You are my mother.

LUCY: I heard you writing.

KATY: You heard me?

LUCY: Writing.

KATY: You heard me?

LUCY: Who was your mother?

KATY: My mother was a hippie. My father was a Panther. I was born in San Francisco in 1962, and I made up stories on the roof of my mouth, at the end of the century, when I sat by myself, on the hot stone floor, inside a prison, across the ocean. And imagined my lost mother.

(The ensemble of women gather around the conference/banquet table.)

KATY: Some people have been in prison so long they don't want to go out, they don't know how to survive outside. In fact, they don't know they're in. Do you know that you are there? In the next cell? Do you know that that is where you are? Scratch your name, your story, into the stone. Scratch it with your blood, your nails, anything. If you hear me, scratch your name. Your story. I'll sew it into the rest.

(Esther takes her brown paper bag and pours the ashes of her daughter onto the table. The bag is passed down the table and into the hands of each female ensemble member until a single line of ashes runs from Esther all the way to Molly.)

END OF PLAY

RIGHTS INFORMATION